The Civil War Guerrilla

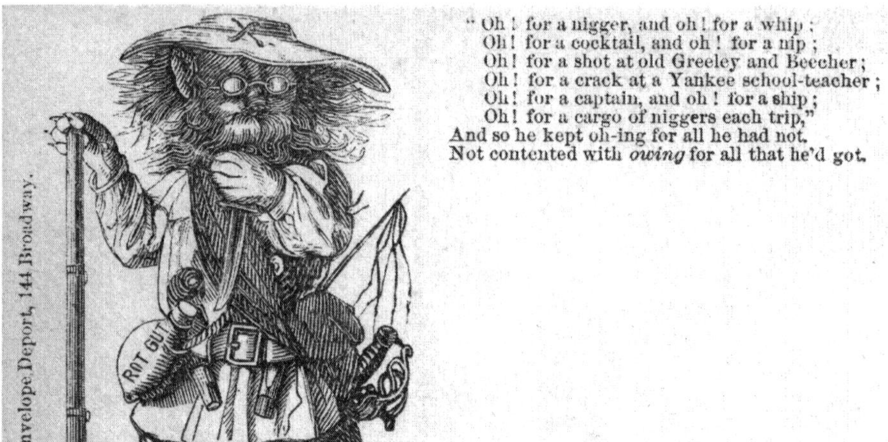
"Oh! for a nigger, and oh! for a whip;
Oh! for a cocktail, and oh! for a nip;
Oh! for a shot at old Greeley and Beecher;
Oh! for a crack at a Yankee school-teacher;
Oh! for a captain, and oh! for a ship;
Oh! for a cargo of niggers each trip,"
And so he kept oh-ing for all he had not.
Not contented with *owing* for all that he'd got.
New-York Union Envelope Depot, 144 Broadway.
ROT GUT
A Southern GORILLA, (Guerilla)

The Civil War Guerrilla

Unfolding the Black Flag in History, Memory, and Myth

Edited by
Joseph M. Beilein Jr.
and
Matthew C. Hulbert

UNIVERSITY PRESS OF KENTUCKY

Paperback edition 2018

Scholarly publisher for the Commonwealth,
serving Bellarmine University, Berea College, Centre College of Kentucky, Eastern Kentucky University, The Filson Historical Society, Georgetown College, Kentucky Historical Society, Kentucky State University, Morehead State University, Murray State University, Northern Kentucky University, Transylvania University, University of Kentucky, University of Louisville, and Western Kentucky University.

Editorial and Sales Offices: The University Press of Kentucky
663 South Limestone Street, Lexington, Kentucky 40508-4008
www.kentuckypress.com

Frontispiece: "A Southern Gorilla (Guerilla)." (Library of Congress, Prints and Photographs Catalog)

Library of Congress Cataloging-in-Publication Data

The Civil War guerrilla : unfolding the black flag in history, memory, and myth / edited by Joseph M. Beilein Jr. and Matthew C. Hulbert.
pages cm. — (New directions in Southern history)
Includes index.
ISBN 978-0-8131-6532-5 (hardcover : alk. paper) — ISBN 978-0-8131-6534-9 (pdf) — ISBN 978-0-8131-6533-2 (epub)
1. United States—History—Civil War, 1861–1865—Underground movements. 2. Guerrilla warfare—United States—History—19th century. 3. Guerrillas—United States—History—19th century. I. Beilein, Joseph M., Jr., editor, author. II. Hulbert, Matthew C., editor, author.
E470.C594 2015
973.7'3—dc23 2014043439

ISBN 978-0-8131-7576-8 (pbk. : alk. paper)

This book is printed on acid-free paper meeting the requirements of the American National Standard for Permanence in Paper for Printed Library Materials.

Manufactured in the United States of America.

Member of the Association of University Presses

Contents

Foreword

Inside Fellman's War

Christopher Phillips

"War is hell and people are shits." Such was my first introduction to my longtime friend Michael Fellman.

The year 1991 was a heady one for me, a published yet unminted PhD student of southern history finishing my dissertation while teaching full-time as an instructor at the University of Georgia. My first book had been issued the previous year, a study of a controversial federal army commander in a slave state—Missouri—barely linked in prevailing scholarship either to southern history or to the Civil War's metanarrative. Born as an MA thesis, the book's contention was that Nathaniel Lyon's rash actions in 1861 in this ostensibly neutral state helped to precipitate a chaotic, internecine conflict there by shifting fragile allegiances of innumerable hitherto-moderate Missourians, especially in rural areas, away from the federal government. The book was put into production in the summer of 1989 and published the following spring—too late, as it turned out, to consider Michael's magisterial *Inside War: The Guerrilla Conflict in Missouri during the American Civil War,* released by Oxford University Press in May 1989. His book not only established Michael's stature as a leading Civil War historian but launched a new genre of Civil War writing—war studies, which integrated civilians into the realm of military history. More, it redefined the history of the Civil War in Missouri and, to some degree, elsewhere. Unexpectedly, it linked Michael's book and mine and sparked a friendship that would last well over two decades.

My introduction to Michael came that fall at a conference in Springfield, Missouri, where, improbably, I presented on the plenary panel alongside Michael and Jim McPherson, whose *Battle Cry of Freedom* had received the Pulitzer Prize in 1988. Midwesterners all, our session served as my introduction to the full-contact sport known as academia. Both Michael and Jim had recently reviewed my book in prominent journals and had fully articulated their criticisms of it. Predictably, Jim questioned my notions of Lyon's personalized motivations over any ideological impetus while Michael targeted my insertion of Lyon into the origins of Missouri's inside war. His understanding of irregular warfare located it as the truest and fullest expression of the human stain—savagery lying just beneath the veneer of civilized codes of conduct, whether social or personal. Because guerrilla warfare is unregulated and violates nearly all the self-styled "laws of war" (in fact, during the American Civil War, it led directly to the first-ever written form of such law in the United States, namely the Lieber Code), such violence provides a mirror into human nature and only confirms Michael's view of war as the exemplar of man's inhumanity to man. Fittingly, Michael's guerrilla war in Missouri was nihilistic, sociopathic, Manichean, and fully immoral. His lodestar, as he stated at the conference and then often afterward, was America's war with Vietnam, the foreign conflict and domestic counterconflict that had shaped his beliefs while a student at the University of Michigan and Northwestern University in the late 1960s. A long academic career at Simon Fraser University in Vancouver, Canada—"seeing clearly from clear across the border," as he put it—deepened his sense of America as a tragic nation of "glittering abstractions" whose residents' "perpetually naïve idealism" convince them that their country is exceptional.

Michael's principal complaint with my book was that no single act, or actor, could have initiated such a brutal conflict as raged in Missouri from 1861 to 1865. Indeed, it emanated from the depth and breadth and height of depravity, the human soul requiring no spark to enflame other than the presence of war itself. His view of war—and of men—led him both inevitably and rightly to rewrite the prevailing narrative of guerrillas not as cryptoheroes or warrior chieftains but as common people, farmers, neighbors, and even friends, who behaved only slightly less commonly under the duress of uncivil war. *Inside War* taught that, under such pressure, all of us are guerrillas—or easily could be.

Similarly, Michael's reviews, not only of my book but of those of many others, conformed to his view that although war is never binary, individualized warfare must be so. Thus his reviews were often warlike—combative, biting, often brilliant, and always trenchant and honest. Similarly, his disagreements with historians whose interpretations differed from his—or who differed with his interpretations—were epically ad hominem. I suffered the lash after blurbing T. J. Stiles's fine book on Jesse James, which he appreciated, although he was largely unconvinced by its argument for the politics of slavery rather than personal pathology as underpinning Missouri's inside war and catalyzing its most iconic inside warrior. Yet, near the end of his life, during a long phone conversation about my latest book manuscript, on the long and expansive border war (which he read in draft in its entirety, offering an essential critique that cued its successful revision), he conceded privately the possibility of an ideological dimension and even basis for guerrilla warfare.

As much as he had once criticized my suggestion that any single individual played so prominent a role in the genesis of Missouri's inside war, he was persuaded by my treatment of Lyon as a flawed individual who used war to exercise—more than to exorcise—inner demons. His own work would soon move to biography in the form of portraits of two of the war's most prominent military figures, William Tecumseh Sherman and Robert Edward Lee. In them, he would display a similar aversion to hagiography as he psychologized his subjects. "I disbelieve in heroes," he claimed to a Vancouver journal, "searching as I do to understand the motives and actions of human beings rather than to present stylized paragons of good and evil." Indeed, Michael became versed in psychoanalytic theory (enough to be named a board member of his adopted city's College of Psychologists) in part to inform his biographical treatments but in larger part to assess the historical failure of societies, especially American society, to evolve sufficiently morally to prevent primal passions from erupting in individualized violence and collectivized war. Just as the personalized warfare he explored in *Inside War* became a model for his understandings of Sherman and Lee, so did it lead to his later interest in terroristic violence, individual and state, as a recurrent presence in American history.

Michael's fascination with what he would later call "the dark side of American history" ultimately led him back to what drew him initially to guerrilla warfare. In one of his last public talks, in November 2012, as part of a workshop and public conference in Lawrence, Kansas, and Kansas City, Missouri, he described the Missouri-Kansas conflict, as with so many over the last five hundred years, as a "war of all against all"—a pithy variant of what he argued for the Missouri conflict a quarter century earlier in *Inside*

War. Although many, including myself, disagree with this characterization because it fails to contextualize conflicts as contingent and ideologically rooted, thus robbing them of lasting meaning and making militarized violence a human constant, one could not but marvel at the scope of his subject, his breadth of knowledge of the past, his nimble mind and thoughtful delivery, and the consistency of his interpretive trajectory. Fundamentally, Michael had not much moved from his beliefs about the inhumanity of guerrilla wars except to argue similarly about all wars, and with it all men.

Interpretive disagreements being the lifeblood of academic labor, Michael's was truly seminal, foddering a rich stable of topics for debate, inquiry, and research, resulting in a more expansive—and expansively understood—inside war. His book anticipated a number of tropes now central to historians' understandings of the Civil War, not simply in Missouri but nearly everywhere, and on both sides: guerrilla warfare as collective terrorism, hard war as spontaneous violence and military policy, class dynamics as a litigant of civilian and military responses, women and slaves as victims and participants in wartime, the evidentiary value of the Union provost marshal records, societal reconstruction in non-Reconstruction states (or "the war after the war"), guerrilla memoirs as historical narrative and mythological basis, war memory as an interpretive lens.

This volume, whose essays (including mine) more challenge than accept his conclusions about guerrilla warfare, serves as a fitting tribute not simply to Michael's incalculable contribution to this subject but to his limitless intellectual curiosity that produced it. None of these authors contest Sherman's claim that war is hell. But perhaps the authors' collective regard for Michael's life work might have convinced him that not all people are shits. I can attest fully that, with rare exception, he was one who certainly was anything but.

Introduction

Of Black Flags and History, Authentic and Apocryphal

Joseph M. Beilein Jr. and Matthew C. Hulbert

In the spring of 1864, Union soldiers were restringing telegraph line through Cross Hollow, Arkansas, when they spotted something strange. Hanging over the road—in these otherwise deserted woods—fluttered a black flag. And upon closer investigation, they discovered a note pinned to the banner. According to the Union officer's transcription, the message read, "We will kill all men that pass this road, and woe be the man that takes down this flag. J. W. Cooper, Captain, Bush." In no uncertain terms, Captain Cooper's note communicated the fundamental meaning of the flag: no quarter.[1]

The authenticity of *this* flag notwithstanding, apocryphal accounts abound of flags flying over the heads of bushwhackers, jayhawkers, and all forms of nonconventional combatants in between. As a case in point, the infamous journalist and mythmaker John Newman Edwards, in describing the September 1864 guerrilla massacre at Centralia, reported that "at the head of [Major A. V. E. Johnston's] column a black flag was carried" and "so also was there one at the head of Todd's column." Today the description of dueling flags may seem symbolic at best and melodramatic at worst—in 1877, however, Edwards represented his account as historically accurate. Even in the immediate aftermath of the war, such was the reputation of the black flag that the old propagandist employed it to warp understandings of the bloody scene to better suit his pro-Confederate brethren in Missouri. But at Centralia and myriad other locales where guerrillas and their enemies clashed, men didn't need the visual confirmation of an emblem or banner to recall the intentions of their enemies—or to know the intentions in their own hearts and minds.[2]

Rooted in reality and shrouded in myth, the black flag has long been associated with the Civil War's guerrilla conflict. When raised, the flag allegedly signaled a war without mercy, fought to the death, without exception. It was meant to instill terror in an opposing belligerent; it held the power to paralyze men before an attack had even commenced; and, more than anything, it reminded men of their own mortality—of the utter finality and loneliness of death on a battlefield. Prior to the 1860s, such emblems had made iconic appearances throughout Western history—waving high atop the masts of a buccaneer's ship or morbidly announcing the ultimate purpose of Santa Anna's army as it battered the Alamo's dwindling defenders into submission. Yet despite the apparent prevalence of the black flag on the oceans and battlefields of history, much doubt still arises over just how common such flags were along Civil War guerrilla fronts ranging from South Carolina and Virginia to Missouri, Kentucky, and even New Mexico. As far as historians can tell, there are no such flags in existence today, in any archive or museum, North or South, public or private, which might confirm their physical existence during the war.[3]

Besides historical questions regarding how widely the black flag might or might not have been used during the Civil War, there are other reasons why the association of guerrilla warfare from that period with a flag of *any kind* is altogether ironic. While conventional armies marched about in formation, signaled, charged, retreated, and otherwise maneuvered with literally hundreds of emblems and standards waving overhead, we rarely, if at all, stop to ponder the staggering multitude of flags employed by the formal armies of the Union and the Confederacy. For its part, the guerrilla war was largely a flagless one. Owing to the nature of irregular violence—a strain of warfare devoted to stealth, ambuscade, camouflage, and terror—these sorts of communicative banners were virtually nonexistent among the guerrilla ranks.

Occasionally, white flags were unfurled in one form or another. A handkerchief, shirt, sheet, or whatever was handy at the time might make an appearance from the window of a burning building or be dangled from above a rocky outcropping. (And even these white flags, as symbols of surrender and thereby of expected quarter, were relatively uncommon among most guerrillas too.) It is more than a little interesting, then, that while use of the white flag may have outweighed that of the more chic black, the ghastly acts of violence typically associated with the latter have been permanently grafted onto general perceptions of the guerrilla war. For all the instances of mercy withheld, there are others where a reprieve from death was granted; and, even minus the flags and trumpets and uniforms, the lack of mandated military structure or frequent lapses from the rules of war did not mean, inherently, that order was impossible or even temporarily uncommon. Nonetheless, these intricacies of time and place have long been hidden by the looming shadow of the black flag.

Together, the essays here cast new light into the shadows—focusing upon both the figures and places of the guerrilla conflict, as well as the historians, ideas, and mores that have shaped their popular perception since the nineteenth century. Our essayists reveal the guerrilla to be a fighter who was not the bloody monster associated exclusively with the black flag. In many of the cases that follow, the long-held perception that the guerrilla was a merciless, apolitical fiend is directly challenged. Equally important to understanding the nature of guerrilla violence is constructing a foundational definition of just who were Civil War guerrillas, what made them so, and how understandings of the war and nineteenth-century society become infinitely more complex as that definition becomes increasingly inclusive.[4]

Thereby the "flagless" warriors that appear in each essay range from the bushwhackers of the border states that have been traditionally associated with guerrilla warfare to Native American raiders in the Old Southwest to the ghostly apparition of a postwar guerrilla who haunted his old homestead along a winding Texas creek. You will also find the irregulars of wartime fiction and a guerrilla war survivor promoting his recollection of time spent with the likes of "Bloody Bill" Anderson. Even a historian makes his debut as a guerrilla, imitating the essence of his subject matter by way of his research tactics.

More important still, the public's almost reflexive association of Civil War guerrillas with the oft-abstract principles of the black flag has obscured the history of irregular warfare for more than a century. During the war, great controversy erupted on both sides concerning the legal status of guerrillas and noncombatants on the home front—the allegorical waters have been muddied ever since. In the first two years of the war, a handful of Union commanders, most notably General Henry Halleck, shifted their attention away from the formal fields of battle and refocused it on the bodies and homes of men who were not technically of the Confederate army but fought on its behalf from the bush. As the head of the Department of

Missouri—in many ways the epicenter of the "irregular crisis"—Halleck issued two orders: one in December 1861 and the other in March 1862. Together, the proclamations declared guerrillas to be brigands or common criminals and denied them the protections offered to official soldiers by the laws of war.[5]

By 1863, when the code developed by Francis Lieber was fully articulated and circulated about the Union army, Halleck's Missouri-based initiative had become a hard and fast policy for dealing with guerrillas in the field. Thus, as the war dragged on, these policies allowed Federal forces to push deeper into enemy households, freeing slaves, confiscating property, and dealing with rebel women however they saw fit in the process. As touted by the media of Halleck's day, the justifications for this turn to hard war were even more heinous acts of violence perpetrated by the guerrillas and their womenfolk. Halleck himself, however, made no such claims. He was much more concerned with bridge burning and the destruction of telegraph wires than with any acts of home-front violence.[6]

Even as Union policies regarding guerrilla activity are now coming into sharper focus for historians, the portrayal of irregulars as freakish anomalies, unknowable enigmas, land pirates, or the inventors of an unprecedented, all-out, "no-holds-barred" approach to war has lingered in the American historical consciousness for more than 150 years. As an emblem, the black flag has enabled this portrayal of Civil War guerrillas; it has flown, frequently unchallenged, as a symbol of ahistorical generality, mythologizing, and widespread misunderstanding. We propose to address these issues here and now—to unfold the deeper meanings of the black flag and to revisit the startlingly broad collection of people, places, and events it has enveloped and the history it has distorted.

One issue before all others is that of terminology. As the frontispiece of this volume illustrates, the guerrilla has not only been misrepresented as a "second-class" belligerent but also labeled with a misspelling. Here "guerrilla" is replaced with "Gorilla." There is no mistaking the intended purpose of the moniker. As made clear by the rotgut whiskey, the overgrown whiskers, and the abundance of weapons, including an upturned dagger and a cat-o'-nine-tails, it draws an immediate parallel between the nonconventional southern solider and a brand of warfare deemed unacceptable—and even simian—by Victorian standards.

Although this caustic propaganda no longer holds much sway over serious scholars of the Civil War, the all too frequent (mis)spelling of the subject continues to appear in historical literature; as a result, the guerrilla is marked as a sideshow or, in keeping with the half-man, half-critter featured in the image, a veritable freak. On this envelope, the printer offers his version of the correct spelling—"guerilla"—with a single "r." This is in fact incorrect. Yet this single-r version of the word also abounds in both amateur and scholarly works on the subject. Sometimes these appear as mere typos; other times, however, the frequency of use suggests a belief that this is the correct spelling. Much more than just a grammatical quibble, this incorrect spelling of the word *guerrilla* denotes a deeper level of misunderstanding as to the identities of these soldiers. Certainly, we do not imagine them as furry caricatures. But it is nevertheless important to remember that they were guerrillas, not "guerillas" and certainly not "gorillas."

As this collection lays bare the complexities of the guerrillas and their environment(s), a truer sense of their identities becomes manifest. These guerrillas were men and boys, and sometimes women, who eschewed the conventionality of formal military service. Oftentimes the choice to wage this more flexible brand of warfare was the product of necessity. Therein, a fight to be made but no time for dispatches, staff meetings, and brass buttons—the stuff of army manuals and the parade ground. For others the guerrilla lifestyle was an extension of preexisting cultural norms; *petit guerre* was their regular war, while the Jominian hordes stood out as alien and irregular. Guerrillas fought for the Union, the Confederacy, their ethnic groups, their tribes, and their families. They killed in ways unlike traditional soldiers, but no more or no less savagely. When the final results of the violence are juxtaposed, a pistol shot to the head of an enemy—armed or unarmed—appears no more or no less grotesque than canister mowing down a line of oncoming men, obliterating their bodies beyond recognition by even their closest comrades.

Thus, while guerrillas have been considered more destructive than Billy Yank and Johnny Reb, much of this perception arises from the idea that they were violent not only against "official" combatants but also against persons considered to be noncombatants by the formal armies. While perhaps more in keeping with mainstream understandings of the war in which it's assumed that combatants and civilians existed in mutually exclusive fronts, the various guerrilla theaters of the South offered no such separation—nor did most irregulars have the luxury of waiting for high commands to decide who and what necessitated destruction. Because more than anything else, a guerrilla was a self-constituted fighter—a self-made killer and a self-justified destroyer—who negotiated his or her own terms of service while simultaneously sustaining him- or herself and his or her people without aid from the leviathan institutions of the mid-nineteenth-century war machine.

As it grapples with the results of a society colliding head-on with irregular violence on an unprecedented scale, this volume marks the rise of a new generation of guerrilla scholars. In the years leading up to this collaboration, guerrilla studies has become an *en vogue* subfield of Civil War history, southern history, and American history. Recent meetings of the Southern Historical Association and the Society of Civil War Historians have featured panels exploring the guerrilla conflict in the Civil War, and entire symposia are now being convened to examine irregular warfare and violence on the wartime home front. Scholars and students want to know who guerrillas were, what motivated them, why they fought in the ways that they did, and what roles they played in the outcome of the war. We are in the midst of a watershed moment in guerrilla studies and Civil War studies more generally.

The new paths cut by our essayists wouldn't be possible, however, without certain foundational interpretations of the Civil War guerrilla. As Chris Phillips indicates in his foreword, much of the historical revision that follows either began with Michael Fellman's *Inside War* or has been greatly influenced by it. As a forbearer to the "dark turn" in Civil War scholarship, Fellman's irregular conflict was one of utter chaos. He painted a graphic portrait of swirling cycles of violence and aimless, but seemingly unstoppable, bloodshed. The guerrillas who mark the pages of *Inside War* begin the struggle as peaceful Christians but are quickly swallowed up by a genocidal mania when the governing limits of society are shattered and the inherently base, savage qualities of men rise to the surface.[7]

In the wake of *Inside War,* Daniel Sutherland provided a much-needed dose of military legitimacy to guerrilla studies.[8] He strove to underscore how pervasive irregular violence had really been in the 1860s and, as a result, how it could no longer be condemned by historians to a few border states or outlier locales: mainly Missouri, Kentucky, and Appalachia. While still brutal and, at times, out of control, the guerrillas of Sutherland's *A Savage Conflict* are no longer bloodlust-infected brigands or apolitical sociopaths; they wage a series of local insurgencies throughout the Union and the Confederacy that ultimately play a major—or decisive, as Sutherland puts it—role in determining the overall outcome of the war.

This newfound importance came with a double edge, however. On the one hand, it made studies of irregular violence immediately pertinent to our broadest understandings of the war through sheer volume and magnitude. In doing so, it has helped bolster a wide range of scholarship dealing with everything from the intersection of financial fraud and irregular violence to studies that blur the division between battlefront and home front once and for all. On the other hand, working on such a broad scale comes with consequences; it requires very broad strokes and much in the way of more local, state, and regional character, nuance, and detail has been necessarily lost.

The next phase of guerrilla studies will involve harnessing the importance granted irregulars by Sutherland but wielding it in more pragmatic scopes of study, as first implemented by Fellman, to not only color the remaining gray space but to reassess that which has already been colored. And so it is with this task of exploring, dissecting, and reassessing the Civil War guerrilla's place in American culture and history that we, as editors, charged our essayists. And without exception, they have raised Mencken's own proverbial black flag on its myth-ridden cousin.

In "The Hard-Line War: The Ideological Basis of Irregular Warfare in the Western Border States," Christopher Phillips surveys the interconnected factors that steered men away from regular army or militia service in Missouri and Kentucky and toward a less "official" life in the bush. While many historians have been content with the notions that independent guerrillas were either nihilists, brigands, or sociopaths (or a volatile cocktail of all three unsavory qualities), Phillips provides a more intricate look at the "inside war" of the western border states. His essay pieces together a much broader, but also nuanced, glimpse at the seemingly more "regular" social, political, and economic ideologies—ranging from ethnic tension and emancipation backlash to draft evasion and socioeconomic deprivation—that fueled the irregular war; and, in the process, by expanding our understanding of *why* guerrillas became guerrillas, Phillips throws crucial new light on how historians might also begin to rethink *who* these men and women actually were and might have been.

On the surface, Andrew William Fialka's essay, "Controlled Chaos: Spatiotemporal Patterns within Missouri's Irregular Civil War," would appear to make the other seven essays in this collection obsolete. From the 1860s to the present, historians and the public alike have understood the unpredictable, uncontrollable, altogether chaotic nature of irregular warfare as universal—this is especially true in the case of Missouri, the stomping grounds of Quantrill, "Bloody Bill" Anderson, and a host of other seasoned killers. But by way of ArcGIS and cutting-edge mapping techniques, Fialka illustrates how, in many cases, the movements and strategies employed by guerrillas corresponded precisely to the position of Union garrisons, occupation efforts, and troop movements. On its own, the essay helps bring a new sense of order to historically fragmented and independent acts of violence at the state level; however, in conjunction with the other essays here, it underscores how different types of guerrillas from locale to locale operated with varying degrees of strategic uniformity and organization. In other words, it illuminates the folly of ever having attempted to understand the guerrilla warfare during the Civil War as a monolithic, homogenous entity in the first place.

Writing from England, David Brown and Patrick J. Doyle expand the geographic parameters of guerrilla history in more ways than one. Their essay, "Violence, Conflict, and Loyalty in the Carolina Piedmont: A Comparative Perspective," provides the first comparative case study of guerrilla warfare in the Piedmont zones of South Carolina and North Carolina during the Civil War. For decades the irregular violence of the Border West has garnered the lion's share of historical consideration and, after that, most remaining attention has been diverted to the raiders of Virginia or Kentucky. But Brown and Doyle reject these traditional geographic boundaries of study; they methodically piece together the factors that created and motivated instances of guerrilla war in the Piedmont, running the gamut from political dissent and economic ruination to outright social upheaval. At the same time, their essay ultimately poses broader questions about how the results of this juxtaposition may force future historians to rethink who and what constituted a guerrilla in the Civil War South.

Megan Kate Nelson's essay incorporates new demographic and ethnic groups into the guerrilla equation—but it abandons the traditional irregular epicenter of the Border West *and* the scholarly emphasis on white guerrillas like William Clarke Quantrill and John Singleton Mosby. Instead, in "Indians Make the Best Guerrillas: Native Americans and the War for the Desert Southwest, 1861–1862," she chronicles how Native American raiders made the war an especially hellish experience for Federals and Confederates attempting to operate in the sweltering badlands and villages of the New Mexico Territory. Scholars have long accepted Indians as the inventors of guerrilla warfare in North America but too often do so in passing or anecdotally. Not only does Nelson innovatively affirm the importance of "home court" advantage in irregular warfare, but she also reveals how and why the Utes, Navajos, and Apaches, among others, kept a deadly pre-Columbian tradition (and a reputation for "savagery") alive in the desert Southwest.

On September 27, 1864, William "Bloody Bill" Anderson and a band of several hundred bushwhackers arrived in the sleepy town of Centralia, Missouri. By the time they bolted the scene that same evening, the guerrillas had pulled off two stunning massacres of Union troops and left roughly 170 dead men—many scalped or otherwise mutilated—in their wake. Matthew C. Hulbert's essay, "The Business of Guerrilla Memory: Selling Massacres and the Captivity Narrative of Sergeant Thomas M. Goodman," tells the story of the only Federal intentionally spared at Centralia. Moreover, it outlines how the published memoir of Thomas Goodman, who inexplicably survived his weeklong stint with "Bloody Bill" and company, fit within a surprisingly prevalent but unavoidably odd niche of the Civil War "memory industry." More than anything, however, Hulbert highlights how pro-Union propagandists, and especially regular soldiers caught up in the irregular conflict, attempted to push back against the increasingly dominant, pro-Confederate guerrilla mythologies emerging from the Border West.

In "Tales of Race, Romance, and Irregular Warfare: Guerrillas Fictionalized, 1862–1866," John C. Inscoe explores how the public began to assess and understand guerrilla warfare through fictional literature and via the stage in the 1860s—in some cases before the Civil War had even concluded. His essay traces the plots and production of a Richmond-based play, *The Guerrillas* (1862), along with a pair of Boston-based novels, *Cudjo's Cave* (1864) and *Among the Guerillas* (1866). In doing so, Inscoe illuminates how northerners and southerners approached wartime irregular violence in the Eastern Theater; and more importantly (as he puts it), how "these much romanticized and heavily biased treatments of individuals and families caught up in the brutality and traumas of this irregular conflict served as important forms of patriotic propaganda, while embracing a wide range of issues related to race, class, and gender, along with astute commentary on civilian and military atrocities, on the nature of Civil War loyalties, and on the larger meanings of the war."

Myriad Americans are familiar with the names of Missouri bushwhackers-turned-bandits like Jesse and Frank James or Cole Younger. Far fewer, however, remember the likes of Manse Jolly, a guerrilla from Anderson, South Carolina, who refused to hang up his guns at war's end. In his essay, "In Search of Manse Jolly: Mythology and Facts in the Hunt for a Post–Civil War Guerrilla," Rod Andrew Jr. traces Jolly's story from humble beginning to mysterious end and, on the one hand, explores how the social bandit's tale was used to explain defeat and rehabilitate manhood in the state that had likely done more to bring the ruinous war upon southerners than any other. On the other hand, though, Andrew also raises a number of critical, methodological questions concerning how scholars of the guerrilla war can and should work with and around silences in the historical record to extract traces of veracity from decades-old myth.

Joseph M. Beilein Jr.'s essay, "'Nothing but Truth Is History': William E. Connelley, William H. Gregg, and the Pillaging of Guerrilla History," explores the construction of the early histories of the guerrilla war in Missouri and the process through which Confederate guerrillas like William C. Quantrill have been wrapped in myth and hyperbole. In particular, his essay focuses on the relationship between historian William E. Connelley and former Confederate guerrilla William H. Gregg. While Gregg intended his story to set the record straight concerning Quantrill and company, Connelley ultimately used his firsthand accounts to demonize Quantrill and to condemn the Confederate cause. Here we see how a self-styled historian utilized guerrilla tactics—in a literary or scholarly context—to produce one of the first histories of the guerrilla war in Missouri and pillaged outright one of the richest sources of early guerrilla history in the Border West. Digging into the unpublished Gregg manuscript, correspondence between Gregg and Connelley, and Connelley's own notes, Beilein excavates the shaky foundation on which much of Missouri's guerrilla history has been built.

In its own distinct way, each essay here pushes us closer to an understanding of how myriad men, women, and children experienced the Civil War as a conflict of irregular wills and tactics. Whether they realized it at the time or not, the survivors of the "wars within the war" that raged from Virginia to New Mexico would not find an easy home within mainstream narratives of 1861–1865. But this "guerrilla experience" encompasses much more than just the war years, however novel or traumatic they may seem. It also involved—and, it bears mentioning, it *continues* to involve—how countless Americans have remembered, forgotten, learned about, hated, revered, and historically contextualized guerrillas long after William Quantrill, Manse

Jolly, or their Apache counterparts had faded from the wartime spotlight. In other words, to understand the guerrilla experience is to trace both guerrillas and our perceptions of them from history to memory to myth; to do this is to unfold the black flag.

Notes

1. U.S. War Department, *The War of the Rebellion: A Compilation of the Official Records of the Union and Confederate Armies* (Washington, D.C.: Government Printing Office, 1880–1901), ser. 1, vol. 34, pt. 3, p. 658 (hereinafter cited as *OR*).

2. Ibid.; John Newman Edwards, *Noted Guerrillas; or, The Warfare of the Border* (St. Louis: Bryan, Brand, 1877), 296.

3. There is some doubt as to whether flags representing no quarter were always black or if they were sometimes red—the color of warning. Such was the case at the Alamo. See Phillip Thomas Tucker, *Exodus from the Alamo: The Anatomy of the Last Stand Myth* (Havertown, PA: Casemate, 2009), 165. See also Colin Woodard, *The Republic of Pirates: Being the True and Surprising Story of the Caribbean Pirates and the Man Who Brought Them Down* (New York: Harcourt Books, 2007), 233.

4. That the dominant textbook characterizes the guerrilla war as "a no-man's land of hit-and-run raids, arson, ambush, and murder" provides a good gauge on the general perception of the guerrillas. See James McPherson, *Battle Cry of Freedom: The Civil War Era* (New York: Oxford University Press, 1988), 292.

5. *OR,* ser. 1, vol. 8, pt. 1, pp. 463, 463–64, 611–12.

6. Ibid; John Fabian Witt, *Lincoln's Code: The Laws of War in American History* (New York: Free Press, 2012). While Witt contends that the Lieber Code was really about the abolition of slavery, the straight line between Halleck's struggle with guerrillas and the Lieber Code cannot be denied. On August 6, 1862, Halleck wrote to Lieber to get his views on the usages and customs of war, "especially to the matter of guerrilla war." The screed that was Lieber's response provided the rough outline and catalyst for General Orders No. 100, or the Lieber Code. See *OR,* ser. 3, vol. 2, pt. 1, pp. 301–9.

7. Michael Fellman, *Inside War: The Guerrilla Conflict in Missouri during the American Civil War* (New York: Oxford University Press, 1989).

8. Daniel Sutherland, *A Savage Conflict: The Decisive Role of Guerrillas in the American Civil War* (Chapel Hill: University of North Carolina Press, 2009). For other important contributions to the recent wave of literature dedicated to the study of the guerrilla war, see Robert Mackey, *The Uncivil War: Irregular Warfare in the Upper South, 1861–1865* (Norman: University of Oklahoma Press, 2004); Barton Myers, *Executing Daniel Bright: Race, Loyalty, and Guerrilla Violence in a Coastal Carolina Community, 1861–1865* (Baton Rouge: Louisiana State University Press, 2009); Brian McKnight, *Confederate Outlaw: Champ Ferguson and the Civil War in Appalachia* (Baton Rouge: Louisiana State University Press, 2011).

The Hard-Line War

The Ideological Basis of Irregular Warfare in the Western Border States

Christopher Phillips

"Jeb Stuart's Ride around McClellan?" mocked Confederate veterans of the trans-Mississippi theater of their more eastern counterparts when attending postwar national encampments and reunions. "Hell, brother, Jo Shelby rode around MISSOURI!"[1]

The proudly invoked reference was the 1863 cavalry raid into southern and western Missouri led by Confederate colonel Joseph Orville "Jo" Shelby. His eight hundred horsemen covered fifteen hundred miles in forty-one days; killed or captured some eleven hundred Federal troops, six hundred guns, and six thousand horses and mules; inflicted $800,000 worth of property damage; and destroyed more than a million dollars' worth of Federal military supplies and equipment, all while evading or fighting Federal forces in the state numbering some eighty times his own. Befuddled Federal commanders futilely tried to catch and defeat Shelby's gray ghosts. Rather than surrender at the war's end, Shelby, by then a major general, and his loyal Iron Brigade sank their flags in the Rio Grande and crossed into Mexico.[2]

More than a fawning tribute to one of the war's most brilliant tactical commanders, these rebel veterans' quip was a barbed reminder of the largely forgotten war west of the Mississippi. Yet, another remembering—of the western border states' desperate war—could not have eluded them. By 1863, brutal, destructive, and ideological warfare raged there, anticipating what the broader war would soon become and likely convincing Shelby and his men to raid Missouri and not to return to it after the war.

War-weary contemporary Americans have become aware of modern insurgents' keen reckoning of benchmark dates and of their use of them to initiate new violence for partisan effect. Likely not coincidentally, Shelby's Great Raid commenced on September 22, 1863, the one-year anniversary of Abraham Lincoln's announcement of his Preliminary Emancipation Proclamation. That it commenced barely a month after the brutal attack on Lawrence, Kansas, by William Quantrill's partisan band, itself a response to the infamous Order No. 11 that depopulated nearly four Missouri counties in order to undercut the guerrillas' "domestic supply line" by making war on disloyal civilians, confirms the western dimension of the now-accepted trajectory toward what historian Mark Grimsley has called a "hard war" that began late in the summer of 1862 in the lower Mississippi Valley and was carried and intensified by Federal troops as they pushed farther south into the Confederacy.[3]

But what in fact occurred in these western border states was even more intrusive, encompassing, and enduring than what would be witnessed in the Confederacy later in the war. A hard-line war raged there, in which the politics of slavery were entwined with the actions of armies, Federal and Confederate, and civilians in states reputedly least dependent on the peculiar institution; by many historians' measure, these states were politically sensitive enough for a conciliatory form of warfare to be Congress's and the Federal armies' modus operandi there prior to 1864. That Shelby's Raid was conceived and commanded by the man reputed to be the wealthiest in his border state—a Missouri hemp planter and rope manufacturer whose home county, Lafayette, was among the state's largest slave-owning counties, whose family owned collectively nearly 150 slaves, and who, during the Missouri-Kansas Border War, led two forays of proslavery activists into the territory and in 1856 participated in the prior sack of Lawrence, for proslavery western Missourians the self-styled abolitionist capital—suggests an ideological as much as a strategic motive.[4]

Imprecision has long assisted with the politicization of the various shadow warriors in the American Civil War who so bedeviled Federal and state troops, especially in the border states. Usage of the term *guerrilla,* like *bushwhacker,* was—and is—anything but nonpartisan. Wartime Unionists referred indiscriminately to these irregulars—whether draft dodgers, partisans, outlaws, or farmers who roamed the roads at night—as guerrillas, and the Shakers at South Union, Kentucky, routinely used the term for armed Confederates generally. Unionists like George D. Prentice, the irascible editor of the *Louisville Journal* and by 1863 a harsh critic of Lincoln, quickly ridiculed hair-splitting, condemning men like John Hunt Morgan as guerrillas for attacking while disguised in Federal uniforms—a common guerrilla ruse—and often under flags of truce. Southern sympathizers, who saw uniformed horsemen as a modern incarnation of the Revolutionary War's "partizans"—irregular fighters who had in fact won this earlier war of independence—often used the term *partisan* rather than *guerrilla* to refer to these new heroes. Even as some threatened to burn her home, Missourian Elvira A. W. Scott characterized bushwhackers as "good-looking, polite, and intelligent . . . the best and bravest of the land, who have been wronged and outraged beyond endurance and have resolved to avenge their wrongs." By contrast, Confederates and their sympathizers reserved the term *guerrilla* for anonymous night riders who plagued the Unionists of their communities. Burnished into an "irregular Lost Cause" by partisan writers like John Newman Edwards, the folk hero status that emerged for Shelby, John Hunt Morgan, M. Jeff Thompson, and even William C. Quantrill, who blurred the lines between regular and irregular warfare, as for partisan raiders, Confederate cavalry, and guerrillas, firmed distinctions in the postwar years far more than among those civilians who suffered their innumerable intrusions in wartime.[5]

This essay will explore various interpretive strands surrounding the proliferation of irregular warfare in the western border region during the American Civil War, for which guerrillas and partisan cavalrymen have served as the primary vehicle. More specifically, it will argue for collective ideological over individual, personalized motives for these shadowy fighters of the "inside war," as historian Michael Fellman quotably termed the irregular conflict in Missouri. Rather than accept Fellman's discrete portrayals of guerrillas as antiauthoritarian nihilists, draft dodgers and deserters, and retributive vigilantes—tropes that have been used variously to interpret irregular fighters and all of which have basis in fact—this essay will argue for the centrality of slavery and emancipation in precipitating the fullest expression of this form of warfare in Missouri and Kentucky. Chronological evidence suggests a causal link between this region's irregular war and the broader regular war trajectory, by which the end of slavery was ascribed as a military strategy and political goal. This hard-line conflict in the western border states exploded only after Abraham Lincoln declared slavery's end to be among the war's primary objectives. After the fall of 1862, civilians and combatants alike sought more than simple security in what was by then seen widely as a war not simply of invasion but of dispossession. Once the war's scope demanded slavery's end, guerrillas, partisan raiders, and rebel cavalry unleashed collective retribution on Federal troops, militia, and civilians in the border region, largely for ideological purposes—to preserve slavery and terrorize those who sought, and fought, to end the peculiar institution in what historian Daniel E. Sutherland has aptly described as the "desperate side of the Civil War."[6]

Guerrilla warfare in these border slave states did not begin with the Confederacy's Partisan Ranger Act, introduced and supported by border state legislators expelled from the U.S. Congress and passed on April 21, 1862, which authorized Quantrill and others like him to organize and lead quasi-cavalrymen. Nor did it reach its full expression in the war's infant months. To all but the most hard-line of Federal commanders on the ground, the real guerrilla war began slowly in the western border region. By one 1861 estimate, the horsemen who would soon plague widespread parts of Missouri numbered in the hundreds, and few references mention irregular warfare at all in Kentucky prior to the summer of 1862. Indeed, that spring one Kentucky Unionist believed the new provost system would "Keep things in Order . . . a death blow to any thing like 'Guerrilla parties' being formed." Even then it was not a widespread phenomenon, largely contained in the state's Purchase area, where in November one resident claimed his counties were "completely overrun by armed bands of hostile troops and marauders." By then, Missourians had long since witnessed the type of war these Kentuckians had only recently begun to fear. In the days surrounding the defeat at Wilson's Creek in southwestern Missouri in August 1861, reports from local home guards and vigilance committees that thousands upon thousands of armed riders seemingly blanketed the entire state led John Pope and Ulysses S. Grant to question their validity. As much from frustration as from conviction, Pope required his officers to "assume command of all the Home Guards" and other bands amid such rampant rumoring and scattered police forces. Ulysses S. Grant, who had seen guerrilla warfare in Mexico and knew about unreliable intelligence, instructed subordinates to "be careful about crediting reports [about guerrillas] you receive from citizens."[7]

The motivations of these earliest night riders were as varied as their targets of opportunity. Because Lincoln's early suspension of habeas corpus gave latitude to local authorities and military commanders to make widespread arrests of "strong 'Southern Rights' men," retaliatory warfare soon followed. Beyond stealing or pressing horses (by far the most common of civilians' complaints about both guerrillas and Federal squads), night riders' main targets of opportunity were railroads and bridges as well as symbols of Federal authority—trains, riverboats, and stagecoaches, especially those carrying mail. Early in the war, Unionist newspapers offered coverage to robberies of residents by armed men, both on the road and in their homes, but just as often pointed out "Secession marauders who . . . allowed no Union men to 'sass' them." With women and children aboard, they fired on boats or derailed trains, acts that one editor claimed were "degrading to think white men would do." Later in the war, it would occur nearly too often for letter writers to mention.[8]

The irregular war in the western border states gained strength precisely as the Confederacy found itself losing the war in the West. When control of the lower Mississippi Valley became the strategic linchpin in the fall of 1862, Federal troops built a string of defensive outposts in garrison towns through the Ozark plateau and across Kentucky's southern tier—including Cassville, Springfield, Rolla, Pilot Knob, and Cape Girardeau in Missouri and Columbus, Mayfield, Russellville, Hopkinsville, Bowling Green, Lebanon, and Crab Orchard in Kentucky—often defended by blockhouses newly built by impressed slaves. They offered a demarcation of sorts of the southern extent of Federal occupation in these border states. Below was a no-man's-land, largely given up as a buffer zone, with only sporadic cavalry patrols to protect residents from the brigands who roamed it. Above was a Federal frontier with military presences in the cities and along the rivers but less or none in the smaller towns and countryside. County seats were the most regular site for garrison squads, and as pro-Confederate civilians assumed responsibility for defending their communities as well as lashed out at occupying Union troops, they and Unionist residents were soon targets of the growing number of horsemen who ranged well north of the no-man's-land.[9]

Confederate deserters and parolees demoralized by the string of western defeats in 1862 found that the Federal occupation exposed them to harassment, arrest, and even compulsory service in the state militia. Indeed, with Confederate recruitment and enrollment squads operating in their states, many took to the brush to avoid them as much as the Federals. Thomas Ewing estimated in the summer of 1863 that half of the men from the border counties of western Missouri had, "at different times since the war began, entered the rebel service. One half of them are dead or still in service; the other half, quitting from time to time the rebel armies, have returned to those counties . . . [and] have gone to bushwhacking." Many had run once already to avoid service, to Arkansas and Tennessee, only to return to their homes to avoid Confederate service. The largest portion of these "refugee Missourians" hid out, family members shielding them from military authorities. Hilled and mountainous areas, such as the Ozarks and eastern Kentucky, saw the worst, with many deserters there "committing all kinds of mischief, plundering the families of the soldiers who are serving in our [Federal] regiment." An exasperated garrison commander at Mount Sterling, Kentucky, in the "brushy portion" of the state's central counties, as one Unionist put it, claimed bitterly that he was unable to control the "outrages there Committed by them" and "that it was impossible for the Union men of that locality to live in security, while these men remained in their midst." Provost marshals had been releasing captured deserters and "repentant Guerrillas" under oath and bond, forcing the department commander, Jeremiah T. Boyle, to order subordinates to stop. The following summer, John M. Schofield was certain that many such parolees from the lower Mississippi Valley, where the war had by then turned harder, "have come back to Missouri—many of them, doubtless, in the hope of being permitted to remain at their former homes in peace, while some have come under instructions to carry on a guerrilla warfare, and others, men of the worst character, become marauders on their own account, caring nothing for the Union nor for the rebellion."[10]

Sweeps by garrisoning troops resulted in arrest, imprisonment, or exile for many deserters trying to get home to their occupied states. For those who managed it, ostracism and anomie greeted many, making it unlikely that they would remain peaceful, much less loyal. One released Louisville Confederate found little for him in his occupied home. "He could not go to church, without having his horse and saddle taken from him. . . . He was treated at home, by them, as though he was not their equal. . . . He said that he must fight the enemy." Many quietly went back under arms. Jacob Snowden, who had ridden as a guerrilla in 1861 and was paroled in the fall of 1862, boasted when arrested in arms again that "he would be God-damned if he had not been in the brush, and he would be God-damned if he did not go to the brush again . . . that he would bushwhack as soon as the leaves came out." Snowden was sentenced to hard labor.[11]

In combination with a hardening war in the summer of 1862, the implementation of national conscription drove many alienated Federal soldiers out of the ranks and into the brush, in "which only loyal men are the sufferers." Federal deserters, too, found their way home to these border states to take up bushwhacking. When captured as a guerrilla near Lewisport, Kentucky, Martin V. Asher was identified by Federal authorities as a deserter from his Indiana infantry regiment and one who had seen the elephant under the name John Wallace. The backlash against conscription soon drove border slave state Unionists to Lincoln's door, prevailing upon him not to allow enrollment to be implemented in their states for fear of the chaos that would ensue. In January 1863 an anxious president feared that any arms the government might provide Kentucky should Congress authorize the new militia enrollment would result in them being "turned against the government" by the state's angry residents. In Missouri, Schofield's militia draft put off Federal enrollment and state officials wrangled with the Lincoln administration over the question of whether state militia were in fact Federal troops. A similar militia authorization in Kentucky, as well as delaying tactics by the state legislature and its congressional leaders, accomplished much the same, although recruiting even for the home guards lagged badly despite bounty inducements. Drafts thus served border state authorities as threats more than as recruiting tools, and no border state district required a Federal draft before 1864. Once they did, the president of Kentucky's Union League claimed that "every draft . . . puts more men into the rebel than in the Union Army," while a Federal officer concluded that the numerous irregulars in his area were largely "composed of men who were drafted for our service."[12]

Draft evasion, whether Confederate or Federal, also contributed to the rise of guerrilla warfare in the summer of 1862. In Missouri on July 22, John M. Schofield authorized the enrollment of all able men between the ages of eighteen and forty-five into the Enrolled Missouri Militia (EMM) specifically to combat irregulars plaguing parts of the state. By November some seventy regiments had been raised, supported nearly entirely by levies and confiscation of property, including horses, mules, furniture, and valuables. (With horses and mules valued from $125 to $160 each by 1864, such levies were felt deeply.) Schofield's militia call required even the disloyal and Confederate sympathizers, past and present, to report to local posts to take the oath, enroll, and give up all weapons. Although they were then allowed to return to their homes and live out the war so long as they would "in no way give aid or comfort to the enemy," those who refused were often marked as disloyal, and those who paid a ten-dollar commutation tax were regarded with distrust. Harassment often followed. Many left for the Far West or Canada, unwilling either to enter the Confederate ranks or to serve in the state militia. Singly and in groups, many enlisted in the state—or in Kentucky, county—militias or home guards to avoid the Federal draft, to infiltrate and disrupt these militias, or to prevent armed Unionists from targeting their families. Indeed, many men who sought to remain in their home states yet refused to serve either their state or federal governments found themselves with little choice but to take up bushwhacking. Those who sought to remain out of the fight entirely, including returning militia, home guards, or Confederate enlistees, often found themselves beset by guerrilla recruiters. In southeastern Missouri, partisan leader Tim Reeves, a nonslaveholding Baptist minister, conscripted local men into service under threat of execution for refusal. "If a man cannot join one or the other party he has no business here," grimly wrote Missouri's Elvira Scott. "He is between fires . . . [with] nothing left but to choose sides."[13]

Conscription alone did not account for the inside war that raged across the border slave states. Its ideological dimension soon enough became clear. The protection of slavery framed a core dimension of the irregular war nearly at the war's outset, and slavery and civilians were quickly integrated into it. Historians Mark Geiger and Don Bowen have found that slavery framed many western Missourians' early decisions to head for the brush. When federal and state authorities took over the region's banks in late 1861, many pro-Confederate Missourians, hailing disproportionately from the upper strata of Missouri rural society, who had for years been engaging in for-profit commercial agriculture and who had invested heavily in railroad construction during the 1850s in order to gain greater access to national markets, saw their farms and slaves auctioned, denying sons in these dispossessed families their economic and cultural inheritances. Many responded not by enlisting in the Confederate service but by becoming irregulars who would wage war upon those who had robbed them. In Missouri's Boon's Lick, four-fifths of identified "bushwhackers" came from indebted families whose property was sold in the estate sales. The families of guerrillas in one western Missouri county were some three times as likely to have owned slaves and twice as likely to have possessed real wealth, including slaves, as an average white male Missourian. Moreover, their families held on average nearly twice as many bondpeople as the average slaveholding family in their home county.[14]

If the postwar recollections of several former guerrillas are reliable (they certainly are not unbiased), self-styled southern residents who took up arms against the government in the war's first year were responding to more than threats to their capital investments. Many took to the brush as a response to the ideological nature of the war with regard to slavery. After Kansas jayhawkers burned their family's home in western Missouri and state militia murdered and robbed their father, Cole Younger and his younger brother joined William C. Quantrill's guerrilla band. By Samuel Hildebrand's admission, his long-standing antipathy for his southeastern Missouri township's antislavery German American majority, largely antislavery Republicans, began his guerrilla career. "The union men were making war upon me," Hildebrand claimed later, "but I was making no war upon them, for I still wished to take no part in the national struggle." When the vigilance committee in his community "became a machine of oppression," persecuting those judged disloyal, and after an "unscrupulous mob" had driven him from his home, hanged his brother and an uncle for guerrilla activities, and brought down a squad of militia cavalry to ambush him, nearly kill him, and burn his home, Hildebrand rode into the woods. "The die was cast—for the sake of revenge, I pronounced myself a Rebel." He soon "rejoiced" in his killing of German soldiers, often by hanging them. That both Younger and Hildebrand hailed from slaveholding families was likely not mere literary device.[15]

Confederates and their sympathizers and even some Unionists were by then openly casting blame for this desperate war not on roving guerrillas but rather on the federal government—particularly the Federals and militias who occupied the loyal border states. Though an emancipationist, George Caleb Bingham had long been incensed by Kansas jayhawkers' and antislavery militias' "predatory warfare" in Missouri, including the indiscriminate freeing of slaves. "They have made war upon Union Men as fiercely as upon Secessionists," the artist railed, believing federal military policy intended to drive from the state all supporters of slavery. Indeed, in the summer prior to Shelby's Raid, hard-liner Benjamin F. Loan threatened to execute "the first half dozen Secessionists whom he could find nearest to the Spot" of guerrilla depredations and ordered the burning of private dwellings. Identifying the victims as "consisting of women and children chiefly . . . charged with *no offense whatever,*" Bingham complained to Federal commander John M. Schofield that these troops were "turn[ing] peaceable and quiet citizens into desperate guerillas [*sic*]." When Missouri cavalryman and quasi-guerrilla M. Jeff Thompson famously announced that he would "'*hang, draw,* and quarter' a minion of said Abraham Lincoln" for every person that John C. Frémont ordered put to death for carrying arms in the fall of 1861, he also was responding to the Federal commander's infamous emancipation order—to "confiscate the property and free the negroes belonging to the members of the Missouri State Guards." The following spring, a slaveholding Confederate sympathizer saw too that a hard-line war made inevitable the end of slavery. "Jayhawkers were plundering their neighbors, burning their houses, and laying waste the country, stealing Negroes and everything they could lay their hands on," wrote Elvira Scott in March 1862. "People have and will retaliate; it is human nature."[16]

The fall midterm elections in 1862 spurred antiauthoritarian guerrillas to target government officials, federal and county, from postmasters to judges. Understanding the nature of their insurgency, they hunted officeholders or draft board members, who by extension represented the legitimacy of the federal government. Nelson McDowell, a Missouri probate judge, was captured in August 1862 by a band of guerrillas that he estimated to number around five hundred. They forced him to resign his office "by signing an obligation not to hold office &c. under the present rulers of our once happy, but now distracted government." Unionist legislators, regardless of their stance on slavery, were among the first to become actual targets of irregulars. Kentuckian Samuel Haycraft, a former state senator turned clerk of the Elizabethtown circuit court, hid out in the fall of 1862 when John Hunt Morgan's cavalry rode into town, "having searched the Clerks office and some private houses." U.S. congressman Aaron Harding well knew that he was a particular prize for guerrilla bands in southern Kentucky. He too left his Greensburg home for Washington that fall, "lest the guerrillas might fall behind our army and seek an interview with me."[17]

In late summer in 1862, the spreading irregular war in Missouri caused the new Federal commander in the state, John M. Schofield, to devise a new approach to suppressing night riders. Believing the "desperate and sanguinary guerrilla war" to have begun with conscription, Schofield announced his intention to combat guerrillas with renewed ferocity. "The time is passed when insurrection and rebellion in Missouri can cloak itself under the guise of honorable warfare," he declared. Beyond assessments, Schofield's policy called for nothing less than summary justice for irregulars, a revival of Frémont's earlier policy. Those "caught in arms" would be shot down where they were. Citizens were expected to assist the militia in finding and capturing bushwhackers, and they could expect punishment should they not.

While implementation of his hardened war policies in Missouri was soon ensnared in political wrangling (after complaints by the national Union League about Schofield's conservatism, Lincoln relieved him only to reinstate him in 1863), their impact was immediate. One Iowa soldier wrote in February 1863 that his advocacy of hard-line war was a product of the recent explosion of guerrilla warfare. "If I had my way I would devastate the whole region," he spat, "and shoot every man I caught running from the flames of the burning homes. . . . These villains are the cause of it all."[18]

Historians often ascribe the rapid expansion of guerrilla warfare in the spring of 1863 to its national dimension—using the Lieber Code as a reference point. Only recently has it found connection with an antislavery foundation. In late July 1862, Henry W. Halleck, the army's general in chief, solicited Francis W. Lieber, a published expert on international law and war then on faculty at Columbia University, to offer a legal framework for combating the irregular fighters plaguing the occupied portions of the slave states. The general's choice was not born of simple respect for a fellow intellectual. The Prussian-born Lieber had recently published an article emphasizing the centrality of slavery to the war effort and rebuking Federal officers for returning to their owners fugitive slaves who entered Federal lines, according to laws of war they in fact misunderstood. (Lieber traveled to Virginia and met with Benjamin Butler, who famously refused to return slave "contrabands," and sent the article to Halleck, who was persuaded by it.) As a reformed former slaveholder turned practical abolitionist, Lieber would soon deliver a jeremiad to New York's Loyal League entitled "No Party Now but All for Our Country," offering a typology for all-or-nothing patriotism that antislavery Republicans would adopt to wage a hard-line war against home-front dissenters. For Lieber, the self-styled "Genesis" of his code, and the basis for guerrilla war, was the destruction of slavery. In April 1863 Lincoln approved what was issued as General Orders No. 100, a careful categorization of irregular combatants by which to assign punishments. The Lieber Code defined as military necessity all measures "indispensable for securing the ends of the war," which in effect offered constitutional sanction to many of the Lincoln government's hard-line war initiatives—martial law, suspension of habeas corpus, confiscation of the property of the disloyal, and emancipation. Drawing from existing precedent in international law, as Lieber indicated in an 1862 pamphlet, and responding to the blurring of statuses of irregular warriors hastened by the Partisan Ranger Act, Lieber's policies toward guerrillas offered discretion while targeting such fighters and allowing for their capital and summary punishment. Because Lieber's code included the term "guerrilla" among such terms as "robbers, pirates, armed prowlers, and war-rebels," in effect it classified all irregulars as outside the "laws of warfare" and denied them the rights of legitimate soldiers. Moreover, while calling for the military's restraint in administering it, the code made civilians who aided these guerrillas, including women, subject to military punishment. Indeed, as the code's most recent scholar has concluded generally, while establishing firm limits to wartime behaviors of armies and governments, especially to retaliatory targeting of black soldiers and their white officers, it simultaneously "featured the more elastic limit of military necessity" in its response to guerrilla warfare.[19]

Seen as linked with emancipation, the Lieber Code responded particularly to the rapid escalation of guerrilla violence, especially in the West. Evidence drawn from the official reports submitted to the Federal and Confederate war departments by commanders in the field supports the argument for an irregular war in Missouri and Kentucky that escalated rapidly in the summer and fall of 1862, coincident with conscription and especially emancipation. A disproportionate number of reports involving guerrillas or bushwhackers are dated after January 1, 1863, the date on which the Emancipation Proclamation took effect, and the number reached its apex in the spring, summer, and fall of 1864. After combining these totals, just 14 percent of these reports occurred prior to January 1, 1863, while 86 percent of these reports occurred after that date. If this evidence bears merit, a chronology of sorts of the guerrilla war emerges from the reports that coincides with the federal government's hardened war initiatives that began in the summer of 1862.[20]

Quantified evidence about Missouri's irregular war in the Union Provost Marshal Papers only confirms this chronology. Of the 822 (of 933) dated files that include the terms *guerrilla, guerrillas,* or *bushwhackers,* only two are dated prior to 1862. The 1862 and 1863 files, when grouped by month and date, offer a startling pattern. Of the 238 files for 1862, 145 of 238 entries, or 61 percent, occurred *after* Lincoln's announcement of the Preliminary Emancipation Proclamation, meaning that a majority of the year's total guerrilla-related incidents occurred in just the year's final three months. Of the 151 files with guerrilla-related activities for 1863, 108 (or just under 75 percent) occurred in the early spring and early summer, an obvious extension of emancipation-related violence.[21]

If the words of guerrillas and Federals are any measure, emancipation stimulated eradicative tactics by both sides. Within two weeks of news of Lincoln's proclamation, on October 11, 1862, Theophilus H. Holmes, the new commander of the Confederacy's Trans-Mississippi Department, complained to Samuel R. Curtis that the "barbarous" executions of captured guerrillas by Federal troops in Missouri and Arkansas was actually hardening the war in the region. "The war of extermination thus declared against the men of the South is infinitely more such a war when extended to the women and children of the South," he warned. But the real "infamy" was in truth far broader. "The proclamation of your President apparently contemplates, and the act of your officers in putting arms in the hands of slaves seems to provide for, even that extremity. It cannot in such a situation be expected that we will remain passive, quietly acquiescing in a war of extermination against us, without waging a similar war in return." Holmes received an answer just a week later, in the form of John McNeil's mass execution of ten prisoners, uniformed as well as civilian, in Palmyra, Missouri, a reprisal for a Unionist's abduction. It immediately became known widely as the Palmyra Massacre and followed a less well-known execution of eleven prisoners charged with bushwhacking. Starting in 1863, drumhead executions of suspected guerrillas were carried out in earnest throughout Missouri, after the department commander, Henry W. Halleck, had ordered that "predatory partisans, and guerrilla bands . . . are liable to the same punishment which was imposed upon guerrilla bands by Napoleon in Spain and by Scott in Mexico." (The month before, Halleck had ordered that those caught in the act of destroying public property "will be immediately shot." Local commanders eagerly obliged.) Schofield boasted in his diary that in late 1862 guerrillas "were, under my orders executed on the spot when captured, and hundreds of sympathizers banished or imprisoned." (Such banishments were frequently to the free states and continued to the end of the war; for Missourians, the terms often forced them to remove specifically east of Illinois, thus burdening Indiana especially with what one provost marshal claimed were "bad men from Missouri.") Having watched the war in their state turn retributive the previous autumn, in the spring of 1863 two of those who first took out for Missouri's greening woods to ride as guerrillas were Frank and Jesse James.[22]

Once the war changed, guerrillas and partisans sought to shred the fabric of the very society they claimed to protect. Speaking of Morgan's raiders, South Union's Shakers in November 1862 said that "the negroes are often hunted by these soldiers, like wild beasts," and they often were hanged. A few months later, one western Missouri bushwhacker vowed to Curtis that he waged war "for no other cause than being opposed to the negro-thieving policy of the Administration." For this, he would show no quarter. Another vengeful Missouri guerrilla threatened to "kill a Radical for every house that is burnt." Missing mail became a regular source of anxiety for Unionists in particular, especially when their correspondence exposed their political views. In December 1862 one Kentuckian wrote to a county court judge asking why he had received no reply to his recent correspondence, which had discussed "the Presidents Proclamation. . . . I suppose it must have fallen into the hands of the Gorillas." That same month, using familiar language, a prominent Kentucky Unionist, Hiram Carver, a recent candidate for office who had helped to capture three notorious guerrillas only to see them released, claimed they and other residents now "hunted [him] with dogs, like wild beasts," a charge reported by national newspapers as occurring widely in the state, while a western Kentucky congressman claimed that his local circuit judge was "driven to bay, and forted in the court house where he had practiced law and administered justice for twenty years." More than for self-defense, the judge's stance was protective of his office and society. Raiders and guerrillas often destroyed court, tax, and other documents housed in these courthouses. In late January 1863 Benjamin F. Loan, commander of the Enrolled Missouri Militia in central Missouri, wrote to Samuel R. Curtis that "in several counties in the district no courts of record of any kind have held a session for several terms past. . . . The records have been stolen, perhaps destroyed, and the civil officers driven from the country." Of the thirty-five Missouri courthouses destroyed, damaged, or disrupted by Confederates or guerrillas during the war, eighteen, or more than half, were in the southern part of the state, where the Federal presence lessened in the winter of 1862. All but two occurred after the announcement of emancipation. Of the twenty-two Kentucky courthouses burned during the war, nineteen were burned in its last fifteen months. Of them, twelve were destroyed by Confederate raiders, eight by guerrillas, and two by Federal troops, and most were in the western and southern parts of the state. Garrisoning troops, especially militia, were often forced not only to protect civil government but to perform civil functions.[23]

At once hunted and empowered, guerrillas adapted their tactics to evade pursuers and maximize their image as protectors. Some sported leather or embroidered cloth "guerrilla shirts" to advertise their independence and ferocity, but far more simply donned Federal uniforms or civilian garb. Many had recently deserted the militia, so they already possessed uniforms and equipage, with which they preyed upon Unionist citizens at their homes. Although a Confederate wearing a Federal uniform would, if captured, be automatically tried as a spy and sentenced to death, Unionist guerrilla bands did likewise, often while serving in the militia or home guards, leading one Missourian to conclude in 1863 that "one half the Bushwhackers seen is the enrolled militia." Civilians fought back, shooting and often killing night riders who approached their homes and spawning vigilante executions. "Men are shot or hung every few days on the most trivial of pretexts," wrote one Missouri woman in November 1862. "It has become so common that it excites no remark."[24]

When the veteran troops moved south, militia or home guards nearly exclusively manned the various permanent and temporary posts and garrisons in the region. Hard-liners in Missouri and Kentucky, especially German Americans, believed the militia was in fact soft on proslavery residents who were fueling the growing insurgency and urged even stronger measures. Government troops and militia, their ranks now infused with enlistees often "driven from their homes by rebel guerrillas," evinced ferocity by outright abuses of civilians. State guard troops occupying Calhoon, Kentucky, arrested three citizens in the middle of the night and extorted $490 for their release. Missouri militia confronted Frank and Jesse James's stepfather, Reuben Samuel, a slaveholding physician, and briefly hanged him from a tree in the front yard of his Clay County home, until he revealed the nearby hiding place of a guerrilla band. (They then arrested him.) Missouri's governor was forced to defend the EMM against powerful political criticism in the state and in the Lincoln administration, most notably Frank and Montgomery Blair, who called for its disbanding in favor of more controllable Federal troops.[25]

Outraged at the president's act, state and county militia and their officers often waged insurgent warfare against known loyalists. Having remained at home in their states largely for ideological reasons and suspicious of the federal administration's intent, many in these militias dissented against the new war direction even more furiously—and more demonstrably—than did the region's federalized troops. For slaveholding officers like Kentucky-born Odon Guitar, an experienced district commander in northern Missouri, the recruitment of proslavery militia might better gain the trust of locals than would Federals' and militias' hard-line treatment. He soon found otherwise. In February 1863, residents in Chariton County complained that William Moberly, commander of the Thirty-Fifth Enrolled Missouri Militia, ordered his men to arrest Unionists, enrolled former Confederates as officers, abused slaves who expressed support for the government, and confiscated slaves from these same Unionist owners to harvest his tobacco. When antislavery Federal and militia commanders and provost marshals issued free papers to fugitives, proslavery EMM commanders began using their men as uniformed slave patrols. One Callaway County EMM officer, Isaac M. Snedecor, accused of using his men to return freedmen to bondage, replied defiantly to critics that his men "are not negro thieves—they are not fighting to free the negroes. . . . If this be a disloyal act, I can state that the Callaway militia are 'disloyal' . . . less [than] an abolitionist and negro thief and those who are in the name of loyalty endeavoring to overthrowing that Constitution and divert this war from its legitimate object and purpose." Another EMM officer in a neighboring county pulled a revolver on an antislavery resident who obstructed one such kidnapping, calling him a "God damned Dutch Son of a Bitch" and threatening to kill him.[26]

Efforts to purify militias were often ineffective, and southern sympathizers and outright disloyalists in these regiments often acted as regulators. Missouri's provisional government authorized a new militia organization, the Provisional Enrolled Missouri Militia (PEMM), constituted of local men who ostensibly supported the war's new radicalism—including emancipation—to replace the EMM. (State commanders moved some PEMM regiments from the state's northern counties to western and central Missouri.) In several of the northwestern counties, after initially stabilizing sections of the region, within weeks of Order No. 11 two of the PEMM regiments were disbanded for mutiny, the leading officers tried for treason, and the others sent to prison. Hard-liners vilified the Paw Paws, as they were called, for their apparent sympathy with the guerrillas, claiming that some of them were former Confederate soldiers. "After rallying all the forces that could be obtained," wrote one provost marshal in December 1863, "they would declare for the Confederate flag," and as a later writer recalled, they "went to the rebels by whole companies." Many others attacked known "radical[s], as we say . . . from the bushes, or as guerrillas, or as the army of the supposed Confederacy." By war's end in common usage among Unionists in Missouri, the epithet "Paw Paw" was synonymous with latent disloyalty.[27]

After a summer lull in 1863, the ideological inside war exploded anew. On August 21, 1863, William C. Quantrill, claiming a Confederate commission as a partisan ranger, boldly attacked Lawrence, Kansas, the longtime abolitionist capital and army enlistment site for liberated Missouri slaves. Screaming "Jennison!" and "Osceola!"—obvious allusions to destructive jayhawker raids—Quantrill's 450 raiders murdered nearly two hundred of Lawrence's townsmen, often in front of their families, and destroyed virtually all of the town's businesses and a hundred of its private homes, totaling some $2 million of property. The raid served as a shocking indication that the western region's hard-line war would become even deadlier. Revenge-seeking Kansas troops and Unionist militia stationed on the border moved beyond hunting for Lawrence's assailants and targeted bushwhackers and supportive residents both inside and outside the Burnt District. The likelihood that their families would soon become the targets of Federal reprisals immediately increased. In early September, Ewing claimed that his men had killed 220 bushwhackers since he assumed command, "more than have been killed on the border before since the war began." Lincoln himself was among those outraged by the carnage in Lawrence. Within days, writing a letter to a longtime friend that he later read at a massive rally in Springfield, Illinois, Lincoln was given to defend the recent harder turn of the war as a remedy to guerrilla violence. "Let us be quite sober," he intoned. "Civilized belligerents do all in their power to help themselves, or hurt the enemy, except a few things regarded as barbarous or cruel. Among the exceptions are the massacre of vanquished foes, and non-combatants, male and female." Short of this, the president supported targeted reprisals. One Missouri Unionist deplored the resulting robberies, burnings, and even murders of citizens that followed Quantrill's Raid because they induced civilians to see guerrillas as security forces. "The policy pursued has caused hundreds of good men to leave their homes and fly to the bushes for protection," he reported, "while others have actually joined the guerrillas as a measure of safety, believing that they would be less liable to danger there than at their homes.[28]

Only a month later, when Jo Shelby's horsemen entered the state, they were astounded at the devastation they found everywhere. "The southern, southwestern, and some of the middle counties of Missouri are completely desolated," Shelby wrote in his report. "In many places for 40 miles not a single habitation is to be found. . . . On this route every house belonging to a Southern family has been burned, and the family as effectually destroyed." In turn, his vengeful troops preyed upon African Americans, especially those in Federal uniform, and German Americans, Missouri's most consistent antislavery constituency. As retribution for the Federals' burning of nearby Sarcoxie, Shelby burned Bower's Mill, or Oregon, "a notorious pest spot for the militia . . . swept from the face of the earth, to pollute it no more forever." As Shelby's men thundered through Missouri, Quantrill's guerrillas attacked a four-hundred-man garrison at Baxter Springs, Kansas, killing a fourth of the troops—many black, and after they had surrendered—in a scenario that would play out elsewhere in the West with increasing frequency, most notably at Fort Pillow and Poison Springs.[29]

The long-delayed enlistment of African Americans, which began in Missouri in December 1863 and in Kentucky in July 1864, unleashed the irregular war's full ideological fury. Guerrillas attacked escaping slaves while Unionist slaveholders used court writs to retrieve their slave property. According to one Missouri newspaper, a year after the Emancipation Proclamation some 1,987 of Missouri's enlisted Federal soldiers were listed as having deserted from the state's twenty-five infantry regiments, as well as from its batteries and cavalry. In the summer of 1864, Lydia Montague saw firsthand the ideological focus of the guerrilla war in her new western home. A Connecticut native, Montague was sent in June by the American Missionary Association to Jefferson City to open a school for freedpeople. After struggling to find lodgings to rent both for herself and for her school from hostile "Cesesh" residents, Montague settled into a small log house in town. She soon had more than fifty students, who often spilled out into the dusty streets during lessons. Local white boys often threw rocks and broke into her school, and adults (among them, she concluded, the militia commander) routinely cursed her as a "nigger teacher." Their daily slings and arrows were nothing compared with an early September guerrilla raid that targeted her school, her students, and those who supported them and convinced Montague to flee to St. Louis. "The Guerrillas came so near us as to kill one of the boarders and wound another," she wrote unstoically. "The Guerrillas are it seems trying to rid the State of every radical voter. In many instances they have scalped them, after murdering them in the most savage manner. . . . This class of men, have not dared to sleep in their houses this summer." One resident of western Missouri claimed that of the more than thirty guerrilla murders committed in his county during the previous year, "we do not know of but one case . . . of any one having been killed by bushwhackers that was not a *Radical*."[30]

By that time, the guerrilla war had met a fuller hard-line complement. Thomas Ewing would soon extend his border removal strategy to southeastern Missouri, claiming that Federal troops there must "renovate" the region. "In one way or another the worst rebel families . . . must be got out before corn planting." In Kentucky, Eleazer A. Paine and Stephen E. Burbridge were implementing a brutal war against guerrillas and southern sympathizers that Paine styled a "plan of salvation," with execution squads often composed entirely of African American soldiers. As William Tecumseh Sherman prepared to march his army across central Georgia to the sea, anticipating guerrilla resistance that he would counter with "a devastation more or less relentless," the army's judge advocate general, Kentuckian and hard-liner Joseph Holt, gave his blessing to such warfare generally. "Guerrillas are upon the land what pirates are upon the sea," he wrote in August 1864. "They are *hostis humani generis,* and are entitled to no quarter."[31]

Among the spectrum of guerrillas and their individual motivations to wage shadow warfare in the western border states, slavery and emancipation provided a collective ideological basis. But the intertwined nature of irregular warfare, emancipation, and evolving war policy there that resulted in the Lieber Code had an unintended outcome. The western conflict might have anticipated the hard war that Federal forces introduced in the lower Mississippi Valley and Georgia, but this later form of war applied mostly to the targeted destruction of civilian property, the selected exile of civilians, and the emancipation of slaves. However strong their impulse to the contrary, the implementation of the Lieber Code in many ways curbed Sherman's troops' desire to use extensive violence against noncombatants on their infamous March to the Sea before they were unleashed on Columbia, South Carolina, in 1865. This restrained war making in the heart of the Confederacy stood in contrast to a hard-line war that raged in the loyal western slave states, one that was politicized, expansive, enduring, and deadlier than elsewhere. Driven by antislavery Federal troops' responses to intractable proslavery populations and by civilians', cavalry raiders', and guerrillas' responses to emancipation and especially black enlistment, Jo Shelby's famed 1863 ride was conducted as a western way of war that had long since drawn a hard line on the landscape of violence that was the American Civil War.

Notes

1. Daniel O'Flaherty, *General Jo Shelby: Undefeated Rebel* (1954; reprint, Chapel Hill: University of North Carolina Press, 2000), xiv.

2. Jo[seph]. O. Shelby to L. A. MacLean, November 16, 1863, in *The War of the Rebellion: A Compilation of the Official Records of the Union and Confederate Armies* (Washington, D.C.: Government Printing Office, 1880–1901), ser. 1, vol. 22, pt. 1, p. 678 (hereinafter cited as *OR*).

3. Mark Grimsley, *The Hard Hand of War: Union Military Policy toward Southern Civilians, 1861–1865* (Cambridge: Cambridge University Press, 1995).

4. LeeAnn Whites, "Forty Shirts and a Wagonload of Wheat: Women, the Domestic Supply Line, and the Civil War on the Western Border," *Journal of the Civil War Era* 1 (March 2011): 56–78.

5. *Lexington (KY) National Unionist,* November 11, 1864; James A. Ramage, *Rebel Raider: The Life of General John Hunt Morgan* (Lexington: University Press of Kentucky, 1986), 6; *St. Louis Daily Missouri Republican,* August 25, 28, 1863; Daniel E. Sutherland, "Guerrilla Warfare, Democracy, and the Fate of the Confederacy," *Journal of Southern History* 68 (May 2002): 267–69; *South Union Journal,* January 29, 1863, entry, Shakers of South Union, Kentucky, Collection, 1800–1916, Mss. 63, Special Collections and Archives, Western Kentucky University, Bowling Green (hereinafter cited as WKU); Elvira A. W. Scott diary, typescript, Mss. 1053, folder 4, pp. 94–99; folder 7, p. 197, folder 8, pp. 212–16, University of Missouri, Western Historical Manuscripts Collection, Joint Collection—State Historical Society of Missouri/University of Missouri, Ellis Library, Columbia (hereinafter cited as SHSM); [Elizabeth Pendleton Hardin,] *The Private War of Lizzie Hardin: A Kentucky Confederate Girl's Diary of the Civil War in Kentucky, Virginia, Tennessee, Alabama, and Georgia,* ed. G. Glenn Clift (Frankfort: Kentucky Historical Society, 1962), 75, 89; Daniel E. Sutherland, *A Savage Conflict: The Decisive Role of Guerrillas in the American Civil War* (Chapel Hill: University of North Carolina Press, 2009), 167–70; Scott J. Lucas, "'Indignities, Wrongs, and Outrages': Military and Guerrilla Incursions on Kentucky's Civil War Home Front," *Filson History Quarterly* 73 (October 1999): 367–69; James B. Martin, "Black Flag over the Bluegrass: Guerrilla Warfare in Kentucky, 1863–1865," *Register of the Kentucky Historical Society* 86 (Autumn 1988): 370–75; Matthew C. Hulbert, "Constructing Guerrilla Memory: John Newman Edwards and Missouri's Irregular Lost Cause," *Journal of the Civil War Era* 2 (March 2012): 58–81.

6. *Richmond (IN) Broad Axe of Freedom,* February 13, 1864; Scott diary, July 23, 1863 entry, folder 8, p. 212, SHSM; Robert R. Mackey, *The Uncivil War: Irregular Warfare in the Upper South, 1861–1865* (Norman: University of Oklahoma Press, 2004), 205–6; Sutherland, "Guerrilla Warfare," 281–83, 287–88; Sutherland, *Savage Conflict,* 10–11, 16–17, 38–40, 100–101; James C. Scott, *Weapons of the Weak: Everyday Forms of Peasant Resistance* (New Haven, CT: Yale University

Press, 1985), xvi; Stathis N. Kalyvas, "The Ontology of 'Political Violence': Action and Identity in Civil Wars," *Perspectives on Politics* 1 (2003): 482–83; Michael Fellman, *Inside War: The Guerrilla Conflict in Missouri during the American Civil War* (New York: Oxford University Press, 1989), 23; Daniel E. Sutherland, *Guerrillas, Unionists, and Violence on the Confederate Home Front* (Fayetteville: University of Arkansas Press, 1999), 3. On June 17, 1862, Thomas C. Hindman, commander of the Confederate Trans-Mississippi Department, issued an order calling for the organization of partisan rangers to assist conscription in Missouri. Robert E. Lee and other Confederate regulars persuaded Congress to repeal the Partisan Ranger Act on February 17, 1864. For southernized biographies of border state partisan rangers, see especially O'Flaherty, *General Jo Shelby;* Ramage, *Rebel Raider;* Ramage, *Gray Ghost: The Life of Col. John Singleton Mosby* (Lexington: University Press of Kentucky, 1999); and Doris Land Mueller, *M. Jeff Thompson: Missouri's Swamp Fox of the Confederacy* (Columbia: University of Missouri Press, 2007).

7. Sutherland, *Savage Conflict,* 122–52, 154; Martin, "Black Flag over the Bluegrass," 368–70; Benjamin Franklin Cooling, *Forts Henry and Donelson: The Key to the Confederate Heartland* (Knoxville: University of Tennessee Press, 1987), 205–10; Sallie Hendricks to Abram W. Hendricks, September 12, 1862, Abram W. Hendricks Papers, Mss. SC733, Indiana Historical Society Library, Indianapolis (hereinafter cited as IHSL); John Raymer to Orlando Brown, June 3, 1862, Orlando Brown Papers, Mss. A/B879, folder 38a, Filson Historical Society, Louisville, Kentucky (hereinafter cited as FHS); C. D. Bradley to Jeremiah T. Boyle, November 9, 1862, Record Group 393: Records of the U.S. Army Continental Commands, 1821–1920 (hereinafter cited as RG 393), pt. 1, ser. 3514: Letters Received, Department of the Ohio, box 1, National Archives and Records Administration, Washington, D.C. (hereinafter cited as NARA); Don Bowen, "Guerrilla Warfare in Western Missouri, 1862–1865: Historical Extensions of the Relative Deprivation Hypothesis," *Comparative Studies in Society and History* 19 (July 1977): 30; John Pope to Cyrus Bussey, August 10, 1861 (italics mine), and Pope to John C. Kelton, August 4, 1861, both in *OR,* ser. 1, vol. 3, pp. 435–36, 427; Ulysses S. Grant, *Personal Memoirs of U. S. Grant* (New York: Da Capo Press, 1982), 132; Grant to W. E. McMackin, August 12, 1861, *OR,* ser. 1, vol. 3, pp. 438–39. Sutherland suggests the accretion of guerrilla warfare in Kentucky only after the spring of 1863.

8. William E. Gienapp, "Abraham Lincoln and the Border States," *Journal of the Abraham Lincoln Association* 13 (1992): 25; Cicero Maxwell to "To Whom it may Concern," May 6, 1863, and Affidavit of Jacob S. Cave, March 31, 1865, both in RG 393, pt. 1, ser. 2229: Correspondence, Affidavits, and Oaths Regarding Civilians Charged with Disloyalty, Department of Kentucky, box 1, NARA; "Sarah Patience," unpublished typescript, Martha W. Dorsey Papers, Mss. SC510, folder 2, pp. 47–49, IHSL; Oliver P. Morton to Joseph Hooker, January 11, 1865, RG 393, pt. 1, ser. 3349: Letters Received, Northern Department, box 2, NARA; H. Smith to J. J. Key, September 2, 1862, RG 393, pt. 1, ser. 3514: Letters Received,

Department of the Ohio, box 2, NARA; *Pomeroy (OH) Weekly Telegraph,* May 26, 1864; Nancy C. Mann to J[ohn]. Preston Mann, November 19, 1863, Mann Family Papers, Coll. 111, box 2, Southern Illinois University, Special Collections, Morris Library, Carbondale, Illinois; Sallie Hendricks to Abram W Hendricks, September 12, 1862, Abram W. Hendricks Papers, Mss. SC733, IHSL; *Hannibal (MO) Daily Messenger,* September 4, 1861; Thomas G. Morrow to [Stephen G.] Burbridge, October 3, 1864, RG 393, pt. 1, ser. 2173: Letters Received, Department of Kentucky, box 4, NARA.

9. T. J. Stiles, *Jesse James: Last Rebel of the Civil War* (New York: Alfred A. Knopf, 2002), 85–87; [U.S. Pension Office,] *Missouri Troops in Service during the Civil War* (Washington, D.C.: Government Printing Office, 1902), 82–84; Patricia Ann Hoskins, "'The Old First Is with the South': The Civil War, Reconstruction, and Memory in the Jackson Purchase Region of Kentucky" (PhD diss., Auburn University, 2008), 58; John F. Bradbury Jr., "'Buckwheat Cake Philanthropy': Refugees and the Union Army in the Ozarks," *Arkansas Historical Quarterly* 57 (Autumn 1998): 248–49; [William Barclay Napton,] *The Union on Trial: The Political Journals of Judge William Barclay Napton, 1829–1883,* ed. Christopher Phillips and Jason L. Pendleton (Columbia: University of Missouri Press, 2005), 204; Stephen V. Ash, *When the Yankees Came: Conflict and Chaos in the Occupied South, 1861–1865* (Chapel Hill: University of North Carolina Press, 1995), 76–107.

10. Bruce Nichols, *Guerrilla Warfare in Civil War Missouri, 1862* (Jefferson, NC: McFarland, 2004), 34–38; Dennis K. Boman, *Lincoln's Resolute Unionist: Hamilton R. Gamble, Dred Scott Dissenter and Missouri's Civil War Governor* (Baton Rouge: Louisiana State University Press, 2006), 222–23; Scott diary, folder 5, p. 144, SHSM; Thomas Ewing to C. W. Marsh, August 3, 1863, *OR,* ser. 1, vol. 22, pt. 2, pp. 428–29; Jeremy Neely, *The Border between Them: Violence and Reconciliation on the Kansas-Missouri Line* (Columbia: University of Missouri Press, 2007), 108–9; Bradbury, "Buckwheat Cake Philanthropy," 241–43; Richard Nelson Current, *Lincoln's Loyalists: Union Soldiers from the Confederacy* (Boston: Northeastern University Press, 1992; reprint, New York: Oxford University Press, 1994), 153–54; [Thomas W. Parsons,] *Incidents and Experiences in the Life of Thomas W. Parsons, from 1826 to 1900,* ed. Frank Furlong Mathias (Lexington: University Press of Kentucky, 1975), 94–95, 121, 139; Gordon Granger to Jeremiah T. Boyle, November 28, 1862, and John W. Foster to Boyle, November 28, 1862, both in RG 393, pt. 1, ser. 2173: Letters Received, Department of Kentucky, 1862–69, box 1, NARA; J[ohn]. M. Schofield to Abraham Lincoln, August 28, 1863, *OR,* ser. 1, vol. 22, pt. 2, pp. 482–84; Statement of Thomas Burris, August 16, 1864, RG 393, pt. 1, ser. 2229: Correspondence, Affidavits, and Oaths Regarding Civilians Charged with Disloyalty, Department of Kentucky, box 2, NARA.

11. Notations of Military Commission Hearing of Jacob Snowden, undated [May 1863], RG 393, pt. 1, ser. 2620: General Orders, Department of the Missouri, 1862–64, 5 vols., 2:19–21, NARA; James M. Fidler to James M. Fry, June

20, 1864, Fidler to R. G. Samuel, December 15, 1862, and Fidler to William Mattingly, September 10 [1864], all in RG 393, pt. 1, ser. 2137: Letters Received, Department of Kentucky, boxes 1, 3, 4, NARA; Phil[ander]. B. Price, January 18, 1864, Hunt-Morgan Family Papers, Mss. 63M202, box 17, folder 1, University of Kentucky, Special Collections and Archives, Margaret I. King Library, Lexington; Cora Owens Hume journal, transcript, September 15, 1864, entry, Mss. A/H921, vault C, 3 vols., 2:20–22, FHS.

12. Yancey Wilson to James B. Meriwether, March 24, 1865, and enclosures, RG 393, pt. 1, ser. 2229: Correspondence, Affidavits, and Oaths Regarding Civilians Charged with Disloyalty, Department of Kentucky, box 2, NARA; J[eremiah]. T. Boyle to W. P. Anderson, November 10, 1863, RG 393, pt. 1, ser. 3514: Letters Received, Department of the Ohio, box 3, NARA; Reid Mitchell, *The Vacant Chair: The Northern Soldier Leaves Home* (New York: Oxford University Press, 1993), 33–34; *St. Louis Daily Missouri Republican,* September 2, 1863; Correspondence, Orders, and Returns Relating to Operations in Missouri, Arkansas, Kansas, the Indian Territory, and Department of the Northwest, from January 1 to December 31, 1863, *OR,* ser. 1, vol. 22, pt. 2, pp. 109–10; *Journal of the Senate of the State of Missouri, at the Adjourned Session of the Twenty-Second General Assembly* (Jefferson City, MO: J. P. Ament, Printer, 1863), 656; J. H. Collins to William S. Rosecrans, February 10, 1864, RG 393, pt. 1, ser. 2593: Letters Received, Department of the Missouri, NARA; Scott diary, folder 4, p. 144, SHSM; J[ohn]. M. Schofield to Abraham Lincoln, August 28, 1863, *OR,* ser. 1, vol. 22, pt. 2, pp. 482–84; Boman, *Lincoln's Resolute Unionist,* 176–77; E. Merton Coulter, *The Civil War and Readjustment in Kentucky* (Chapel Hill: University of North Carolina Press, 1926; reprint, Gloucester, Mass.: Peter Smith, 1966), 189–94; Abraham Lincoln to Green Adams, January 7, 1863, in Roy F. Basler, ed., *The Collected Works of Abraham Lincoln* (Springfield, IL: Abraham Lincoln Association, 1953; reprint, New Brunswick, NJ: Rutgers University Press, 1988), 6:42; O. F. Miner to A. M. Stout, February 9, 1865, *OR,* ser. 3, vol. 4, p. 1188; Peter Levine, "Draft Evasion in the North during the Civil War, 1863–1865," *Journal of American History* 67 (March 1981): 819, 825n19; Fellman, *Inside War,* 26–31; Le Roy Fitch to David D. Porter, June 11, 1864, *OR,* ser. 1, vol. 39, pt. 2, p. 102; General Order No. 2, August 8, 1864, Edward Henry Hobson Papers, Mss. 51M41, University of Kentucky, Special Collections and Archives, Margaret I. King Library, Lexington; General Order No. 2, August 8, 1864, David. L. Thornton Papers, Mss. 61M256, box 1, University of Kentucky, Special Collections and Archives; [Record and Pension Office, War Department], *Organization and Status of Missouri Troops (Union and Confederate) in Service during the Civil War* (Washington, D.C.: Government Printing Office, 1902), 53; *Annual Report of the Adjutant General of Missouri for 1864* (Jefferson City: W. A. Curry, 1985), 38; Lowell H. Harrison, *The Civil War in Kentucky* (Lexington: University Press of Kentucky, 1975), 95. Although in August 1864 the Confederate War Department ordered mandatory enlistment in western Kentucky for all men between the ages of seven-

teen and forty-five, and conscription for those who evaded, far more would in fact become guerrillas than Confederates. According to the 1866 Kentucky adjutant general's report, 12,486 individuals served in the Kentucky militia system during the Civil War. This figure includes all soldiers called to duty in Kentucky in 1861 by Robert Anderson, those who continued service in the Kentucky State Guard (1861–1864), and those 4,519 men who served in the ten Kentucky Active Militia Battalions (also called Kentucky State Troops Proper) from 1864 to 1866. This total does not include 114 regiments of the Kentucky Enrolled Militia authorized by the Militia Act of 1860 (with eight hundred to eleven hundred men authorized to fill each regiment but whose totals are unrecorded), or the various home guard units, county and municipal, that historian Lowell Harrison has estimated as having exceeded ten thousand men. Aggregation of men who served in Missouri's various militias is even less easily determined. Although Missouri state militia enrollment was capped at ten thousand, it actually exceeded thirteen thousand in 1862 before being reduced by disbanding and consolidating some regiments. Later some militia units were opened to recruiters for the Federal volunteers. By September 1862, over twenty Enrolled Missouri Militia (EMM) regiments had been formed in the city and county of St. Louis, representing approximately seventeen thousand men. By the end of 1862, sixty-nine regiments, three battalions, and fifty-eight independent companies had been organized, with a total of 52,056 officers and enlisted men, and ultimately eighty-five regiments, sixteen battalions, and thirty-three independent companies were organized. The 1864 Missouri adjutant general's report includes monthly aggregates of active EMM units, with the peak coming in October at 24,164 and the low the previous May at 339. The median figure for active militia during these months is 2,448. As in Kentucky, these figures likely do not include home guards, Six-Months' Militia, Provisional Enrolled Missouri Militia (PEMM), or other independent companies and battalions. Any listing of enrollment assumes the risk of overcounting because men, and their enrollment figures, transferred from organization to organization. (For example, the provisional versions of the EMM, especially the PEMM, were often the same men who had enrolled in the original EMM.) My thanks to Brandon Slone, Military Records and Research Branch, Kentucky Department of Military Affairs, and Steve Mitchell, Missouri State Archives, for their assistance with the various militia units in Kentucky and Missouri.

13. Report of Brig. Gen. John M. Schofield, U.S. Army, of Operations in Missouri and Northwestern Arkansas, April 10–November 20, 1862, *OR,* ser. 1, vol. 13, p. 12; [Record and Pension Office, War Department], *Organization and Status of Missouri Troops,* 53; William E. Parrish, *Turbulent Partnership: Missouri and the Union, 1861–1865* (Columbia: University of Missouri Press, 1963), 91–94; Stiles, *Jesse James,* 84; Scott diary, folder 5, pp. 138–39, folder 8, pp. 214–15, SHSM; *Frankfort (KY) Tri-weekly Commonwealth,* March 25, 1863, March 16, 1864; Stephen V. Ash, *Middle Tennessee Society Transformed, 1860–1870: War and Peace in the Upper South* (Baton Rouge: Louisiana State University Press, 1988), 148–51;

Sutherland, "Guerrilla Warfare," 271–72, 284–85; Fellman, *Inside War,* 153–55; W. Randolph to Stephen G. Burbridge, December 1, 1864, Stephen Gano Burbridge Correspondence, Mss. C/B, FHS; Nichols, *Guerrilla Warfare in Civil War Missouri,* 43–44; Diary of Johanna Louisa (Underwood) Nazro, typescript August 2, September 22, October 23, 1864, entries, Johanna Louisa (Underwood) Nazro Collection, Mss. SC 1709, WKU; "Sarah Patience," unpublished typescript, Martha W. Dorsey Papers, Mss. SC510, folder 2, p. 54, IHSL; James M. McPherson, *Battle Cry of Freedom: The Civil War Era* (New York: Oxford University Press, 1988), 602–6; Jennifer L. Weber, *Copperheads: The Rise and Fall of Lincoln's Opponents in the North* (New York: Oxford University Press, 2006), 88; Cora Owens Hume journal, transcript, September 4, 1864, entry, Mss. A/H921, vault C, vol. 2, p. 13, FHS; "Enrollment of Disloyal men or those who have sympathized with the Rebellion between the ages of 18 and 45 years" and "Enrollment of Disloyal men and those who have sympathized with the Rebellion over the age of 45 years living in Andrew County," both in Andrew County Civil War Document Collection, box CW2, file 15, Missouri State Archives, Jefferson City. To pay for EMM enlistments, in March 1863 Missouri's General Assembly authorized Gamble to issue $1 million of "Union Military" bonds, payable in twelve months at 6 percent interest, and when that proved insufficient, it authorized another $1.5 million the following November. One southern Indianan characterized home guards as "men who could not enlist for service in the field." Many more chose to evade enlistment by serving in these units.

14. Mark W. Geiger, *Financial Fraud and Guerrilla Violence in Missouri's Civil War, 1861–1865* (New Haven, CT: Yale University Press, 2010); Geiger, "Indebtedness and the Origins of Guerrilla Warfare in Civil War Missouri," *Journal of Southern History* 75 (February 2009): 49–82; Bowen, "Guerrilla Warfare in Western Missouri," 43–51; Neely, *Border between Them,* 108–10. The sample in Bowen's study is a group of 194 identified guerrillas who lived in or near Jackson County, Missouri.

15. Special Orders No. 10, September 29, 1861, *OR,* ser. 2, vol. 1, p. 284; Fellman, *Inside War,* 252–53; Samuel S. Hildebrand, *Autobiography of Samuel S. Hildebrand, the renowned Missouri "bushwacker" and unconquerable Rob Roy of America: Being his complete confession, recently made to the writers, and carefully compiled by James W. Evans and A. Wendell Keith; together with all the facts connected with his early history* (Jefferson City, MO: State Times Book and Job Printing House, 1870; reprint, Woodbridge, CT: Research Publications, 1985), 27–28, 35, 37, 41–51; Kirby Ross, "James O. Broadhead: Ardent Unionist, Unrepentant Slaveholder," posted December 6, 2002, Civil War St. Louis, http://www.civilwarstlouis.com/History2/broadheadprofile.htm; T. Coleman Younger, *The Story of Cole Younger by Himself: Being an Autobiography of the Missouri Guerrilla Captain and Outlaw* (Chicago: Henneberry, 1903), 4–5; Neely, *Border between Them,* 108–9.

16. George Caleb Bingham to Ja[me]s. S. Rollins and W[illia]m. A. Hall, January 22, February 12, 1862, in Rollins, ed., "Letters of Bingham to Rollins," pt.

5, "Letters: January 22, 1862–November 21, 1871," *Missouri Historical Review* 33 (October 1938): 47, 52, 56, 59; Nancy Rash, *The Painting and Politics of George Caleb Bingham* (New Haven, CT: Yale University Press, 1991), 177–83, 188; Bingham to H[amilton]. R. Gamble, June 8, 1863, Hamilton R. Gamble Papers, folder 10, Missouri Historical Society, St. Louis; "History of South Union, Ky., No. 16 [November 28, 1862]," *Manifesto (1884–1899)* 25 (February 1895): 25–28; Bingham to John M. Schofield, June 4, 1863, Correspondence: Letters Received, ser. 1, 1861–1875, John M. Schofield Papers, box 2, folder B4–30, Library of Congress, Washington D.C.; General Orders No. 32, December 22, 1861, *OR,* ser. 1, vol. 8, p. 463–64; Stiles, *Jesse James,* 74–75; *St. Louis Daily Missouri Republican,* November 10, 1861, in Silvana Siddali, ed., *Missouri's War: The Civil War in Documents* (Athens: Ohio University Press, 2009), 82; Scott diary, folder 4, pp. 94–99, SHSM; Jon G. Taylor to Robert Neil, September 21, 1863, Robert Neil Family Papers, Mss. 259, Ohio Historical Society, Columbus.

17. Sutherland, *Savage Conflict,* 152; Nelson McDowell to Hamilton R. Gamble, August 3, 1862, Record Group 3.16: Records of Hamilton Rowan Gamble, box 1B, folder 9, Missouri State Archives, Jefferson City; J[eremiah]. T. Boyle to E[dward]. M. Stanton, August 21, 1862, *OR,* ser. 3, vol. 2, p. 431; Samuel Haycraft journal, typescript, October 10, 20, 1862, entries, pp. 26–27, Mss. A/H414, FHS; Lucas, "Indignities, Wrongs, and Outrages," 357; A[aron]. Harding to Dear Jack, November 16, 1862, and Sallie A. Harding to John and Samuel Harding, December 4, 1862, both in John Harding Collection, Mss. A/H263, folder 6, FHS.

18. Report of Brig. Gen. John M. Schofield, U.S. Army, of Operations in Missouri and Northwestern Arkansas, April 10–November 20, 1862, *OR,* ser. 1, vol. 13, p. 12; Adam I. P. Smith, *No Party Now: Politics in the Civil War North* (New York: Oxford University Press, 2006), 69; Fellman, *Inside War,* 137–38, 161–62.

19. Fellman, *Inside War,* 82–84; Smith, *No Party Now,* 3; Henry W. Halleck to Francis Lieber, August 6, 1862, and response (undated), both in *OR,* ser. 3, vol. 2, pp. 301–9; Sutherland, *Savage Conflict,* 126–29; Grimsley, *Hard Hand of War,* 11–13; John Fabian Witt, *Lincoln's Code: The Laws of War in American History* (New York: Free Press, 2012), 170–249; Matthew J. Mancini, "Francis Lieber, Slavery, and the 'Genesis' of the Laws of War," *Journal of Southern History* 77 (May 2011): 326–39; [Francis W. Lieber,] *No Party Now but All for Our Country* (Philadelphia: Crissy and Markley, Printers, 1863), 3–5, 10–12; Burrus M. Carnahan, "Lincoln, Lieber and the Laws of War: The Origins and Limits of the Principle of Military Necessity," *American Journal of International Law* 92 (April 1998): 213–15; Sutherland, "Guerrilla Warfare," 288.

20. Searching the term "guerrilla" in the digitized version of *OR* volumes, the contents of which were themselves culled from the original War Department records (and thus they are not complete), and narrowing the search to reports specific to commands located or events occurring in Missouri and Kentucky, yields 64 individual reports dated on or before July 18, 1862, the date Lincoln issued

his initial call for three hundred thousand additional troops. By contrast, 358 such reports dated thereafter are contained in the volumes. A similar search of the term "bushwhacker" yielded 4 reports prior to the implementation of the draft and 121 after it. Using only the term "guerrilla," 17 percent of its usage appears in the reports prior to July 18, 1862, as compared with 0.3 percent for the term "bushwhacker." This sampling is of course limited, possibly more suggestive of the resources committed by Federal military authorities in these states by way of individual reports about irregulars than the breadth of their activities.

21. Fellman, *Inside War,* 82; *Annual Report of the Adjutant General of Missouri for 1864,* 38; John N. Edwards, *Shelby and His Men* (Cincinnati: Miami Printing and Publishing Co., 1867), 197. This quantification is based upon the Missouri State Archives' complete indexing of extant Missouri cases in 394 microfilm reels of Record Group 109, War Department Collection of Confederate Records, housed at NARA, organized as *Union Provost Marshals' File of Papers Relating to Individual Citizens* (three hundred microfilm reels, dated 1861–1866) and *Union Provost Marshals' File of Papers Relating to Two or More Civilians* (ninety-four microfilm reels, dated 1861–1867). These records were assembled in the U.S. War Department from documents that were extracted from the files of the Union army provost marshals and from other records of army territorial commands. This sampling derives from the online database index compiled by the staff of the Missouri State Archives in 2000–2009. Staffers included 66,129 case files originating in the state of Missouri drawn from 378 reels of both of the NARA collections, which thus are included in this sampling. See http://www.sos.mo.gov/archives/provost/, accessed December 3, 2009. My thanks to Lynn Morrow, director of the Local Records Program at the Missouri State Archives, who supervised the provost marshal project and provided me with the database of case files that the archives compiled for this sampling.

22. Th[eophilus]. H. Holmes to Samuel R. Curtis, October 11, 1862, *OR,* ser. 1, vol. 8, pp. 726–28; J[ohn]. M. Schofield to Colonel [John] McNeil, June 12, 1862, *OR,* ser. 1, vol. 13, p. 427; Joseph A. Mudd, *With Porter in Northeast Missouri* (Washington, D.C.: National Publishing, 1909), 299–310; Scott E. Sallee, "Porter's Campaign in Northeast Missouri, 1862, Including the Palmyra Massacre," *Blue and Gray* 17 (February 2000): 6–20, 44–51; William E. Parrish, "'The Palmyra Massacre': A Tragedy of Guerrilla Warfare," *Journal of Confederate History* 1 (Fall 1988): 259–72; Daniel Berry to Mary B. Crebs, November 28, 1862, Daniel Berry Letters, Misc. Vol. 53, Southern Illinois University, Special Collections, Morris Library, Carbondale; Stiles, *Jesse James,* 86–88; "Diary of Events in Department of Missouri, 1863," August 26, 1863, entry, John McAllister Schofield Papers, box 1, Library of Congress; Milo T. Haswell to Ambrose E. Burnside, May 19, 1863, RG 393, pt. 1, ser. 3514: Letters Received, Department of the Ohio, box 3, NARA; J. B. Meriwether to G. M. Bascom, March 11, 1865, and E. B. Burnett to Provost Marshall, Louisville, March 11, 1865, both in RG 393, pt. 1, ser. 2229: Correspondence, Affidavits, and Oaths Regarding Civilians Charged

with Disloyalty, Department of Kentucky, box 1, NARA; Sutherland, *Savage Conflict,* 59–63; General Orders No. 1, January 1, 1862, *OR,* ser. 1, vol. 8, pp. 476–78; General Orders No. 32, December 22, 1861, *OR,* ser. 2, vol. 1, p. 237. Curtis claimed in a subsequent letter to Holmes that he had no knowledge of the Palmyra execution until afterward and regarded it as "a kind of police resentment . . . by an indignant and outraged community." Curtis to Holmes, December 24, 1862, *OR,* ser. 1, vol. 22, pt. 2, pp. 860–61.

23. "History of South Union, Ky., No. 16 [November 28, 1862]," *Manifesto (1884–1899)* 25 (February 1895), 25–28; Nazro diary, February 18, 1863, entry, WKU; Joseph A. Eppstein to J[ohn]. M. Schofield, March 16, 1862, Record Group 109: War Department Collection of Confederate Records, Union Provost Marshals' File of Papers Relating to Individual Citizens, Mss. M345, microfilm reel 269, NARA; Fellman, *Inside War,* 137–38, 161–62; Lucas, "Indignities, Wrongs, and Outrages," 358–59; Benjamin F. Loan to Samuel R. Curtis, January 27, 1863, *OR,* ser. 1, vol. 22, pt. 2, p. 80; W. Anthony to Judge Jesse W. Kincheloe, December 3, 1862, Kinchloe-Eskridge Families Papers, Mss. A/K51, folder 2, FHS; *New York Daily Times,* November 8, 1863; Hiram Carver to J[eremiah]. T. Boyle, December 22, 1862, Leonidas Metcalfe to Boyle, December 14, 1862, and James M. Fidler to J[ames]. B. Fry, June 10, 1864, all in RG 393, pt. 1, ser. 2173: Letters Received, Department of Kentucky, boxes 1, 3, NARA; *Speech of Hon. George H. Yeaman, of Kentucky, on the President's Proclamation, Delivered in the House of Representatives, December 18, 1962* (Baltimore: John Murphy and Co., 1863), 17; Marian M. Ohman, *Encyclopedia of Missouri Courthouses* (Columbia: Curators of the University of Missouri, 1981). Three Missouri courthouses were destroyed or damaged by Federal troops or state militia, while another nine were damaged by occupation. Only two were in the western part of the state, where the guerrilla war was perhaps most vicious but also where garrisons in county seats were larger.

24. Fellman, *Inside War,* 31–32; Lucas, "Indignities, Wrongs, and Outrages," 370; Scott diary, folder 6, pp. 163–65, SHSM.

25. Speed S. Fry to Lewis Richmond, May 9, 1863, RG 393, pt. 1, ser. 3514: Letters Received, Department of the Ohio, box 3, NARA; D. Little to J[eremiah]. T. Boyle, December 20, 1862, RG 393, pt. 1, ser. 2173: Letters Received, Department of Kentucky, box 1, NARA; Parrish, *Turbulent Partnership,* 94–97; Stiles, *Jesse James,* 87–90.

26. William E. Parrish, *A History of Missouri,* vol. 3, *1860–1875* (1973; reprint, Columbia: University of Missouri Press, 2001), 54–55; Stiles, *Jesse James,* 85, 98; George R. Todd to Thomas J. Bartholomew, February 2, 1863, newspaper clipping, Isaac D. Snedecor to Mr. Editor, April 10, 1863, and J. Wendall Keiter to Thomas Armstrong, March 19, 1863, all in Record Group 109: War Department Collection of Confederate Records, Union Provost Marshals' File of Papers Relating to Two or More Citizens, ninety-four microfilm reels, file 3899, reel M416, and file 19533, reel 73, NARA; Stiles, *Jesse James,* 85.

27. *Macon (MO) Weekly Argus,* January 31, 1866; Preston Filbert, *The Half Not Told: The Civil War in a Frontier Town* (Mechanicsburg, PA: Stackpole Books, 2001), 116–21; Special Orders, No. 255, September 18, 1863, *OR,* ser. 1, vol. 22, pt. 2, pp. 542–43; [Record and Pension Office, War Department], *Organization and Status of Missouri Troops,* 82–86, 230; Petition of John Osborne et al., February 26, 1864, RG 393, pt. 1, ser. 2593: Letters Received, Department of the Missouri, box 14, NARA. Missouri raised eleven regiments of PEMM. On September 18, 1863, the Tenth and Eleventh Provisional Regiments mutinied and were disbanded by Special Order No. 255 on November 1, 1863. The PEMM was formally disbanded by act of the legislature on March 12, 1865. The term "Paw Paw Militia" has been attributed variously to the brushy bottoms of the region and to the more pejorative reference to these militias' sympathy with the guerrillas who commonly hid out in these areas.

28. Bowen, "Guerrilla Warfare in Western Missouri," 47; Thomas Ewing Jr. to Thomas Ewing Sr., September 22, 1863, Ewing Family Papers, box 17, Library of Congress; Abraham Lincoln to James C. Conkling, August 26, 1863, in Basler, *Collected Works of Abraham Lincoln,* 6:407–8; Ira Berlin, Barbara J. Fields, Stephen F. Miller, Joseph P. Reidy, and Leslie S. Rowland, eds., *Freedom: A Documentary History of Emancipation, 1861–1867,* ser. 1, vol. 1, *The Destruction of Slavery* (Cambridge: Cambridge University Press, 1985), 407; Kalyvas, "Ontology of 'Political Violence,'" 481.

29. Jo[seph]. O. Shelby to L. A. MacLean, November 16, 1863, *OR,* ser. 1, vol. 22, pt. 1, pp. 670–79.

30. *St. Louis Daily Missouri Republican,* September 2, 1863; George Candee to George Whipple, June 14, 24, July 11, 1864, Doc. Nos. 73530, 73540, 73555; L[ydia]. H. H. Montague to Rev. Mr. Streby, June 20, 1864, Doc. No. 73533; Montague to Rev. Mr. Jocelyn, September 7, 1864, Doc. No. 73593, all in American Missionary Association Archives, 1839–1882, 261 microfilm reels, Amistad Research Center, New Orleans, Louisiana, reel 1: Missouri; Tenth U.S. Census, 1880, Population Schedule, St. Louis City, NARA; Joe M. Richardson, *Christian Reconstruction: The American Missionary Association and Southern Blacks, 1861–1890* (Athens: University of Georgia Press, 1986); Julie Roy Jeffrey, *The Great Silent Army of Abolitionism: Ordinary Women in the Antislavery Movement* (Chapel Hill: University of North Carolina Press, 1998), 226; Elijah Buchanan et al. to Alfred Pleasanton, July 16, 1864, RG 393, pt. 1, ser. 2593: Letters Received, Department of the Missouri, box 12, NARA.

31. Lee Kennett, *Marching through Georgia: The Story of Soldiers and Civilians during Sherman's Campaign* (New York: Harper Collins, 1995), 265; J[oseph]. Holt to E[dwin]. M. Stanton, August 5, 1864, *OR,* ser. 3, vol. 4, p. 577.

Controlled Chaos

Spatiotemporal Patterns within Missouri's Irregular Civil War

Andrew William Fialka

At the Battle of Spotsylvania Courthouse in May 1864, Private Thomas Roche witnessed a fellow Confederate "throw down his musket and pick up a hatchet. As a Federal c[ame] at him with a bayonet, he pushed it aside with his left hand, while with the hatchet in his right he brain[ed] his opponent. . . . The Federals shrank from the sickening scene."[1] Historians who analyze fierce accounts such as Roche's do so in the larger context of battle. Individually, Roche's rendition of the fighting at Spotsylvania seems chaotic. However, when cartographers inscribe Roche in a square labeled "Sixteenth Mississippi" and place that square in a battle line on a map, Roche's individual report melds into the overall strategy of Robert E. Lee. A map's expansive scale allows historians to interpret evidence in different ways; geographically speaking, Roche's brutal actions give way to Lee's tactical genius when viewed on a larger scale.[2] Guerrilla warfare requires the same spatial insight to be comprehensively understood. The usual historiographical overview of the Civil War's irregular conflict in Missouri portrays guerrilla warfare as chaotic, disorganized, and savage—but how much of that is simply a product of *how* the information is typically presented? We have never mapped guerrilla violence; we have mapped Gettysburg hundreds of times over. Of course, Gettysburg has an order to it; we have seen it repeatedly with a bird's-eye view. Scholars of the guerrilla conflict have tended *only* to use a qualitative approach, which certainly succeeds in richly illustrating how individual civilians and Union troops experienced irregular warfare. However, this approach, especially at its more anecdotal extremes, fails to *make sense* of guerrilla violence; it does not consider guerrillas' actions in relation to one another, to the Union army's location and force, and to the terrain and time in which guerrillas operated. In short, irregular warfare has been seen as altogether *irregular,* as if there are no patterns within it.[3]

Viewing the guerrilla war through a spatiotemporal lens will allow us to reinterpret seemingly chaotic events and uncover an organized infrastructure and logic animating guerrillas' violent actions. This essay draws on digital methods—specifically, animated maps created in ArcGIS and Neatline—to illuminate patterns within guerrilla violence.[4] Better than text, a map can lay bare the interactions and correlations of spatial phenomena. Better than static maps, animated maps with synchronized timelines, zoom functions capable of transcending multiple scales, and the ability to embed packages of information onto the map can help us to see patterns where once we saw disorder. Instead of looking at evidence individually, with an animated map I can simultaneously view guerrilla warfare's participants as they appeared in time and space: instances of guerrilla violence emerge on the day and in the space they occurred, while the Union army materializes in specific locations during scheduled times of permanent and temporary occupation. This essay is most specifically concerned with the correlation between instances of guerrilla violence and the spatial and temporal locations of the Union army in Civil War Missouri's central counties.[5] Such visualizations reveal what we could not see without them—that guerrilla violence was not wholly *irregular* but instead worked in the wake of temporary Union occupation. Guerrillas were opportunists, were ordered, and were smart; they chiefly targeted Union war industries—small garrisons, Unionist militias, railroads, telegraph lines, and supply trains—and mainly operated in locations previously occupied by small outfits of Union troops. Similarly, the Union army, in Missouri and especially later in the war, drafted specific policies to legitimize waging war on guerrillas, which reflects a more conventional pattern of protracted skirmishes in other theaters of war. Studies of the Civil War's irregular conflict must consider seriously these patterns within what is still too often seen as anarchic guerrilla violence.[6]

Placing the irregular conflict on a map will only enrich our current appreciation for the importance of the guerrilla theater. Daniel Sutherland's *A Savage Conflict* is the broadest survey of guerrilla warfare we have, extending across the border states and the trans-Mississippi and lower South regions. Sutherland's comprehensive work proves that the guerrilla experience was typical rather than exceptional for civilians throughout war-torn states and argues persuasively for the decisive rôle of guerrillas in the Civil War by clarifying the spatial extent of their influence. Sutherland, moreover, is undoubtedly right that fighting in both irregular *and* regular theaters was to some extent "savage" but in neither theater was it "chaotic," and we will better see the similarities and differences between the two theaters when we *treat them the same methodologically,* especially by mapping them.[7] Of course, Sutherland's depiction of irregular warfare does not incorporate a spatiotemporal approach partly because, unlike a conventional battle, the guerrilla war in Missouri began in the 1850s and lasted well after General Lee's surrender at Appomattox Court House.[8] Moreover, guerrilla violence did not occur on specific battlefields but throughout the entire landscape in accordance with irregulars' small, disjointed numbers and hit-and-run maneuvers. Due to the longevity and scale of guerrilla warfare in Missouri, traditional interpretations and static maps that might appear in a book cannot fully depict the irregular conflict.

My digital and spatiotemporal approach to Missouri's guerrilla war confronts two major methodological problems. First, maps tend to impose order on turbulent events and experiences. Few, if any, individuals in war experienced the order that a battle map projects. Moreover, guerrillas utilized unpredictability and the perception of chaos to their advantage in employing surprise, mobility, and stealth as an effective strategy against Union forces. These tactics allowed a small number of guerrillas to combat thousands of Union troops. In this way, seemingly disorganized acts of guerrilla violence did not lack ideological underpinnings. Second, an animated map created at state, county, and city levels faces issues of scale already existent in the historiography. An anecdotal approach to the irregular conflict applies conclusions drawn at one scale—from individual guerrillas—to the Civil War's irregular conflict at a state and national levels. Scholars who use inferences drawn from one scale to make historical claims at a different scale commit the ecological fallacy. This essay's predominantly spatiotemporal approach to Missouri's Civil War neglects personal experiences and neighborhood relations.[9] Consequently, I do not attempt to argue what motivated guerrillas at an individual level, nor do I impute cause-and-effect relationships to quantitative evidence that is merely correlative. The presence of Union armies is not the only factor that contributed to guerrilla violence. However, a digitized map does serve as a predictor of guerrilla warfare by illustrating the proximity of irregular violence to cities temporarily occupied by Union troops. In fact, instances of irregular violence occurred in predictable locations and against expected targets.

Union occupational strategies presaged patterns of guerrilla violence. An in-depth examination and comparison between the city of St. Louis and Missouri's central counties illustrates that the presence of large and consistently occupied garrison towns effectively quelled guerrilla violence while smaller communities that experienced temporary occupation by Federal companies, detachments, and foraging squads acted as magnets for violence and instigated guerrilla activity. The large urban center of St. Louis boasted a population of over 160,000 people and contained a Federal arsenal, multiple barracks, hospitals, prisons, and a largely Unionist German American citizenry.[10] Moreover, the city's location at the junction of the Missouri and Mississippi Rivers made it a strategic military point. St. Louis was Missouri's largest garrison town and the Union's most important foothold in the state; consequently, the Union occupation in St. Louis was consistently robust. Two to six regiments were stationed within the city limits from June 12, 1861, to June 1, 1865, and never abandoned their occupation of the city. Soldiers constantly drilled in the streets, manned fortifications, and pervaded the city's social ranks. Union forces rarely left the city in large numbers and did so only in short stints. Very few instances of guerrilla violence occurred in the surrounding counties, and none penetrated the city's limits. Ultimately for St. Louisans, a continual Union presence provided a zone of protection against guerrillas for the entirety of the war.[11]

In contrast, most civilians in Missouri's central counties suffered from violent guerrilla warfare due to temporary and inconsistent Union occupation. Central Missouri counties experienced sporadic Federal expeditions, contained no large garrison towns, and witnessed a mass exodus of Union troops after 1862 (see map, "Central Missouri counties"). Moreover, Missouri's location on the western frontier distanced the state from most Confederate and Union strongholds. While the Union military stationed some regiments in towns for months on end, a majority of soldiers manned temporary locations for only days or weeks at a time, and no town played host to the Union army for the entirety of the war. Quantitatively speaking, Missourians experienced temporary Union occupation for almost 60 percent of the war: the ratio between stationary and temporary Union troops

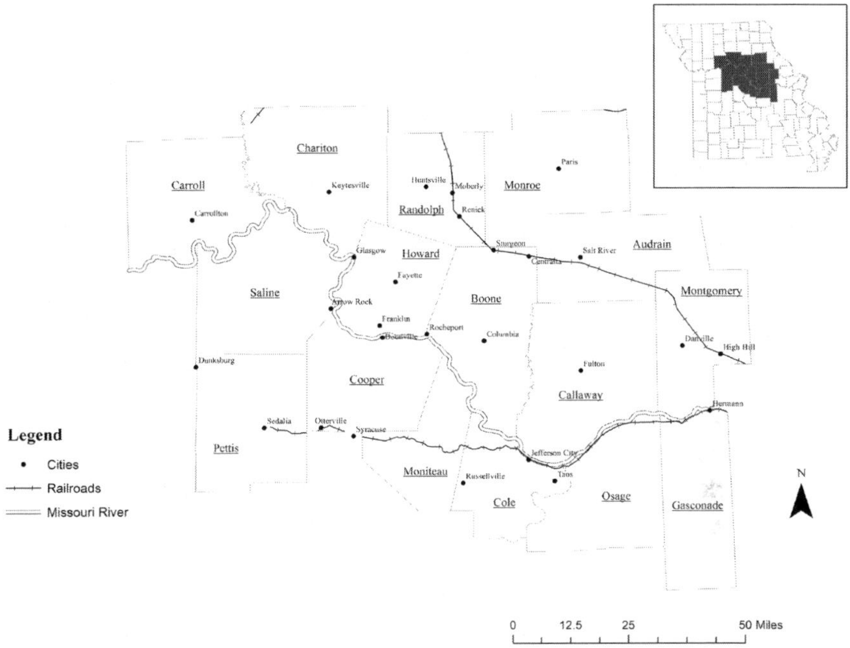

Central Missouri counties. (Andrew Fialka)

in the central counties was 37:49. Furthermore, a vast majority of stationary occupations occurred in 1861.[12]

Missourians' personal recollections and official reports detailing Union operatives shed light on the effects of "temporary" Union occupancy. Numerous civilians with Unionist and southern sympathies claimed that Federal forces were "dreaded even by loyal men nearly as much as bush-whackers, as their officers seem[ed] to exercise but little control over them." Scholars affirm this assessment of the Union military's draconian practices against civilians in areas of guerrilla activity. In his watershed work, *Inside War,* Michael Fellman argues that the guerrillas' hit-and-run ambushes, their ability to conceal themselves within the civilian population, and their practice of mutilation dictated Union troops' vengeful response to Missouri's civilians and unleashed a downward spiral of retaliation between guerrillas, Union troops, and noncombatants. Clay Mountcastle, in *Punitive War,* argues that "the Union army was enticed into using punitive war because of frustration brought on by guerrilla violence." Correspondence between Missouri's top military officials—Major General William Rosecrans, General Clinton B. Fisk, and Colonel J. P. Sanderson—in the case of J. W. Terman confirms that the Union army covered up multiple occurrences of murder, robbery, larceny, and arson among its "detectives," who utilized guerrilla tactics against civilians.[13] It is safe to assume that some Union troops who temporarily occupied towns in Missouri conducted themselves in a similar manner.[14]

Reading evidence on guerrillas in Missouri through a spatiotemporal lens reveals three fundamental characteristics in the relationship between temporary Union armies and guerrilla violence. First, Federal troops' use of excessive force against civilians in violation of official Union policy instigated guerrilla violence. The documented actions of small Union foraging squads created anxiety and fear rather than security among civilians and encouraged them to look elsewhere or take up arms for their own safety. Second, garrison towns' effectiveness depended on their size and longevity. The mercurial presence of Union armies in Missouri's central counties created large numbers of Union supply trains and company-sized skeleton crews that were unable to offer protection to civilians and actually became targets for guerrillas. Furthermore, Washington regularly called on regiments in Missouri to serve in the Eastern Theater during the last two years of the war. As the numbers of Union troops dwindled, guerrillas took advantage of the vacuum to instigate more attacks. Last, guerrillas chiefly targeted the Union army and Unionist militias, not civilians; instances of guerrilla violence overwhelmingly appear in the former locations of temporary Union occupiers where skeleton crews and ad hoc militias remained. The ratio between guerrillas' attacks against Union property and those against civilians in central counties was 40:18; that is, guerrillas in this region targeted Union troops over two times as often as civilians.[15] Guerrillas did not choose their victims at random but carefully targeted the Union army and its supporters. They sought out the Union army's logistical network, and most destruction of civilian property was collateral damage of more organized attacks. In these ways, the Union army's presence shaped patterns of guerrilla violence.

Placing evidence in time and space throughout central Missouri clearly illustrates the effects of stationary *and* temporary Union occupation. The nature of guerrilla warfare in central Missouri directly reflected changes in the nature and size of Union occupation. In 1861, stationary Union posts outnumbered temporary ones by a ratio of 2:1, and *no* instances of guer-

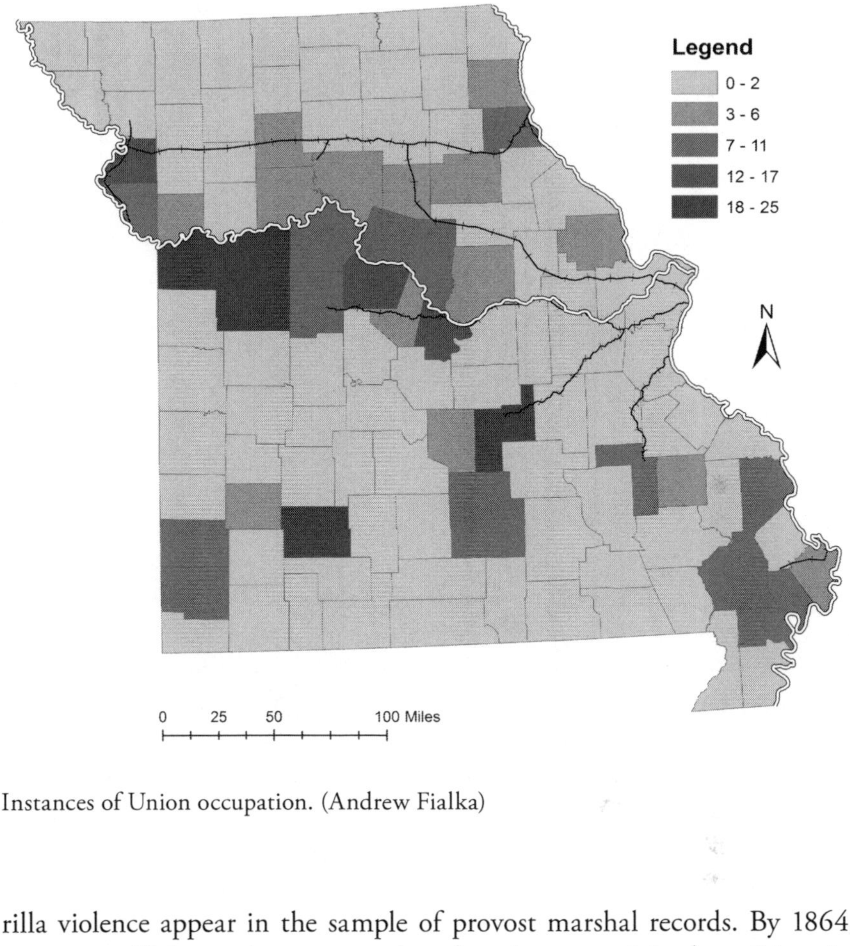

Instances of Union occupation. (Andrew Fialka)

rilla violence appear in the sample of provost marshal records. By 1864, temporary Union actions outnumbered stationary activity by a 5:1 ratio. The Union's occupational strategy changed because of limited manpower and resources and the relative unimportance of Missouri's countryside to the larger war effort. Concurrently, guerrilla violence in central Missouri exploded during the summer of 1864 (see map, "Instances of Union occupation").[16]

Although guerrillas were not prevalent in Missouri's central counties until 1864, the Union army's locations in 1861 foreshadowed a pattern of violence. Despite some instances of stationary Union occupation in 1861—most notably in Taos, Jefferson City, Franklin, Otterville, and Columbia—most Federal regiments conducted short excursions into small communities and planted the seeds of retaliatory violence.[17] For example, the Twenty-Second Indiana Infantry and Seventeenth Kentucky Infantry pursued guerrillas during one- and two-week stints, respectively, in Cooper and Howard Counties in early June, while the Thirty-Seventh Illinois Infantry pulled a similar four-day jaunt in Saline, Howard, and Cooper Counties in September.[18] Likewise, Boone County experienced a short occupation at the hands of the Fourteenth Missouri Infantry from December 12 to December 14.[19] The most populated and trade-oriented towns in these counties—Rocheport, Arrow Rock, Glasgow, Centralia, Boonville, and Fayette—became synonymous with guerrilla violence later in the war. This evidence demonstrates the presence of temporary Union occupation in towns later associated with the irregular conflict. Moreover, the towns associated with stationary Union occupation—Taos, Jefferson City, Franklin, Otterville, and Columbia—maintained a steady presence of Union outfits and experienced markedly less irregular violence later in the war.

The nature of Union occupation in central Missouri steadily changed from stationary to temporary as the war progressed into its second year.[20] Beginning in March, Union occupational strategy relocated thousands of troops to other states and subsequently assigned insufficient numbers of troops to short stints in small communities, as opposed to long, stationary positions at well-manned fortifications. Consequently, temporary Union expeditions outnumbered stationary duties at a 7:2 clip for the remainder of the year. Remnants of the Fifth Ohio Artillery, First Missouri Cavalry, and Eleventh Iowa Infantry pulled out of central Missouri on March 7, 1862, en route to more conventional service. In the same month, a local outfit known as the Boonville Cavalry ran operations in neighboring Saline County for four days while Companies A and C of the Sixth Missouri Infantry led a similar four-day expedition through Moniteau County and engaged in skirmishes with guerrillas while on patrol.[21] Similarly, the first documentation of guerrillas' actions in the provost marshal papers began in March 1862 and did not waver through the outburst of violence in 1864.

May 27, 1862, marked the first reported instance of violence among civilians in central Missouri, an event that highlights the difficulties inherent in interpreting the irregular conflict. Randolph County Sheriff John Hanstren indefinitely held Bob Sweeny, a southern-sympathizing citizen of Moberly, in custody without a trial for "kill[ing] a Union man."[22] The available information in this case cannot positively determine whether Sweeny was an overzealous southern sympathizer or a guerrilla himself, nor can the

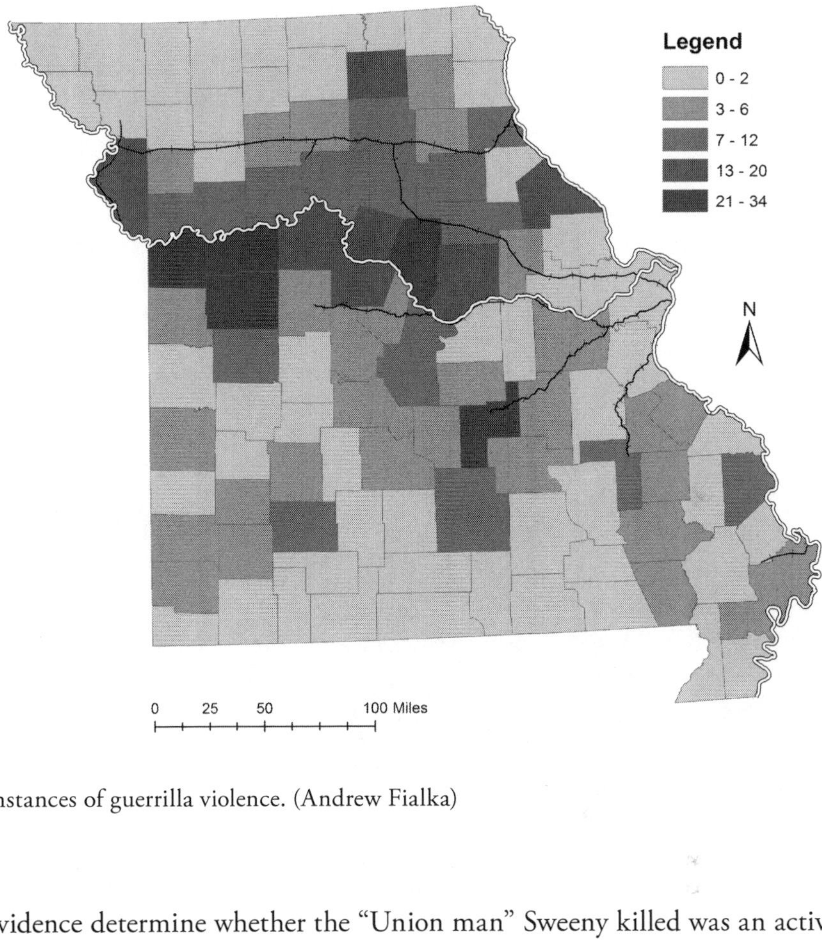

Instances of guerrilla violence. (Andrew Fialka)

evidence determine whether the "Union man" Sweeny killed was an active militia member or not. However, a digital map can prove that Sweeny's hometown lay less than twenty miles away from two counties—Howard and Boone—in which temporary Union occupation existed prior to Sweeny committing murder. A spatiotemporal lens places Sweeny's actions within the context of the Union's shifting occupation strategy and consequently provides a deeper understanding of violence that complicates historians' current portrayal. Although Sweeny's individual motives remain opaque, his actions are consistent with the spatial proximity of violence and temporary Union occupation (see map, "Instances of guerrilla violence").[23]

From May to September 1862, temporary posts typified the Union occupation of central Missouri. From May 30 to July 12, a regiment listed only as "3 years Service" organized a pursuit of guerrillas in Howard and Cooper Counties.[24] Companies of the Sixth Missouri Cavalry carried out operations and scouting expeditions in Pettis and Saline Counties for less than a week in late July.[25] Detachments of the same regiment rode all the way to Johnson County in western Missouri to temporarily man an outpost between August 30 and September 14, while the Fifty-Third Missouri Infantry scouted Ralls County for six days in mid-September.[26] Moreover, between twenty-five and fifty Federal regiments gathered in Boonville between May 30 and June 11 before moving to the Eastern Theater of war. Not coincidentally, these towns and counties experienced repeated guerrilla assaults in 1864.

In 1863 very few Union detachments roamed the countryside, and almost no guerrilla bands targeted Union war industries for the entire year because Missouri's guerrillas coordinated across regions of the state in response to developments in the regular war effort during this time period. The Union and Confederate armies' presence in western Missouri in late 1862 and 1863 attracted most guerrillas to the Kansas-Missouri border. In this way, guerrilla activity in Missouri developed in the context of the larger war; the fate of Missouri's southern-sympathizing civilians was inextricably tied to that of the Confederate army. Not only did the guerrillas chiefly target Union war industries, but they also cooperated with the Confederate army when given the opportunity. A spatiotemporal consideration of guerrilla violence in relation to the presence of the Confederate army further reveals patterns within the irregular conflict.[27]

For example, guerrillas assisted the Confederate army's recruiting efforts in western Missouri in the summer and fall of 1862. Confederate forces under Colonels Gideon W. Thompson and John T. Hughes recruited in central and western Missouri in hopes of strengthening their depleted forces in the Trans-Mississippi Theater. On August 11, Thompson and Hughes joined forces with William Quantrill's guerrillas and routed the Union cavalry operating out of Independence. Four days later, Union troops again clashed with a combined force of guerrillas and the Confederate army in Lone Jack. Although the Rebels forced Union soldiers under Emory S. Foster off the battlefield, the formal Confederate forces quickly retreated to Arkansas after failing to expand their numbers. The Union cavalry's defeat at the hands of the departed Confederate army left guerrillas to continue the battle in Missouri unaccompanied by Rebel soldiers.[28]

Furthermore, guerrillas utilized their informal kinship networks across county lines to respond to the chief threats from the Union army. In the spring of 1863, Brigadier General Thomas Ewing Jr.—commander of the newly created District of the Border—vowed to root out the bushwhackers in Missouri and targeted the guerrillas' female family members to achieve this goal. A Kansas City jail holding female relatives of well-known guerrillas collapsed on August 13, fatally crushing four women and severely injuring eight others. To make matters worse, the next day Ewing signed into law General Orders No. 10, which called for "the forced removal of bushwhacker families and friends and their exile from west Missouri." Before Union troops could carry out these orders, Missouri's guerrillas responded to Ewing's actions brutally and swiftly. Leaving central Missouri vacant, 450 bushwhackers infamously sacked Lawrence, Kansas, to "have revenge" on the Union army a little over a week after the jail collapse and Ewing's issuance of General Orders No. 10. Afterward, most guerrillas migrated to Texas for the winter of 1863–1864, while General Ewing issued General Orders No. 11 on August 25, which forced "approximately 20,000 people [in western Missouri] to evacuate their homes, almost all of which then were burned."[29] With General Orders No. 11, the Union army had destroyed or dislocated guerrillas' households, forcing the evacuation of their women and destabilizing their domestic line of supply, making it impossible for them to operate in Missouri's western counties.[30]

These examples of guerrillas' statewide interconnections in late 1862 and 1863 unveil their hidden organizational network throughout the state. In central and western Missouri, violence was not random but widely organized and carefully orchestrated against guerrillas' primary threats. The absence of sources depicting guerrilla violence in central Missouri coupled with the noted increase of regular and irregular violence in western Missouri during 1862 and 1863 illustrates guerrillas' willingness to coordinate with Confederate forces and their priority in opposing the Union army.[31]

The guerrillas who raided Lawrence, Kansas, and subsequently rode to Texas returned to the central part of Missouri in the summer of 1864 because of the swift enforcement of General Orders No. 11. Overwhelmingly, these guerrillas concentrated in towns previously associated with temporary Union occupation. Due to a lack of troops, the Union army responded to the increase of guerrillas by enacting five times as many temporary expeditions as stationary occupations. Moreover, guerrillas targeted the Union army two and a half times more often than they did civilians.[32] Reading evidence of central Missouri's irregular conflict in 1864 from a digitized map uncovers violence in previously occupied counties and towns from 1861 to 1862 and allows us to identify patterns of violence in these spaces.

For example, on June 1–12, 1864, J. W. Terman—a Union detective operating under the guise of Captain Harry Truman—led a twenty-man detachment through Chariton County with soldiers from the Ninth Cavalry, Missouri State Militia. Truman and his men disguised themselves as guerrillas to entrap southern sympathizers into admitting their inclusion in guerrillas' domestic supply line.[33] While in and around the town of Keytesville, Truman and men under his command murdered seven men, robbed ten homes, and burned down one man's house before fleeing the county.[34] Two days after Truman's exit, local southern sympathizers *or* guerrillas murdered between four and nine Unionist civilians who had offered Truman assistance.[35] In response, the Thirty-Fifth Missouri Infantry scouted Chariton County from July 27 to July 30, and Unionist civilians (whether acting alone *or* in cooperation with the Thirty-Fifth Missouri Infantry) "burned down . . . the dwellings of nearly every citizen against Truman" between June and December.[36] This extraordinary example details the muddy nature of historical sources concerning guerrilla warfare. Read at an individual scale and without knowledge of the spatial dimensions of Chariton County's previous Union occupation, this example leads historians to assume that a spontaneous and endless cycle of retaliation characterized Missouri's Civil War. Information concerning Truman's "scouting expedition" cannot positively determine whether Chariton County's southern-sympathizing and Unionist civilians murdered each other in cold blood or whether Confederate-sympathizing guerrillas and local Unionist militias squared off at every opportunity, nor can it even draw a clear line between southern sympathizers and guerrillas or between Unionists and legitimate militia members. However, the fact that these instances of violence followed temporary Union occupation is clear: Chariton County experienced Union occupation starting in 1861 and also attracted large amounts of guerrilla and Federal violence in 1864. Violence began only after occupation became intermittent and destabilized the fabric of this space.

A monthly depiction of violence throughout the summer of 1864 illustrates the proximity of guerrillas' actions to Union occupiers. During July, most violence occurred in Randolph County and along a twenty-five-mile stretch of the Missouri River in Boone, Cooper, and Saline Counties. Along the river on July 1, guerrillas skirmished with Federal forces temporarily stationed at Arrow Rock, a town the Union army had temporarily occupied in October 1861.[37] This skirmish suggests that Federal companies remained in the city and acted as an easy target for guerrillas. Federals injured or exhausted from the fight presumably fled to a temporary garrison at Boonville to lick their wounds, while guerrillas under George Todd immediately occupied the abandoned town of Arrow Rock and "confiscate[d] 40 horses and $20,000" the same day.[38] Moreover, guerrillas fired upon Federal steamboats passing Rocheport sometime between the beginning of the month and July 20, while the First Oregon Cavalry carried out orders to attack guerrillas in Boonville on July 20 and August 17.[39]

Violence in Randolph County followed a similar pattern. Guerrillas targeted Federal troops, railroads, telegraph lines, and Unionist militias in Huntsville, Moberly, and Renick. The vast majority of these attacks involved guerrillas and the Union army or militia, yet some civilians did experience violence during the spree. For example, Bill Anderson "torture[d] a 72-year-old former judge" for information in Huntsville on July 30 because the judge was the father of the Union officer commanding the local garrison.[40] While such an act is certainly brutal, Anderson did not choose his victim at random. He directed his ruthlessness at carefully chosen civilians to gain information on the Union war effort.[41]

Throughout August, Union detachments continued to scout familiar territory while guerrillas mainly operated in temporarily occupied counties bordering the Missouri River: Carroll, Saline, Howard, Chariton, Boone, and Cooper. Guerrillas under Bill Anderson's command took multiple Unionist home guardsmen prisoner, killed between sixteen and twenty-three Federal troops, and lost thirty-five of their own to Union soldiers under Major Matlock throughout these counties.[42]

Nearly all guerrilla activity in September 1864 materialized in neighboring Audrain, Boone, Cole, Howard, and Randolph Counties, in close proximity to Union soldiers. On September 1 a band of guerrillas "assault[ed a] Federal wagon train" and "kill[ed] 25 Federals" near Rocheport.[43] A member of the group, Hamp Watts, concurrently "led a detachment of guerrillas who collected a contributory tax" from the town's civilians.[44] The record does not indicate whether those civilians held Unionist or Confederate loyalties. In either case, this example demonstrates that guerrillas often victimized civilians in conjunction with more organized attacks against Union troops and pro-Union militias. Due to the civilian nature of home guards and militias, reports of looting, the taking of prisoners, robberies, and murder usually coincided with coordinated guerrilla attacks on Federal occupiers, Unionist home guards, and Unionist militias. Moreover, guerrilla aggression against Union troops resulted in large numbers of deaths, while civilian victims commonly lost their fences, food, money, and sense of protection—not their lives.

Guerrillas belonging to Bill Anderson's band camped in Rocheport for the first two weeks of September, subsisting off southern sympathizers' support, goods stolen from Unionists or "contributory taxes," and even merchandise from "capture[d Federal] tug boats." Moreover, they clashed regularly with nearby Federal forces north of the Missouri River.[45] On September 12 a "25-man mounted patrol of [the] 9th Missouri State Cavalry" attacked and killed five guerrillas just north of Columbia.[46] These same forces skirmished again on September 23 less than thirty miles northwest of Columbia in the town of Fayette. Union troops held the upper hand again as they took one guerrilla prisoner and "killed and scalped" six others.[47] Guerrillas demonstrated their strength and mobility by "plunder[ing] and burn[ing a] . . . train of 18 wagons escorted by 80 members of [the] 3rd Missouri Militia" in between Columbia and Fayette the same day. An "unknown number" of Federals died, while guerrillas "execute[d]" twelve.[48] Swollen with confidence, guerrillas under Bill Anderson and George Todd abandoned their usual tactics and attempted to sack the newly established Federal garrison at Fayette the next day. Uselessly firing upon Union troops who had barricaded themselves in the town's brick courthouse, the guerrillas suffered a "humiliating defeat": eight guerrillas lost their lives, and twenty-four more rode away with ghastly wounds.[49] Some guerrillas retreated to Glasgow while others vented their frustration by "tear[ing] down several miles of telegraph wire" along the railroads near Allen, Renick, and Moberly.[50]

The Union response to September's bloodbath unfolded in temporarily occupied towns and in stark similarity to events surrounding the Lawrence Massacre. On September 26, General Clinton B. Fisk, disgruntled that central Missouri's civilians had harbored and enabled guerrillas throughout the month, "instructed the Federal commander [at Rocheport] . . . to 'let the rebels in that region to understand that there is something besides Bill Anderson['s] power in North Missouri.'" Union troops "moved from house to house and building to building, obeying their orders with ruthless precision. When they rode away, flames engulfed all of Rocheport." Fisk reported to his superiors that the fire was "accidental."[51] Much like the collapse of the Kansas City jail and the Union's enforcement of General Orders No. 11, the Federal troops' temporary presence in and subsequent burning of Rocheport redoubled guerrillas' efforts to oppose punitive Union policies.

Guerrillas understood that the ultimate protection of their households and slave society from Federal force rested with the presence of a regular Confederate army. In September and October 1864, irregulars under Bill Anderson sought out the railroad depot at Centralia to gain information on General Sterling Price's last attempt to invade Missouri.[52] Instead of news pertaining to Price's upcoming raid through Missouri, guerrillas intercepted a passenger train carrying civilians and twenty-three Federal soldiers on furlough from Sherman's army in Georgia. They then proceeded to rob the civilians, strip the soldiers, execute all but one of Sherman's men, and send the empty train barreling back to Sturgeon shrouded in flames. When 155 men of the Thirty-Ninth Missouri Infantry under the command of Major A. V. E. Johnston saw the train, they immediately headed to Centralia from the east. Blinded by his anger, Johnston led his men directly into an ambush and one of the most lopsided engagements of the war. Guerrillas under Bill Anderson, John Thrailkill, Tom and George Todd, and Si Gordon suffered only a handful of casualties while inflicting 123 of their own. Guerrillas then mutilated more than one hundred of the Federal corpses.[53] The massacre at Centralia bookended a month of unparalleled violence within the state's borders.

Sterling Price's ambitious 1864 raid through Missouri shaped guerrillas' actions in the fall, and the lack of irregular violence following the Confederate army's exit from the state further demonstrates that there was strategic purpose to guerrillas' activities. Sterling Price believed that "tens of thousands of Missourians springing up from the land to join him in his crusade" would swell his force of twelve thousand men enough to capture St. Louis.[54] However, sporadic engagements with Union troops and Price's mishandling of guerrilla support undermined his efforts. His downfall at the Battle of Westport on October 23 effectively ended his Missouri campaign and, more importantly, eased the widespread guerrilla violence throughout the state despite the continuation of the regular war for six months after his retreat.[55] After Price's departure, from November 1 to the end of the war only two instances of guerrilla violence appear in my sample of provost marshal records.[56] Widely considered the last hope for a Confederate Missouri by its civilians, Price's failed attempt to take St. Louis registered defeat in the eyes of a vast majority of guerrillas. Beginning in April 1865, most guerrillas surrendered to Federal authorities or simply laid down their arms and returned home. Others—most infamously Jesse and Frank James—continued their criminal activity and sealed the guerrillas' reputations in historical memory.[57] Despite exaggerated exceptions like the James brothers, Missouri's guerrilla war ended with the lost possibility of a regular Confederate presence.

Comparing spatiotemporal analyses of St. Louis, western Missouri, and central Missouri complicates our understanding of the Civil War's irregular conflict. Most importantly, obvious patterns of guerrilla violence existed within the state. Violence regularly occurred in towns that experienced temporary Union occupation, while it rarely happened in towns that experienced consistent occupation throughout the war. The presence of Union and Confederate armies directly influenced the presence of guerrilla warfare in Civil War Missouri. Union occupiers induced guerrilla violence throughout the state. Guerrillas carefully selected the towns and people they attacked in direct relation to Union occupation and orchestrated offensives with Confederates forces when possible. Moreover, the size, style, and frequency of guerrillas' attacks depended on the local nature of Union occupation. The presence of temporary Union detachments and official policies affecting guerrillas' female family members elicited brutal retaliation from guerrillas, while permanent Union regiments created spheres of relative peace. These findings challenge historians' current definition of guerrilla warfare by adding aim, intent, and purpose to guerrillas' violent actions and by demonstrating the capabilities of digital maps (see map, "Union occupation and guerrilla violence").

Furthermore, a spatiotemporal examination of Missouri's irregular conflict redefines what it meant to be a Civil War guerrilla.[58] A majority of those civilians who took up arms outside of the conventional army did not kill and plunder for pleasure. In fact, guerrilla operations depended upon a common enemy and a domestic supply line of female-headed households. Missouri's guerrillas orchestrated violence in recognizable patterns and shared goals with the conventional Confederate army. Finally, the size and intensity of guerrillas' actions directly reflected the Union army's occupational strategy. This essay is not an attempt to excuse the guerrillas' brutal deeds, only to illuminate the logic behind their actions.

Historians' employment of this developing methodology remains problematic for several reasons. First and foremost among these is the use of

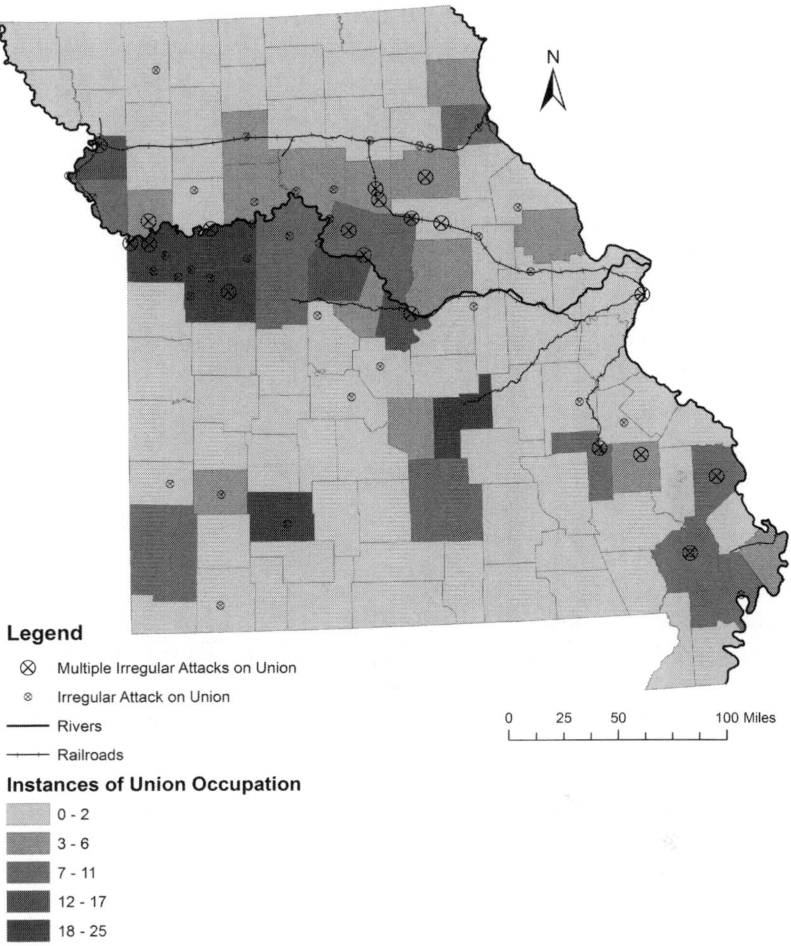

Union occupation and guerrilla violence. (Andrew Fialka)

technology combined with more traditional historical methods. The uncertainty, ambiguity, and human nature of historical sources do not easily wed with computer software's calculated and rigid code. Datasets and spreadsheets allow little room for diverse psychological motives, controversial definitions, cryptic messages, and incomplete evidence. Historians who attempt to quantify, measure, and map subjective evidence open the door for criticism and dissent. Therefore, scholars need to incorporate digital methods' advantages within their already effective social, cultural, and gendered approach to better understand the past.[59]

By discovering where instances of violence occurred in relation to the people present in the built and natural environment, we can highlight patterns within guerrilla warfare, see a clearer picture of the irregular conflict, and better explain why law-abiding citizens resort to violence in certain locations and time periods. To debate whether or not it was more acceptable to lose twenty thousand lives on a predetermined field under a national flag than it was for a band of guerrillas to kill a teenager and burn down a house would be to miss the point of this essay. Instead, we must try to understand the chaos and brutality that characterized America's Civil War. If we can understand how the guerrilla war became such hell, perhaps we can understand war in all its hellish forms, whether it took place in the bush of Missouri, the trenches at Spotsylvania Courthouse, the beaches at Normandy, the jungles of Vietnam, or the mountains of Afghanistan.

Notes

1. Thomas T. Roche, "The Bloody Angle: A Participant's Description of the Fiercest Combat of the War," *Philadelphia Weekly Times,* September 3, 1881.

2. The most popular Civil War narratives in existence heavily lean on battle maps to better illustrate instances of violence. For example, Shelby Foote, *The Civil War: A Narrative, Fort Sumter to Perryville* (New York: Vintage Books, 1958) contains forty-four battle maps and features a full-color map of the United States on the front endpaper. Bruce Catton, *Terrible Swift Sword* (New York: Doubleday, 1963) uses fifteen battle maps and also features a full-color map on the front and back endpaper. More recently, James McPherson, *Battle Cry of Freedom: The Civil War Era* (New York: Oxford University Press, 1988) uses twenty-three battle maps.

3. Some classic titles emphasizing this viewpoint include Richard S. Brownlee, *Gray Ghosts of the Confederacy: Guerrilla Warfare in the West, 1861–1865* (Baton Rouge: Louisiana State University Press, 1958); and Michael Fellman, *Inside War: The Guerrilla Conflict in Missouri during the American Civil War* (New York: Oxford University Press, 1989). More current examples include Albert Castel and Tom Goodrich, *Bloody Bill Anderson: The Short, Savage Life of a Civil War Guerrilla* (Lawrence: University Press of Kansas, 1998); Robert R. Mackey, *The Uncivil War: Irregular Warfare in the Upper South, 1861–1865* (Norman: University of Oklahoma Press, 2004); Clay Mountcastle, *Punitive War: Confederate Guerrillas and Union Reprisals* (Lawrence: University Press of Kansas, 2009); and Daniel E. Sutherland, *A Savage Conflict: The Decisive Role of Guerrillas in the American Civil War* (Chapel Hill: University of North Carolina Press, 2009). For

the best historiographical review of guerrilla studies, see Daniel E. Sutherland, "Sideshow No Longer: A Historiographical Review of the Guerrilla War," *Civil War History* 46, no. 1 (March 2000): 5–23.

4. ArcGIS and Neatline are two software programs that allow users to build digital maps. For more information see, ESRI Software Products, "ArcGIS," ESRI, http://www.esri.com/software/arcgis, accessed December 27, 2013; and Scholars' Lab, "Neatline: Plot Your Course in Space and Time," University of Virginia Library, http://neatline.org/about/, accessed October 23, 2012.

5. Research for this essay was derived from my master's thesis, Andrew William Fialka, "Reassessing Guerrillas: A Spatial and Temporal Analysis of Missouri's Civil War" (master's thesis, West Virginia University, 2013). "Reassessing Guerrillas" takes into account instances of guerrilla violence, the Union army, and the women heading southern-sympathizing households that made up guerrillas' domestic supply line throughout the entire state of Missouri. It argues that guerrilla warfare was carefully organized along a web of rebel households *and* in the wake of temporary Union occupational locations. "Reassessing Guerrillas" tracks Missouri guerrillas who sympathized with the Confederacy and does not explore the no-less-important role of Union-sympathizing guerrillas. For example, Kansas jayhawkers commonly raided Missouri using guerrilla tactics and contributed to instances of guerrilla violence within the state. Union-sympathizing guerrillas deserve further scholarly attention. Moreover, my focus on central Missouri in this essay does not depict nuanced trends of guerrilla violence throughout the state's different regions.

6. This essay is part of an ongoing project to map guerrilla warfare in the Civil War entitled *Of Methods and Madness: A Spatial History Approach to the Civil War's Guerrilla Violence.* A majority of the quantitative evidence in this essay comes from Fialka, "Reassessing Guerrillas." However, the University of Georgia's Center for Virtual History currently hosts an expanding version of the datasets and maps used in this essay. For more information and to view the animated maps discussed in this essay, please visit *Of Methods and Madness,* eHistory, http://www.ehistory.org/projects/of-methods-and-madness.html.

7. Sutherland, *Savage Conflict,* 28–29.

8. For examples of the guerrilla conflict before and after the Civil War, see Albert Castel, *Civil War Kansas: Reaping the Whirlwind* (Lawrence: University Press of Kansas, 1997); and Fellman, *Inside War,* 3–22, 231–66.

9. I was unable to plot evidence at the neighborhood level because the State Historical Society of Missouri's collection of Missouri county plat books begins in 1875, far too late to provide an accurate reference, considering the mass displacement of civilians during and after the Civil War. A similar spatiotemporal approach in other states that contain wartime plat maps is necessary to confirm or complicate my findings.

10. William C. Winter, *The Civil War in St. Louis* (St. Louis: Missouri Historical Society Press, 1994).

11. Analyzing the Union occupation of St. Louis from a wide spatial scope simplifies the complex divisions and dissension present within the city. For an example of the Union's difficult management of St. Louis civilians, see LeeAnn Whites, "'Corresponding with the Enemy': Mobilizing the Relational Field of Battle in St. Louis," in *Occupied Women: Gender, Military Occupation, and the American Civil War,* ed. LeeAnn Whites and Alecia P. Long (Baton Rouge: Louisiana State University Press, 2009), 103–16; and LeeAnn Whites, "Home Guards and Home Traitors: Loyalty and Prostitution in Civil War St. Louis," in *Gender Matters: Civil War, Reconstruction, and the Making of the New South* (New York: Palgrave Macmillan, 2005), 65–83.

12. This ratio steadily changed in favor of temporary occupation throughout the war, with yearly ratios of 18:10, 10:13, 3:9, and 6:17. Using Frederick H. Dyer, *A Compendium of the War of the Rebellion: Regimental Histories* (New York: Sagamore Press, 1908), I categorized Federal regiments as "stationary" or "temporary" based on the amount of time they spent in a given location *and* on the words Dyer used to describe their actions. Any troops who remained in one location for over a month are "stationary," while those staying under a month are "temporary." Moreover, soldiers who permanently "moved," those on "campaign," "duty," or "relief," and those "stationed" and "organized" classify as "stationary." Those on "guard," an "expedition," "scout," "operations," or "reconnaissance" and those involved in a "skirmish" or "actions" classify as "temporary." Unfortunately, these ambiguous descriptors depicting the Union army's activities are typical in Dyer's *Compendium* and highlight the gap between official Union policy and Union troops' actions *on the ground.*

13. Assistant Provost Marshal Charles D. Ludwig to Lieutenant A. J. Harding, Fulton, September 2, 1864, in U.S. War Department, *The War of the Rebellion: A Compilation of the Official Records of the Union and Confederate Armies* (Washington, D.C.: Government Printing Office, 1880–1901), ser. 1, vol. 41, pt. 3, p. 35 (hereinafter cited as *OR*); Fellman, *Inside War,* 123; Mountcastle, *Punitive War,* 1; and Case against J. W. Terman, Series: Court Martial Case Files, compiled 12/1800–10/1894, U.S. National Archives, Washington, D.C., 226–28.

14. Mark Grimsley provides abundant examples of Union troops who abused their orders to forage and targeted civilians. Although Grimsley posits that this was the exception to the rule, Union actions in Missouri stand in contrast to his argument. Moreover, Grimsley credits the orders of Union generals for imposing restraint and ignores the difference between official orders and Union troops' actions *on the ground.* See Mark Grimsley, *The Hard Hand of War: Union Military Policy toward Southern Civilians, 1861–1865* (New York: Cambridge University Press, 1995). Also see Stephen V. Ash, *When the Yankees Came: Conflict and Chaos in the Occupied South, 1861–1865* (Chapel Hill: University of North Carolina Press, 1995), 76–107; and Phillip Shaw Paludan, *A People's Contest: The Union and Civil War, 1861–1865* (Lawrence: University Press of Kansas, 1988), 76–84. For examples of Union actions in Missouri, see Fellman, *Inside War,* 29–37.

15. This figure actually inflates the number of civilian targets, in opposition to my argument. For this essay I did not finely differentiate between guerrillas' attacks on the Union army and on pro-Unionist militias. Nor did I delve into each particular case, reading between the lines of cryptic interrogations and survival lies to discover the true sympathies of civilian casualties. More careful analysis is needed on this subject. Pro-Unionist militias often operated as "well-led 'mobs'" and practiced extralegal violence. Guerrillas often felt justified in treating pro-Unionist militias as an extension of the Union military, while some Unionist civilians categorized violence against militia members as unjustified attacks against civilians. I pool pro-Unionist militias in with civilians because to do the opposite would unfairly ignore guerrillas' actions against civilians. Still, this figure shows guerrillas' heavy slant toward targeting the Union army. See Fellman, *Inside War,* 238.

16. To discover the Union army's location, I utilized a digitized version of Dyer's *Compendium,* the most comprehensive description of the entire Union army's spatial location throughout the war. Scholars at Tufts University's Perseus Digital Library digitized Dyer's *Compendium* and allow users to download their version as an XML file. Known and unknown errors exist in Dyer's *Compendium.* Dyer mainly worked at the regimental level and did not include many company-level movements in his work. This poses a problem, as the Union military sent many companies on search-and-destroy missions targeting guerrillas in Missouri. Dyer drew much of his evidence from *The War of the Rebellion;* any errors or omissions in that source transmitted to Dyer's work. A large amount of guerrilla violence enacted against civilians targeted members of local Unionist militia companies. Dyer seldom accounts for local home guards or civilian militias. This omission further leads historians to assume that guerrillas attacked civilians randomly. Most importantly, Dyer was a Union veteran, and Union subjectivity must be taken into account. For example, Andrew William Fialka, "Captain Harry Truman: A Case Study of the Union Military's Use of Guerrilla Tactics against the Civilian Population in Civil War Missouri" (honor's thesis, University of Missouri–Columbia, 2010), argues that the Union military funded "detectives" and indirectly ordered them to murder guerrillas and their supporters. Such "detectives" do not show up in Dyer's *Compendium,* and their actual numbers are unknown. Errors also exist in the Perseus rendition of Dyer's *Compendium.* Most importantly, not every location in Dyer's work is sufficiently geotagged and therefore locatable on a map. The University of Richmond's Scott Nesbit wrote the necessary code to organize the digitized XML file in a format compatible with ArcGIS for a project entitled *Visualizing Emancipation.* Once converted into an ArcGIS table, Dyer's *Compendium* lists 1,728 instances of Union occupation within Missouri's borders throughout the war. To view and download this dataset, visit University of Richmond, *Visualizing Emancipation,* http://dsl.richmond.edu/emancipation/data-download/, accessed July 12, 2014. Of the instances of Union occupation in Missouri, 406 include complete spatial information for the central Missouri counties under con-

sideration. Gregory R. Crane, "Perseus Digital Library," Tufts University, http://www.perseus.tufts.edu/hopper/, accessed December 6, 2012. I am especially grateful to Scott Nesbit for his expertise and insight concerning data manipulation and available resources for digital historians.

17. The Second U.S. Cavalry was stationed in Taos from April 1 to September 30. The Ninth Iowa Infantry guarded a railroad station in Franklin from October 11 to December 31, while the Fifth Ohio Artillery, First Missouri Cavalry, and Eleventh Iowa Infantry barricaded Jefferson City and Otterville from mid-October until well into 1862. Moreover, companies from the First Missouri reinforced the garrison at Jefferson City throughout the months of June and September. See "Second United States Regiment Cavalry Service," http://localhost/omeka-1.5.3/items/show/1528; "Ninth Iowa Regiment Infantry Service," http://localhost/omeka-1.5.3/items/show/1571; "Fifth Ohio Independent Battery Light Artillery Service," http://localhost/omeka-1.5.3/items/show/1572; "First Missouri Regiment Cavalry Service," http://localhost/omeka-1.5.3/items/show/1578; "Eleventh Iowa Regiment Infantry Service," http://localhost/omeka-1.5.3/items/show/1579; and "First Missouri Regiment Cavalry Service," http://localhost/omeka-1.5.3/items/show/1557, all in Fialka, "Reassessing Guerrillas." Citations such as those above refer to material from Neatline databases that are part of my master's thesis, Fialka, "Reassessing Guerrillas"; the URLs are item identifiers, not publicly accessible website addresses. These materials will be made publicly available at the *Of Methods and Madness* project site on eHistory.org at the University of Georgia's Center for Virtual History. The names in quotations refer to case files in the Missouri Union Provost Marshal Papers, evidence from previously noted secondary source material, or titles given to Union army regiments by Tufts University from Dyer's *Compendium.* In addition, several companies of Union troops guarded the University of Missouri in Columbia and the capitol building in Jefferson City for the length of the war. Although these companies remained stationary for almost the entire war and successfully dissuaded guerrillas, they do not appear in Dyer's *Compendium* because of their size.

18. "Twenty-Second Indiana Regiment Infantry Service," http://localhost/omeka-1.5.3/items/show/1533; "Seventeenth Kentucky Regiment Infantry Service," http://localhost/omeka-1.5.3/items/show/1532; and "Thirty-Seventh Illinois Regiment Infantry (Fremont Rifles) Service," http://localhost/omeka-1.5.3/items/show/1570, in Fialka, "Reassessing Guerrillas."

19. "Fourteenth Missouri Regiment Infantry Service," http://localhost/omeka-1.5.3/items/show/1589 in Fialka, "Reassessing Guerrillas."

20. Between 1861 and 1862, the ratio between stationary and temporary Union occupation went from 2:1 to 2:7.

21. "Boonville State Militia Cavalry Battalion (Epstein's Cavalry)," http://localhost/omeka-1.5.3/items/show/1611; and "Sixth Missouri Regiment Infantry Service," http://localhost/omeka-1.5.3/items/show/1614, in Fialka, "Reassessing Guerrillas."

22. "Sweeny, Bob," http://localhost/omeka-1.5.3/items/show/1917 in Fialka, "Reassessing Guerrillas."

23. To locate instances of guerrilla violence, my map uses data from the Missouri Digital Heritage project's Missouri Provost Marshal Database and selected personal diaries and secondary sources. The Missouri Provost Marshal Database contains over seventy-two thousand entries, including citizen complaints, petitions, investigations, and loyalty documentation. I used a sample of these records that included only entries with complete spatial information and those containing the words "guerrilla" or "bushwhacker." Missouri's Union Provost Marshal Papers are still an imperfect source because they are incomplete and disorganized. Many of the papers omit locations and dates from their record. Moreover, provost marshals existed in a limited number of cities. Some citizens who made a report had to travel to a central location in order to do so, calling into question the validity of the recorded dates and locations. For a thorough description of Missouri's Union Provost Marshal Papers and to view the online database, see "Missouri's Union Provost Marshal Papers: 1861–1865," State Historical Society of Missouri, Missouri State Library, www.sos.mo.gov/archives/provost, accessed December 5, 2012. I also drew spatial information from personal diaries and secondary sources in regard to Missouri's most notorious guerrillas: William Quantrill, "Bloody" Bill Anderson, and Samuel S. Hildebrand. Those that included the best spatial information include O. S. Barton, *Three Years with Quantrell: A True Story Told by His Scout John McCorkle* (New York: Buffalo-Head Press, 1966); Samuel S. Hildebrand, James W. Evans, and Abraham Wendell Keith, *Autobiography of Samuel S. Hildebrand, the Renowned Missouri "Bushwhacker"* (Jefferson City, MO: State Times Printing House, 1870); and Castel and Goodrich, *Bloody Bill Anderson.* In total, the sample includes 572 instances of guerrilla violence.

24. "3 years Service," http://localhost/omeka-1.5.3/items/show/1624, in Fialka, "Reassessing Guerrillas."

25. "Sixth Missouri Regiment State Militia Cavalry Service," http://localhost/omeka-1.5.3/items/show/1627; and "Sixth Missouri Regiment State Militia Cavalry Service," http://localhost/omeka-1.5.3/items/show/1628, in Fialka, "Reassessing Guerrillas."

26. "Sixth Missouri Regiment State Militia Cavalry Service," http://localhost/omeka-1.5.3/items/show/1635; and "Fifth-Third Missouri Regiment Enrolled Militia Infantry," http://localhost/omeka-1.5.3/items/show/1638, in Fialka, "Reassessing Guerrillas."

27. For a description of guerrillas' actions in western Missouri throughout 1863, see Albert E. Castel, *William Clarke Quantrill: His Life and Times* (Norman: University of Oklahoma Press, 1962), 101–21.

28. Jay Monaghan, *Civil War on the Western Border, 1854–1865* (New York: Bonanza Books, 1955), 255–56, 323–32.

29. Thomas Goodrich, *Bloody Dawn: The Story of the Lawrence Massacre* (Kent, OH: Kent State University Press, 1991), 20–25; Castel and Goodrich,

Bloody Bill Anderson, 26–27; Barton, *Three Years with Quantrell,* 78–79; Brownlee, *Gray Ghosts of the Confederacy,* 124; Sutherland, *Savage Conflict,* 194; and Fellman, *Inside War,* 95.

30. Guerrillas' domestic supply line consisted of the women in their households who supplied them with food, clothing, shelter, resources, and information. I classify these women as militarized civilians and suggest that they enabled guerrillas to operate and served as the conduit for guerrilla warfare. For the leading argument that "women were an integral part of the war of occupation" and domestic supply line, see Whites and Long, *Occupied Women.* The spatiotemporal locations of guerrilla violence—and lack thereof—in central and western Missouri during 1863 and 1864 bolster Joseph Beilein's argument that "General Order No. 11 . . . effectively destroyed the logistical side of [guerrillas'] . . . entire rebel supply line" and stands in stark contrast to Albert Castel's claim that General Orders No. 11 "had no such effect . . . of making it impossible for the guerrillas to maintain themselves in th[e] region." See Joseph Beilein, "Household War: Guerrilla-Men, Rebel Women, and Guerrilla Warfare in Civil War Missouri" (PhD diss., University of Missouri, 2012), 77–78; and Castel and Goodrich, *Bloody Bill Anderson,* 31.

31. For more examples of guerrillas cooperating or attempting to cooperate with the Confederate army, see Brownlee, *Gray Ghosts of the Confederacy,* 76–91, 206–22.

32. For the years 1861 to 1864, the ratios of stationary to temporary Union occupation are 2:1, 2:7, 0:2, and 1:5, respectively. For 1864 the ratio between guerrillas' attacks on the Union army and those against civilians is 2:1. However, evidence suggests that some of the civilians under attack belonged to Unionist militia organizations. Categorizing those incidents as attacks on the Union army brings the ratio to 3:1. I selected the halfway point in arguing that guerrillas were "two and a half times as likely" to target the Union war machine. Guerrilla attacks that targeted the Union army as opposed to civilians increased from an 1861–1863 ratio of 0:6 to an 1864 ratio of almost 3:1.

33. 1864 Missouri Union Provost Marshal File for Two or More Individuals, file 10159, Ellis Library Special Collections, Columbia, MO.

34. Case against J. W. Terman, Series: Court Martial Case Files, compiled 12/1800–10/1894, U.S. National Archives, Washington, D.C., 226–228. Terman/Truman's case indicates that he was found guilty on seven of nine murder charges, three of nine robbery charges, seven of twelve larceny charges, and one arson charge.

35. Ibid., 221; *OR,* ser. 1, vol. 34, pt. 4, p. 372.

36. "Thirty-Fifth Missouri Regiment Enrolled Militia Infantry," http://localhost/omeka-1.5.3/items/show/1724, in Fialka, "Reassessing Guerrillas"; *OR,* ser. 1, vol. 41, pt. 4, p. 815.

37. "John McCorkle," http://localhost/omeka-1.5.3/items/show/131, in Fialka, "Reassessing Guerrillas."

38. "George Todd," http://localhost/omeka-1.5.3/items/show/24, in Fialka, "Reassessing Guerrillas."

39. "Bill Anderson & Gang," http://localhost/omeka-1.5.3/items/show/34; and "First Oregon Regiment Cavalry," http://localhost/omeka-1.5.3/items/show/1717, in Fialka, "Reassessing Guerrillas."

40. "Bill Anderson & Gang," http://localhost/omeka-1.5.3/items/show/41, in Fialka, "Reassessing Guerrillas."

41. Similarly, Union soldiers often targeted and tortured civilians for information about deserters and guerrillas. For example, see Phillip Shaw Paludan, *Victims: A True Story of the Civil War* (Knoxville: University of Tennessee Press, 2004).

42. "Bill Anderson & Gang," http://localhost/omeka-1.5.3/items/show/43; "First Missouri Regiment State Militia Cavalry Service," http://localhost/omeka-1.5.3/items/show/1718; "Bill Anderson & Gang," http://localhost/omeka-1.5.3/items/show/50; "Major Matlock," http://localhost/omeka-1.5.3/items/show/53; "Bill Anderson Raids Howard and Boone Counties," http://localhost/omeka-1.5.3/items/show/52; and "Bill Anderson & Gang," http://localhost/omeka-1.5.3/items/show/55, in Fialka, "Reassessing Guerrillas." Instances of violence appeared elsewhere—in Cole, Gasconade, and Monroe Counties—at a much lower frequency. Bill Anderson "strip[ped] and whip[ped] a man because he was a Union man" in Russellville on August 2. On August 11, H. Clay Price, a member of the "Davis band of guerrillas," robbed Captain W. E. Foukes, the sheriff of Monroe County. The next day, guerrillas in Anderson's band killed the "captain and four soldiers of [a] Union militia company" in Fredericksburg. See "Bill Anderson," http://localhost/omeka-1.5.3/items/show/45; "Price, H. Clay," http://localhost/omeka-1.5.3/items/show/1279; and "Bill Anderson & Gang," http://localhost/omeka-1.5.3/items/show/47, in Fialka, "Reassessing Guerrillas."

43. "John McCorkle," http://localhost/omeka-1.5.3/items/show/134.

44. "Hamp Watts," http://localhost/omeka-1.5.3/items/show/58, in Fialka, "Reassessing Guerrillas."

45. "Bill Anderson & Gang," http://localhost/omeka-1.5.3/items/show/57, in Fialka, "Reassessing Guerrillas."

46. "Widow Turner," http://localhost/omeka-1.5.3/items/show/59, in Fialka, "Reassessing Guerrillas."

47. "Cave Wyatt," http://localhost/omeka-1.5.3/items/show/61, Fialka, "Reassessing Guerrillas."

48. "Bill Anderson & Gang," http://localhost/omeka-1.5.3/items/show/60, in Fialka, "Reassessing Guerrillas."

49. "Tom Benton," http://localhost/omeka-1.5.3/items/show/12; and "Defense of Fayette," http://localhost/omeka-1.5.3/items/show/63, in Fialka, "Reassessing Guerrillas." For a detailed description of the failed guerrilla attack on Fayette, see Castel and Goodrich, *Bloody Bill Anderson,* 60–61.

50. "Bill Anderson & Gang," http://localhost/omeka-1.5.3/items/show/64, in Fialka, "Reassessing Guerrillas."

51. Castel and Goodrich, *Bloody Bill Anderson,* 105.

52. Albert Castel and Tom Goodrich contend that Bill Anderson went to Cen-

tralia because it "had stores, and those stores had money, plunder, and whiskey. . . . He did not particularly care about Price—his was a different war both in purpose and kind." The lure of a passenger train loaded with civilians carrying "jewelry, greenbacks, and real money in the form of gold and silver" may have also provided Anderson a "profitable as well as enjoyable" experience. See Castel and Goodrich, *Bloody Bill Anderson,* 70. Although guerrillas regularly targeted Unionist civilians, militia members, and home guards, I argue that they did so more often with larger implications and in conjunction with attacks on the Union army. Guerrillas did not lazily congregate in towns with railroads, waiting to rob random civilians of their money and liquor. Their tactics were built on speed and stealth. While Anderson certainly preyed on civilians across central Missouri, he did not do so solely for random profit and enjoyment. He subjected carefully chosen targets to savage actions in order to gain an advantage against the Union army.

53. For the most authoritative account of the Centralia Massacre, see Castel and Goodrich, *Bloody Bill Anderson,* 79–99.

54. Ibid., 112.

55. For information on Sterling Price's exploits in Missouri, see Monaghan, *Civil War on the Western Border,* 307–45.

56. Of course, more than two instances of guerrilla violence occurred after Price's retreat from Missouri. However, it is clear that far fewer incidents occurred than had the previous summer, in 1864.

57. Guerrilla warfare's historiography leads readers to believe that the ending of the conventional Civil War somehow turned bloodthirsty heathens back into regular farmers and the world went back to normal. I argue that guerrillas had clear goals in mind, and once the war was over there was no longer a need to fight as bushwhackers. Characters like Jesse James and his postwar criminal antics perpetuate and exacerbate the current historiography's reading of postwar Missouri.

58. Historians have yet to satisfactorily define "guerrilla," and they tease irregulars out of the civilian population with varying degrees of success. This essay uses the nineteenth-century definition of guerrillas as depicted by Francis Lieber: "Self-constituted sets of armed men in times of war, who form no integrant part of the organized army, do not stand on the regular pay-roll of the army, or are not paid at all, take up arms and lay them down at intervals, and carry on petty war chiefly by raids, extortion, destruction, and massacre, and who cannot encumber themselves with many prisoners, and will therefore generally give no quarter." See *OR,* ser. 3, vol. 2, pt. 1, pp. 307–8. Note that this definition differs from that for partisan rangers, "small, elite conventional forces given an unconventional role"—adopted most notably by John S. Mosby and John Hunt Morgan. For the best breakdown of unconventional forces in the Civil War, see Mackey, *Uncivil War,* 3–23.

59. For an excellent example of scholars who are reengaging the possibilities of technology and humanities scholarship, see David J. Bodenhamer, John Corrigan, and Trevor M. Harris, eds., *The Spatial Humanities: GIS and the Future of Humanities Scholarship* (Bloomington: Indiana University Press, 2010). To see how

historians use spatiotemporal methods to revisit old historical problems and the challenges to digital scholarship, see William G. Thomas III and Edward L. Ayers, "An Overview: The Differences Slavery Made; A Close Analysis of Two American Communities," *American Historical Review* 108, no. 5 (December 2003): 1299–1307. For examples of how historians have attempted to wed digital and textual arguments, see Anne Kelly Knowles, *Past Time, Past Place: GIS for History* (Redlands: ESRI Press, 2002); William G. Thomas III, *The Iron Way: Railroads, the Civil War, and the Making of Modern America* (New Haven, CT: Yale University Press, 2011); and University of Richmond, *Visualizing Emancipation*, http://dsl.richmond.edu/emancipation/, accessed July 28, 2013.

Violence, Conflict, and Loyalty in the Carolina Piedmont

A Comparative Perspective

David Brown and Patrick J. Doyle

W. W. Herbert was fully aware of the potential utility of guerrilla warfare for the southern cause. A resident of the South Carolina Piedmont who had spent much of the late 1850s in Kansas devoting himself "to the advancement of the interests of the South," Herbert wrote to several influential acquaintances in Fairfield District with a new project in mind as the secession crisis deepened in the winter of 1860–1861. This venture was to be "a company of mounted men, which shall be *independent* of all other military organizations," raised with the intention to "wage a war upon our enemies upon the principle adopted by the 'Swamp Fox' [Francis Marion] of S. Carolina, during the Revolutionary struggle." Surely influenced by his experiences in Kansas, Herbert concluded that "this mode of warfare will be more . . . destructive than any other which can be adopted."[1] Yet Herbert's vision of a partisan cavalry unit never came to fruition. Indeed, Herbert's proposed collaborator in organizing the company, William S. Alston, seemingly gave up hope of establishing such a unit, quickly accepting a role as sergeant in Captain James M. Gadberry's First Regiment South Carolina Volunteers on January 12, 1861.[2]

Herbert's proposal provides an interesting counterpoint to how the North and South Carolina Piedmont actually experienced the war. While Herbert had envisioned guerrilla tactics as being the most effective way for the South to achieve independence, localized skirmishing against official Union forces never took place in the Piedmont. This owed much to the basic absence of the enemy in the region, with invading Federal forces arriving only during the final acts of the war. The insulated nature of the Carolina Piedmont meant that not only would local citizens avoid physically encountering the dreaded Yankees face to face, but they would remain subject to the control of the Confederacy and their state governments for almost the entirety of the war. As such, the bitter irregular conflicts between Union forces and Confederates over contested power and territory that blighted other portions of the South, particularly in its western and border regions, would not be replicated in the Piedmont.[3] Instead, the violence waged there would be, to borrow Robert R. Mackey's typology, between "guerrillas"—armed citizens, including draft dodgers and deserters, who acted independently of federal military supervision—and Confederate forces marshalled to suppress their activities.[4] Although distant from the major theaters of war and the Union army, some parts of the Carolina Piedmont nonetheless witnessed a bitter inner Civil War.

Other parts of this Confederate heartland, by contrast, avoided the stresses and strains of irregular warfare. Guerrilla violence would be a lot less widespread in South Carolina than in other parts of the Piedmont and, when it occurred, was confined to the more hilly and mountainous sections located in the extreme northwest of the state. Moreover, this sporadic violence was more benign in South Carolina, lacking the animosity that typified conflict in some Piedmont counties of the Tar Heel State. State lines and other geopolitical borders are man-made constructions that can mean little for the day-to-day experience of ordinary people. The growth of a market economy in western North Carolina, for instance, followed well-worn routes across borders rather than being constrained within the state line.[5] During the Civil War, however, the state border seemed to genuinely divide two regions, one blighted by internal conflict and one in which a significant guerrilla problem never fully materialized, despite some flashpoints of violence. This essay explores this discrepancy. Why and how did a pervasive and belligerent opposition—"communities of dissent" as Victoria E. Bynum has described it—develop in the North Carolina Piedmont but not in South Carolina?[6] Taking a comparative approach, this essay outlines the origins, form, and consequences of irregular conflict in the Carolina Piedmont. Local studies of individual communities and counties have offered the "most revealing recent explorations of the South's wartime experience," but a process of comparison is the most effective way to explore the ways in which loyalty, discontent, and community dynamics differed, ultimately producing violence in some places and not others.[7] From a comparative perspective, fundamentally different views of the Confederacy in the North and South Carolina Piedmont explain the contrasting nature of irregular conflict. North of the state line questions about the legitimacy of the new southern nation would remain divisive and routinely provoke internal conflict. Conversely, an overwhelming majority of Piedmont South Carolinians supported the Confederate cause, even if worsening social conditions caused some to grow tired of war.

A central thread in recent guerrilla warfare historiography is the critical importance of prewar conditions. Conflict was a product not only of wartime strains and fluctuating power structures but also of antebellum socioeconomic conditions: kinship ties, neighborhood dynamics, political affiliations, and the peculiar and often idiosyncratic ways in which communities functioned. Power relations in rural southern localities, especially in a political sense, were formed long before the attack on Fort Sumter in April 1861. The differing socioeconomic complexions of the North and South Carolina Piedmont make the region an intriguing case study. As one historian has noted, the formation of anti-Confederate communities often reflected their geographic position in relation to the South's cotton belt.[8] A lack of engagement with cotton production engendered lesser reliance on slavery and consequently greater scepticism regarding the Confederacy. While not minimizing the importance of outside events such as withdrawal from the Union or Confederate imposition of conscription, we share the approach of recent historians who take the continuities and discontinuities of community dynamics during the late antebellum period and follow them into the war years as the essential starting point for understanding guerrilla violence.

For the Piedmont sections of South Carolina, ubiquitously referred to as the upcountry, cotton was certainly king prior to the Civil War. The cotton boom of the late 1840s had cemented the primacy of the cash crop in the upcountry, even enabling the upper Piedmont districts located among the foothills of the Appalachian Mountains to shift from a self-sufficient form of agriculture to the more commercially engaged production of cotton.[9] There continued to be differences between the upper and lower Piedmont sections of the South Carolina upcountry, with higher rates of slaveholding and cotton production in the latter, but the region was largely united by a dedication to staple-crop production. Pockets of the upcountry, though, remained largely outside the cotton economy. The hill and mountain sections of upper Piedmont districts such as Greenville, Pickens, and Spartanburg predominately concentrated on the production of corn, wheat, and livestock.[10] Spartanburg District provides the best example of the limited nature of economic change in some small sections of the region. According to the agricultural schedules of the 1860 federal census, 63.3 percent of residents in the southern half of Spartanburg were growing cotton compared to 25.8 percent in the northern half. Moreover, cotton farmers in the less hilly southern section of Spartanburg were growing markedly larger quantities of the crop and were thus more deeply entwined with the cotton economy than were those who lived closer to the North Carolina border.[11]

In the North Carolina Piedmont, cotton and slavery were far less important. Border counties such as Anson, Mecklenburg, and Richmond could be described as having cotton economies, but others did not. Indeed, the region as a whole was in the midst of a transformation from self-sufficient farming to a more commercial, market-focused agricultural economy, encouraged by the growth of textiles and other industrial pursuits as well as the arrival of the North Carolina Railroad.[12] The central Piedmont was certainly not reliant on production of one main cash crop, as were many other parts of the South, including the South Carolina Piedmont. Slaves were present in the region, but they were proportionally not more than one-third of the total population, and in many counties they made up considerably less than a third. In 1860 just 15–20 percent of whites in the central Piedmont owned slaves. Even allowing for those who did not own slaves but were involved with slavery (overseers, for example), it is fair to conclude that for about three-quarters of the central Piedmont's white residents, slavery was not central to their immediate economic concerns.[13] As is by now well-known, moreover, central Piedmont counties contained a large Quaker population, and a number of citizens had religious and other ideological concerns about slavery as an institution.[14] In stark contrast, slaveholding among white families in the South Carolina Piedmont averaged 30–35 percent in the hillier upper Piedmont and 55–65 percent in the lower Piedmont in 1860, rates markedly above the southern average of approximately 25 percent.[15]

Whereas in South Carolina secession was decisive and quick, it was a far messier, drawn-out process in North Carolina. For the Palmetto State, unity of economic interests influenced the political process. As South Carolina reacted to the election of Abraham Lincoln in 1860, a widespread response rejected the incoming Republican administration and endorsed

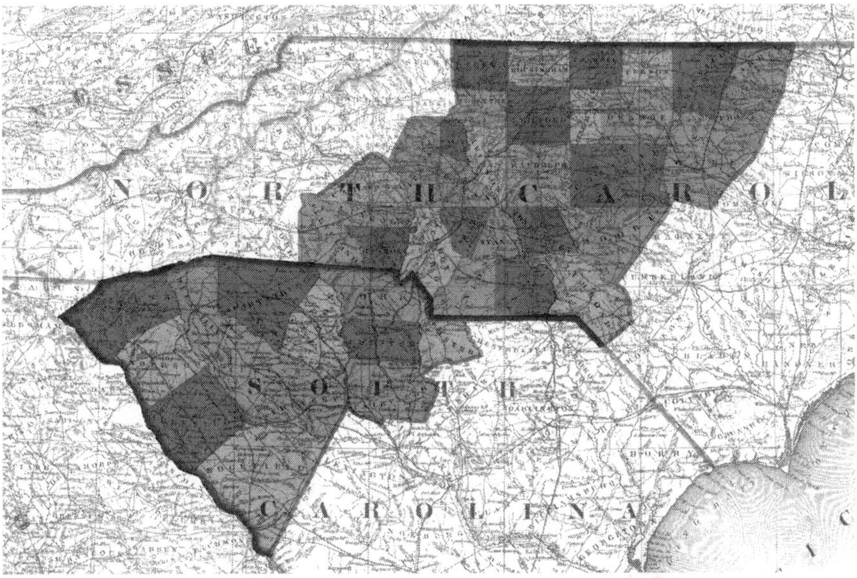

The North and South Carolina Piedmont, 1860. (Original map from A. J. Johnson, *Johnson's New Illustrated [Steel Plate] Family Atlas, with Descriptions Geographical, Statistical, and Historical* [New York: Johnson and Browning, 1860], 26–27. Edited by Paul Waddell.)

disunion. Some parts of the upper Piedmont, however, were not as enthusiastic as elsewhere in South Carolina. William K. Easley, newspaper editor, wealthy slaveholder, and would-be delegate to the 1860 secession convention, was "astonished" by the "perfect indifference" of the citizens of Pickens District toward disunion.[16] As Easley's surprise suggests, however, those doubting the prudence of secession usually did so out of ambivalence or cautiousness rather than outright opposition—despite the upper Piedmont's association with Unionism during previous secession crises and the presence of outspoken Unionist figurehead Benjamin F. Perry in Greenville. As one store owner in Spartanburg District remarked, "The Union men say wait until Lincoln commits an overt act," implying a distrust of the new president among those opposing immediate secession.[17] It is significant, however, that parts of the upper Piedmont that displayed a hesitancy, if not opposition, toward secession were those less involved in cotton production. They would later suffer most acutely from a guerrilla problem. It would be churlish, though, to overemphasize the number or influence of dissenters in the upcountry; most in the South Carolina Piedmont supported secession and would have surely agreed with one newspaper correspondent's declaration that disunion and war were not merely about "rich men's niggers" but "family and home and country."[18]

Secession was far more divisive in North Carolina. Only after the firing on Fort Sumter, with cries of coercion ringing in the ears of Piedmont folk, were Unionists resigned to defeat. Abraham Lincoln's call for troops transformed sentiment across the state, with Piedmont Unionist John Gilmer confessing that he "could do nothing more with the people. My voice was hushed."[19] Gilmer might have conceded, but Colonel Caleb Bohanan, a Yadkin County slaveholder, told his local militia "that no man ought to support" the Confederacy and that he hoped Lincoln found sufficient volunteers because "every secessionist ought to be hung."[20] While most did not go that far, there were numerous displays of Union loyalty in the central Piedmont. These were not just vague anti-Confederate feelings or mild expressions of discomfort regarding the political situation, but deep-seated, defiant, and very public displays of dissent. In Alamance County, a committee of Unionists sent advance notice to secessionist Thomas Ruffin of their intention "to raise the Flag of this Nation" on May 16 at a battle site where the Regulators had famously resisted British troops sent by Governor Tryon on that date in 1771.[21] Later that year, as Alamance elected a new constable, William Ruffin informed his brother that "one of the candidates announced himself as still devoted to the union and his supporters voted for him with ballots having on them the Eagle, as emblematic of their attachment to the Union." The same letter noted "indications of decided disaffection to our new government" when the militia "refused to muster" under the Confederate flag and forcibly "defended themselves from arrest with arms in their hands." Ruffin's characterization of "disaffection" here is insufficient. This was not disaffection, but opposition rooted in an abiding dedication to the Union. It is not incidental that Unionists chose to demonstrate their allegiance during an election, or that they chose to unfurl the Stars and Stripes. These were cherished rituals and symbols of the American Union.[22]

The dynamics of secession in the North Carolina Piedmont served to highlight a number of fractures and would have detrimental effects later in the conflict. First, the February 1861 secession convention election split the region, as central Piedmont counties decisively rejected the call for a secession convention while cotton-producing counties on the South Carolina border supported it.[23] Even more importantly, however, voting reflected regional tensions that had plagued North Carolinian politics, pitting the eastern plantation establishment against the Piedmont and the mountainous west. Within the central Piedmont, this long-standing tension threatened to become a class issue between slaveholders and nonslaveholders. According to historian Robin E. Baker, "the secession delegate election served to polarize the North Carolina electorate along class lines" and imperil the political stability provided by two-party politics maintained within the state long after the demise of the Whigs elsewhere.[24] Second, the fact that the eventual decision to secede was not referred back to voters tarnished disunion as undemocratic. Notably, Jonathan Worth from Randolph County, in conjunction with other Unionist politicians (the majority from the Piedmont), had tried to prevent this from happening by seeking an amendment requiring secession to be ratified by voters.[25] Reflecting back on disunion, Randolph County postmaster Emsley Beckerdite asked, "Was ours a republican government?" Were "the people, the bone and sinew of this once great country . . . ever legitimately consulted upon the question of cession. You would not like to risk your well earned title to intelligence by answering affirmatively."[26] The feeling that secession had been forced upon them encouraged continued devotion to the Union and antipathy toward the Confederacy and enforcement of Confederate rule. A resident of Rowan County explained that he remained with "the Union all the time," for the "secession ordinance was not submitted to the people."[27] Many citizens of the North Carolina Piedmont had trouble regarding the Confederacy as "their" movement. Such a feeling of alienation from the secession movement and subsequent Confederate government has been noted by some scholars of guerrilla warfare as an important antecedent to irregular violence in the South.[28] There is little to no evidence suggesting that Piedmont South Carolinians believed the secession movement in their state to be a conspiracy, despite some recent scholarship portraying the state's secession movement as fundamentally antirepublican, bordering on coercive at times.[29]

Differing responses to secession in the North and South Carolina Piedmont developed into contrasting relationships with the nascent southern nation. In the Palmetto State, with the exception of a very small Unionist minority, citizens felt that the Confederacy represented their best interests and that their former nation had fallen into the hands of abolitionist radicals. In the Tar Heel State, a significant minority refused to sever their emotional ties with the Union, and a larger number held an ambivalent view about their new nation. Respective military enlistment patterns give the historian a clear insight into the divergent loyalties within the two regions. In the South Carolina Piedmont, many were eager to fight. Soon after the first shots of the war had been fired, Confederate president Jefferson Davis called on South Carolina to provide eight thousand men for the provisional army of the Confederate States of America, and the state had little problem in furnishing these men.[30] Wade Hampton III's legion, a complete military regiment comprising infantry, artillery, and cavalry units, amply demonstrates the enthusiasm for military enlistment. The legion, comprising companies from Anderson, Edgefield, and Greenville Districts, filled up rapidly, with Hampton reporting in May 1861 that "there have been already tenders of very many more troops than I am authorized to accept."[31] Such enthusiasm for enlistment was widespread. Even upper Piedmont districts, where some had been uncertain regarding disunion, had little problem furnishing troops. Indeed, one Greenville soldier wrote home to his father declaring the futility of his neighbors and kin following him to Columbia to join his company in the Second Regiment of South Carolina Volunteers. "There is no chance . . . to get in this company," the enlistee warned. "There has not been less than fifty applications in the last day or two."[32] As Charles Edward Cauthen's thorough examination of official records concludes, South Carolina's "response [to military enlistment] was excellent."[33] It was a very different story north of the state line. Historian Charles C. Bolton estimates that fewer than 20 percent of eligible men from the central North Carolina Piedmont volunteered for military service in 1861.[34]

In the South Carolina Piedmont, the small number of Unionists, publicly at least, swiftly came to terms with secession and war. Indeed, considering the mood of the state, rejecting the prevailing opinion of the time could endanger an individual. In Spartanburg District, an abortive Union military company was formed in the wake of South Carolina's secession but quickly disbanded for "fear [of] being hanged." One farmer did note, however, that, despite the demobilization of the unit, "I do not believe their politics are changed," offering possible insight as to why some sections of the district would struggle with violent deserters later in the war.[35] This process of public acceptance during the war's initial phases is encapsulated in the words and actions of Unionist figurehead Benjamin F. Perry. Perry had remained atypically silent in the months following secession. At a meeting on May 20, 1861, in northern Greenville, Perry explained that he had avoided the political occasions of the previous few months because "I was opposed to this great movement which has been made through the Southern states." However, Perry maintained that he "would sustain her [South Carolina]" and urged his listeners to come to terms with the passing of the Union, as the state had acted and they had little choice but to follow. As a gesture of his commitment, Perry, despite being "an old Union man," gave his "son, two horses and a negro boy, and fifty dollars for the support of necessitous families or soldiers" to a local cavalry company that was to be part of Wade Hampton's legion. As Perry himself put it, the state, during the secession crisis and mobilization for war, was typified by a "unanimity never before witnessed."[36]

In North Carolina, by contrast, loyalties were contested from the outset. On the same day that Benjamin Perry delivered his speech accepting secession and supporting war against the Union, B. M. Edney wrote a letter to Governor John W. Ellis painting a picture of anything but unanimity in Henderson County, directly north of Greenville District. Sections of Henderson were "as deadly hostile to our raising volunteers and the whole defence of the South as any portion of Pennsylvania." As in the central Piedmont, violent resistance was threatened from the very outset, and in an excessive form that was more characteristic of the later war years than the first months in most parts of the South. Edney portrayed a home front where the battle lines were already firmly drawn and in danger of being crossed. "Now Sir, the most dreadful apprehensions are felt by our female society at large," he wrote, because loyal men had volunteered for Confederate service and "as soon as we leave that bloodshed house burning & death will commence." Such violence had, in fact, already erupted. "I am in no alarmist but write you the sentiment at the request of all the true men of this neighborhood. Houses, & other buildings have been burned already" and it had become necessary to "hire night guards" for protection. It might be assumed that the writer was indeed an alarmist, but he was actually an important Buncombe County lawyer "with considerable militia experience." Governor Ellis's reply was an early indication of what throughout the war would often prove a fairly ineffective gubernatorial response, save when regular troops were involved: "Say that a committee of safety [be formed] is all I can suggest—the militia of Buncombe may be called out to aid them."[37]

It is the Heroes of America, or the Red Strings as they were known, that best demonstrate the connection between Unionism and violent resistance in the North Carolina Piedmont. Exactly where and when the group became the Heroes of America is uncertain. Necessarily secretive in nature, the group is estimated to have had perhaps as many as ten thousand members. We can say with certainty that the Heroes of America was at its strongest in the central Piedmont.[38] A report describing events in northeastern Davidson County most likely recorded their early formation and motivation. In July 1861, James H. Moore described "a combination of persons opposed to the Southern Confederacy and who openly advocate the Union and express sentiments favorable to the policy of the old government and in favor of the coercion policy of Lincoln," led by John Hilton. Moore estimated the group to include about 150 in total, "some of whom are men of considerable property (not slave owners)," although elsewhere in his letter he admitted that Hilton claimed his group was five hundred men strong. This group refused to accept the Confederacy: "We sent men from this place to their muster ground to take note of the proceedings and they report that the officers of the company openly declared they would muster under the U.S. flag and would kill any man or set of men that should attempt to prevent it." Hilton's men were a persistent thorn in the side of the Confederate authorities and forged links with similarly minded groups within the Piedmont and across, and probably beyond, the state. They attracted deserters, draft dodgers, escaped Union soldiers (from Salisbury Prison in Rowan County), and dissenters, coordinating Unionist families and communities in the goal of mutual protection, armed resistance, and undermining the Confederacy. Their opposition was founded on clear grounds: "Declaring that the state was unconstitutionally carried out of the Union . . . they will never submit to the Southern Confederacy."[39]

The implementation of conscription in April 1862, as much of the historiography on guerrilla warfare has emphasized, was a key turning point in the story of the Carolina Piedmont's inner civil war. While some folks tried to avoid military service throughout the South Carolina upcountry, with one enrollment officer lamenting that Greenville District was "a great country for dodgers and deserters," conscription had a far more significant impact north of the state line.[40] Those in the North Carolina Piedmont who held doubts and concerns about the Confederate cause now faced the prospect of forced enlistment. Unionist sympathizers were placed in an invidious position: reveal their true colors and risk arrest or swallow their principles and fight for a nation they did not recognize.[41] Unsurprisingly, conscription encouraged further anti-Confederate behavior as men sought to avoid enforced military service. R. F. Armfield of Yadkin County noted "a strong feeling against the conscript law amongst uninformed part of the citizens here." Such sentiment was made clear by both the actions and words of local citizens. Armfield fretted that "many of that class swore they would dye at home before they would be forced off and when the time came for them to go, perhaps nearly one hundred in this county took to the woods, lying out day and night to avoid arrest. . . . These skulkers have always had many more active friends than they had and could always get timely information of every movement to arrest them and so avoid it."[42]

The imposition of conscription underscores the highly politicized nature of the home-front fractures blighting the North Carolina Piedmont. Brian Tyson, a yeoman and owner of four slaves from Moore County, emerged as the most articulate Unionist in the central Piedmont. He rejected secession, and his opposition was further galvanized when one-third of the militia was drafted by Governor Clark for the defense of eastern North Carolina in March 1862, a month before the even more controversial Confederate conscription act. Clark's action prompted Tyson to write the pamphlet *A Ray of Light,* asserting that the Confederacy had not been democratically endorsed by voters, that it could not match the industrial might of the North, and that North Carolina should return to the Union before inevitable defeat. This, historian Larry Tise asserts, "articulated the views of a vast number of North Carolinians from the Piedmont region who opposed the war and resisted the efforts of Governor Zebulon B. Vance to prosecute it."[43] Tyson wrote other pamphlets defending his views, which were sent to high-ranking officials in North Carolina and Jefferson Davis's administration. Unsurprisingly, he was eventually arrested, and drafted, but he somehow managed to secure an exemption and returned home. Tyson eventually escaped to the North in the winter of 1863–1864, but Unionism remained defiant in the North Carolina Piedmont despite the loss of one of its figureheads. Confederate policies of conscription, taxation, and impressment swelled the ranks of the Heroes of America with deserters, outliers, and other Piedmont men formerly ambivalent toward the war.[44]

Irregular warfare came later to the South Carolina Piedmont. The summer of 1863 saw parts of the region, particularly the more mountainous sections of the upper Piedmont, afflicted by a guerrilla problem. The clear catalyst in this instance was a spate of desertions from local regiments.[45] In May 1863, South Carolinian soldiers belonging to General Nathan Evans's brigade were ordered to transfer from Charleston to Jackson, Mississippi. However, for soldiers belonging to upper Piedmont regiments, such as the

Sixteenth South Carolina Infantry, which was largely derived from Greenville District, the temptation to visit loved ones proved too great, and they left the train when it passed near their homes.[46] By August 1863, John D. Ashmore, a conscription officer based in Greenville, reported that over five hundred men had "taken refuge in the mountain fastnesses and passes of the districts of Greenville, Pickens, and Spartanburg."[47]

But how did these men transition from deserters to guerrillas? Whereas the North Carolina Piedmont experience suggested many did not have far to go in becoming active dissenters, anti-Confederate sentiment was not nearly as deep-seated in the South Carolina upcountry. While evidence is sparse, perhaps the most plausible explanation is to be found in the specific communities deserters returned to. Guerrilla activity was generally confined to the mountainous portions of the upper Piedmont, the pockets that had been typified by lesser engagement with cotton production and a more tepid response to the secession crisis. As such, perhaps we should not be surprised that the residents here questioned the Confederate cause more quickly than those elsewhere in the South Carolina Piedmont. In fact, military officials squarely blamed local communities for the guerrilla problem's escalation. The state commandant of conscripts was certain that these men intended to return to the army after visiting their families, but "finding among their friends and throughout the country a change of tone, a weariness with the war, a readiness to counsel and encourage desertion, they have but with few exceptions remained at home."[48] As news spread, more men deserted and remained at home. The rugged terrain of their home region also emboldened these deserters, who presumably felt confident that they could evade the instruments of Confederate authority. Without doubt, the isolated passageways and caves of the mountains, coupled with community-level support, made these men very elusive for conscription officials. John D. Ashmore lamented that deserters controlled around 150 miles of terrain, "every foot of which is a mountain country and much of it almost inaccessible," and that his attempt to hold meetings with their leaders had been flatly rejected. Most worrying for Ashmore was the fact that they were very well armed, had a system of "spies and signals" to ensure they were not caught, and were "bold, defiant, and even threatening."[49]

On occasion, matters went beyond intimidation. Writing ten days after first noting the threat posed by the deserters, Ashmore warned that the region was on the cusp of slipping into "lawlessness and crime." Along the border between Greenville and Spartanburg Districts matters had become violent. A Mr. Wright's house was burned to the ground, and the deserters had set up a new encampment near Philip Lester's factory. Lester had been bluntly told that if he resisted their presence they would "burn him up" as well. Consequently, conscript guards and locals were frightened to intervene with the deserters because the "torch and knife is freely threatened by these reckless and lawless men."[50] Such acts of violence, though, were more individualistic and less driven by personal vendetta or political allegiance, in contrast to irregular conflict in the North Carolina Piedmont or other portions of the South. The core motivations for these men were instincts of self-preservation, a clear desire to both provide for their families and evade capture, two mutually compatible goals. In his earlier report, Ashmore confided that "several bands of deserters work on their farms together, traverse the country with traveling thrashing machines, and congregate at still-yards and houses where quantities of liquor are distilled by them, and swear vengeance against any one who approaches with the intention of molesting them."[51] Put another way, the primary objective of these men was to simply dodge service and provide for their families. If that meant robbing or committing arson to ensure silence, so be it.

Though the various military reports on this upsurge of violence took a holistic approach to the problem in the Piedmont, viewing it as an issue that traversed state lines, they also indicate important differences. C. D. Melton, South Carolina's commandant of conscripts, noted that conditions in the Tar Heel State were far more polarized. Melton explained that "the necessities of mutual protection" had divided some regions into "bands."[52] As George W. Lay, a high-ranking officer in the Confederate Bureau of Conscription, explained when discussing the problem of deserters in Iredell, Randolph, and Yadkin Counties, "These men are not only determined to kill in avoiding apprehension (having just put to death yet another of our enrolling officers), but their esprit de corps extends to killing in revenge as well as in prevention of the capture of each other."[53] The nature as well as the causes of violence distinguish the experiences of the North and South Carolina Piedmont during the Civil War.

The response of county and state authorities to deserters and guerrillas in the Tar Heel State certainly fueled these bitter and acrimonious home-front confrontations. Militia, home guard, and Confederate army detachments were used to tackle the problem of lawless activities. If the complaints and lamentations in the governor's papers are anything to go by, however, their conduct only exacerbated the problem. The inner war became vicious in the Piedmont, particularly when regular soldiers, who had little hesitation in using coercive measures, were sent in. Zebulon Vance, elected governor in September 1862, took a much harder line on conscription and desertion, ordering four separate operations in the Piedmont targeting guerrillas and deserters.[54] Those aiding and harboring outliers risked torture, imprisonment, and even execution. These tactics were a direct attempt to reassert Confederate law and order, but largely because of the violence perpetrated, they not only failed to solve the guerrilla problem but failed to reassure the ordinary populace. Indeed, a deserter reported that pro-Union feeling in Randolph County was actually stronger by the end of 1863 than it had been at the beginning of the war, suggesting that official attempts to tackle the problem only hardened, rather than quelled, Confederate opposition.[55]

The escalation of violence in 1862 and 1863 is most closely associated with Brian Tyson's successor. It is assumed, though primary evidence is elusive, that William Owens took control of the Heroes of America after Tyson's exile, leading a vicious rearguard action until his arrest in late April 1864.[56] Owens had volunteered for army service before he could be conscripted in March 1862, but he deserted a few months later. He joined a guerrilla group operating out of northern Montgomery and Moore Counties. Whether Owens was as committed to Unionism as his predecessors is an issue worthy of greater scrutiny. A report from the beginning of the war suggests that Owens's neighborhood, directly adjacent to Randolph County's southeastern border, contained a long-standing renegade band. At the same time that John Hilton was leading a parade under the Stars and Stripes in upper Randolph County, "on the river of lower Randolph county," J. H. Foust observed, "a band of desperate men who have organized them selves into a compact for general purposes of plunder so soon as the volunteers of our county leave for the service of their country." There was no indication that their plans were made to further the Union cause; they were merely "intending to rob our people of property, commit outrages of a gross character on our defenceless citizens." The war had provided an opportunity that the group intended to take advantage of: "So soon as our volunteers leave they intend robbing our wealthiest citizens and committing brutal outrages on our defenceless females."[57]

Earlier incarnations of guerrilla violence in the North Carolina Piedmont had been primarily politically motivated, but the example of Bill Owens and his men is more problematic. Some scholars straightforwardly assert that Owens and his band were Unionists, but contemporary accounts illustrate both the criminal and political motivations of these men.[58] They were "*Abolitionists* and *Lincolnites,* a population that is entirely unsafe amongst us," one resident complained, adding that they threatened the safety of every law-abiding citizen (emphasizing the linkage between disloyalty and criminality).[59] Jason S. Dunn provided a harrowing description of his encounter with the group, who stole guns, food, and horses, as well as burning his barn and threatening further retribution. Dunn had been forced out of bed in the middle of the night. When he refused to hand over his weapon, pistols were raised against his wife and daughter. "If I behaved myself," he said, they promised "to restore me to the Bosom of Abe. Lincoln . . . but if they herd from me anymore they would send me to the Devil where secession came from and my age only saved my life." Rhetorically at least, Owens was willing to utilize highly politicized language. Dunn feared for his life, and the safety of his family and property, and was afraid to report Owens for fear of retaliation. "The wretched and deplorable condition of Treason Rebellion Robery and incendaryism with plundering and ravaging the country all around going on here is incredible."[60]

Owens underscores the problematic nature of neatly pigeonholing Civil War guerrillas. Indeed, while we can attempt to frame guerrilla behavior as either political or criminal, there is of course considerable slippage between the two. Criminal gangs of vagabonds threatened havoc across the South from the war's beginning. Within North Carolina, the strongest evidence comes from Wilkes County, bordering the northwestern edge of the Piedmont. In June 1861 a justice of the peace explained the activities of "a class of men who have been withstanding the common law for five or six years," long before the formation of the Confederacy. Wartime disruption evidently encouraged the escalation of their activities. Not content with stealing meat and other food items, they demanded guns, ammunition, money, gold, and silver and openly proclaimed "defiance to Sheriff[,] constables and law."[61] It is difficult to interpret such violent, criminal rejection of society and authority as not constituting political action. As Noel C. Fisher neatly puts it, rigid distinctions between different forms of partisan conflict can be "somewhat artificial and distorting." After all, "while the distinction between violence motivated by political ends and violence originating in personal grievances is not unimportant, the participants themselves did not always separate the two."[62] Contemporaries, in fact, actively tried to blur such distinctions. "One of the Posse" who ultimately captured the "noted Outlaw" Bill Owens claimed that Owens's abandoned camp was empty, bar a copy of the *Raleigh Standard,* William W. Holden's antiadministration paper. The correspondent was, not so subtly, trying to link criminal behavior and political disloyalty.[63]

The job facing the South Carolinian authorities was comparatively much easier. Indeed, they needed simply to assert their power, not repeatedly reassert it. The plan was to launch a search-and-destroy mission so that "the country shall be cleaned of its malcontents."[64] After one or two unsuccessful minor military forays, Captain John J. Maguire of the Sixth South Carolina Cavalry was detached to round up the absentees and restore order in September 1863. Maguire had an intimate knowledge of some of the men he was dealing with, if not the terrain. Indeed, in August 1863 Maguire rejoined his unit to find twelve men absent, having deserted and returned to Greenville. These men openly refused to come back, and Maguire fretted about the impact such behavior would have on military discipline among the rest of his men. He requested that his commanding officer detach him and thirty or so of his men to round them up and perhaps even bring back some more recruits.[65]

A month later Captain Maguire got his wish, and through the correspondence of the pro-Confederate Neves family of Mush Creek in northern Greenville District, we can see the lengths he went to in tackling the desertion problem. Some members of the Neves family had worried about the deserters prior to Maguire's arrival, with one predicting that "I think they will have to draw all the forces from Charleston and send them up to the mountains a while they have great work trying to sort them from the caves."[66] Maguire showed no mercy to the recalcitrant deserters, much to the glee of the Neves clan, and this no-nonsense approach brought tangible results. The Neves family patriarch wrote to his son that, within days of arriving in the region, the cavalry officer had arrested just under a dozen deserters and had shot one, mortally wounding him. Alsey Albert Neves explained that "I think a few more to get the same fare will bring the torys and deserters to there sences" and that he heard Maguire proclaim that "the man that hurts one of his boys shall have fifty balls through his hide." Still, Neves was perturbed by the arrogance of the deserters in his community. "I hear of there bosting what they will do," explained the farmer before confessing that he heard his neighbor "Sam Tinsly talking yesterday in rather a bostful way I set him down for a tory . . . he says the men that goes to take them will not all get off alive he sais there is fight in them he got rather cold comfort from me."[67] Neves's estimation of Samuel Tinsley as a "tory" was an accurate one and again suggests the permeable barrier between political and criminal actions on the Confederate home front; Tinsley would go on to assist Union forces when they arrived in the region before affiliating with the Republican Party after the conflict's end.[68]

Within a month it seemed that Maguire had fulfilled his objectives. Neves explained in mid-October 1863 that the cavalry officer had captured 284 deserters—2 had been shot and 1 had been hanged—concluding that "the name of Mcguire is a turer to torys and deserters."[69] Maguire's tough stance surely helped nullify the problem. The continued presence of Confederate soldiers must have deterred some from deserting while reassuring the loyal members of communities, enabling them to assist the antideserter forces. The key here in terms of contrasting the North and South Carolina Piedmont is political allegiance. For a majority in the upper South Carolina Piedmont, Maguire represented the best chance of restoring law and order to a disaffected region. For those in the central Piedmont of North Carolina, state and Confederate troops represented an attempt to reassert the political control and legitimacy of a regime that some were opposed to and many others were ambivalent toward—and even those who were pro-Confederate had many reasons to become further disenchanted as the war progressed. However, it would be foolish to suggest that the deserters simply disappeared in South Carolina, and the absentees remained tenacious. A week after mentioning the large number of arrests made by Captain Maguire, the Neves family noted another armed confrontation. Deserters remained a genuine problem in the more mountainous pockets of the South Carolina upcountry.[70]

The summer of 1863 seems to have marked the zenith of the problem in the South Carolina Piedmont. While 1864 would not see a repeat of Maguire's active intervention, the problem certainly did not disappear. Governor Milledge Luke Bonham, concerned by bands of bushwhackers, wrote to Secretary of War James A. Seddon several times in March and April 1864 for aid but seemingly received little response, and Colonel James Chesnut later sent a small detachment of troops up to Greenville District. Chesnut also hoped to pool the reserve forces at his disposal so that he could "make a clean sweep" of the mountain region, but this seemingly never came to pass.[71] Again, these anxieties were directly linked to wide-scale desertions from military units derived from the regions in question. In February 1864 it was reported that a large part of the Fourth South Carolina Infantry and several companies of the Third South Carolina Infantry, units that drew many men from the upcountry generally and the upper Piedmont specifically, had been beset by desertion.[72] As before, local communities helped to sustain these absentees. John Payne, for instance, was prosecuted for providing supplies for his kinsman Richard Payne and another deserter in the Greenville caves during the spring of 1864.[73]

Reports of crime, particularly stealing horses, proliferated throughout the upper Piedmont during 1864, as local communities were seemingly left to face the problems themselves. In March 1864 the *Charleston Courier* reported that organized bands of horse thieves were operating around Pendleton and Walhalla.[74] Several months later, the *Southern Enterprise,* a Greenville newspaper, claimed that deserters "in hundreds" were committing robbery, arson, and murder in the northern parts of the district.[75] As Daniel E. Sutherland has noted, during mid-1864 military absentees had formed gangs that traversed state lines, and these raiders largely came from Tennessee and North Carolina.[76] Residents of the mountainous portions of South Carolina asked for help. In July 1864 J. C. Burgess of Pickens District wrote to the Confederate secretary of war pleading for a regiment of cavalry to "capture or kill" the three hundred deserters who were terrorizing his neighborhood.[77] A month earlier, Angus M. Brown wrote on behalf of his company to James Earle Hagood, the clerk of court for Pickens District, expressing very similar sentiments. "There are a large gang of deserters in the mountains, committing all kind of depridations upon the citizens," explained Brown, before claiming that his cavalry company "could soon rid the country of these rascals." Brown also gave insight into the contagious nature of irregular warfare, as insufficient protection for their loved ones caused soldiers to question the cause. Brown demanded that the powers that be "protect the families of the soldiers who are now battling for our rights to protect the helpless women and children."[78]

Had folks in the South Carolina Piedmont been aware of some of the behavior of antiguerrilla forces across the state line, they may have thought twice about their request for help. What Sutherland describes as "a game of escalating revenge" between Confederate authorities and guerrilla bands seemingly reached a peak in April 1864, when the North Carolina Piedmont witnessed its most notorious event—the torture of Bill Owens's wife.[79] Refusing to reveal the location of her husband, Mrs. Owens was forced to "put down her baby" while men "tied her thumbs together behind her back" and then was suspended by her thumbs "so that her toes could just touch the ground." When the effects of this tactic wore off, her thumbs were placed "under a corner of a fence," whereupon it was usual to apply excruciating pressure by sitting on the fence. For understandable reasons, much scholarly attention has been focused on this incident, although arguably more shocking was Judge Thomas Settle's revelation that such treatment was hardly unique. Settle estimated that as many as 150 women from Chatham, Davidson, and Randolph Counties, "some of them in delicate health and five advanced in pregnancy," had been "dragged from their homes & put under close guard" for periods of weeks. "The consequence in some instances have been shocking. Women have been frightened into abortions almost under the eyes of their terrifiers."[80] Incidents such as these had an escalating, almost infectious, effect.[81] As Paul D. Escott and Jeffrey J. Crow have rightly stated, "Violence of this type could itself become a cause of internal war, for inhumane abuse generates resentment, alienation, and often a desire for retribution."[82] Moreover, escalating violence dragged in the young and the old, whether male or female, in the central North Carolina Piedmont. As Victoria E. Bynum astutely observes, Confederate soldiers "were sent to restore order in a region they were told was under siege by lawless bandits." The reality was that they actually faced "neighborhoods of families and extended kin who resisted with arms the authority of what *they* considered to be a lawless government created in defiance of the will of the people."[83]

For residents of the Carolina Piedmont, their insulated position far away from the major theaters of war and invading armies set their experience of the war apart from that of many other parts of the South. As one South Carolinian newspaper put it after General William T. Sherman had entered the state, "compared to hundreds of other places in the Confederacy" Piedmont folk had had "a very calm and pleasant walk on the highway of life."[84] These circumstances directly affected the way in which the internal dynamics of the conflict played out. In contrast to Missouri and other contested regions, locations that Stephen V. Ash terms "no-man's land," where competing forces could not assert their dominance, the fundamental power structure in the Piedmont remained intact for virtually the entirety of the war.[85] For the interior sections of North and South Carolina, Confederate and state governments remained in control, albeit tenuously at times in the counties of the central North Carolina Piedmont. Levels of violence were not generally on the same scale as the brutal and horrific atrocities routinely carried out in Missouri by the latter stages of the war. Fatalities were common in the worst-affected Piedmont counties, but they usually claimed the lives of men opposing or enforcing Confederate rule. Civilians were caught up in the trouble, of course, but routine indiscriminate killing and other atrocities, public acts often utilized to assert supremacy and dominance elsewhere, would not typify the Piedmont's inner conflict.

The relationship between citizens and the respective power structures would shape the conflict in a different way in the Carolina Piedmont. The issue here was not so much about contested power but the legitimacy of that power. In the upcountry sections of the Palmetto State, a majority had supported secession and, as such, the Confederacy remained legitimate in their eyes, despite growing disaffection due to worsening economic conditions as the war went on. North of the state line, and particularly in the Tar Heel State's central Piedmont districts, an attachment to the Union had endured. A minority were correspondingly hostile toward the Confederacy, while many more were ambivalent. The success of William Holden's peace movement in the North Carolina Piedmont during the war highlights the region's different relationship with the Confederacy. Moreover, the not-unrelated existence of a genuine guerrilla problem in the central Piedmont, whether primarily motivated by political, economic, or social causes (and, as argued, these matters cannot be neatly separated), constituted a bitter struggle over law and order.[86] With this in mind, we should not be surprised that the attempt of state and national authorities to exert control within the North Carolina Piedmont exacerbated long-standing tensions and widened preexisting fissures. In South Carolina, conversely, a clear majority identified with the Confederacy, meaning that violent resistance to the government was less likely to occur and, when it did, the protagonists could not expect the support of local citizens, with the exception of a few sections anomalous within the wider upcountry experience. Gauging matters of loyalty, violence, and power is not easy for the historian; when considered at the local level, especially, such matters are nebulous and impossible to measure with precision. They emerge with more clarity, however, when placed within a comparative context.

Notes

1. W. W. Herbert to Messrs. Woodward, Boyleston and McCants, December 3, 1860, McCants Family Papers, South Caroliniana Library, University of South Carolina, Columbia (hereafter cited as SCL); emphasis in the original.

2. Sergeant William S. Alston, Company E, First South Carolina Infantry (Six Months, 1861), Compiled Service Records of Confederate Soldiers Who

Served in Organizations from the State of South Carolina, National Archives, 1861–1865, Washington D.C.

3. Though not strictly a study of guerrillas, Stephen V. Ash's *When the Yankees Came* remains the most significant study of the impacts of Federal invasion and local resistance across the South. See Ash, *When the Yankees Came: Conflict and Chaos in the Occupied South, 1861–1865* (Chapel Hill: University of North Carolina Press, 1985). A number of more localized treatments of guerrilla warfare have similarly highlighted the role of irregular violence as a method of opposition to Union forces. See, for example, Samuel C. Hyde Jr., "Bushwhacking and Barn Burning: Civil War Operations and the Florida Parishes' Tradition of Violence," *Louisiana History* 36 (Spring 1995), 171–86; Noel C. Fisher, *War at Every Door: Partisan Politics and Guerrilla Violence in East Tennessee, 1860–1869* (Chapel Hill: University of North Carolina Press, 1997); Stephen S. Michot, "'War Is Still Raging in This Part of the Country': Oath-Taking, Conscription, and Guerrilla War in Louisiana's Lafourche Region," *Louisiana History* 38 (Spring 1997), 157–84; Barton A. Myers, *Executing Daniel Bright: Race, Loyalty, and Guerrilla Violence in a Coastal Carolina Community, 1861–1865* (Baton Rouge: Louisiana State University Press, 2009); and Judkin Browning, *Shifting Loyalties: The Union Occupation of Eastern North Carolina* (Chapel Hill: University of North Carolina Press, 2011). Missouri, as a state where political allegiance had been highly fraught during the antebellum period and in which the Union invaded swiftly after the commencement of hostilities, was home to a particularly fierce guerrilla war. Accordingly, it has been the subject of some of the finest studies of Civil War guerrillas, such as Michael Fellman, *Inside War: The Guerrilla Conflict in Missouri during the Civil War* (New York: Oxford University Press, 1989); and Mark W. Geiger, *Financial Fraud and Guerrilla Violence in Missouri's Civil War, 1861–1865* (New Haven, CT: Yale University Press, 2010).

4. Mackey divides irregular combatants into three broad groupings—"guerrillas," as defined in the main text; "partisans," independent irregular soldiers but typically organized into companies and subject to special orders by their government and/or army; and "regular cavalry raiders," regular soldiers who utilize irregular tactics. Robert R. Mackey, *The Uncivil War: Irregular Warfare in the Upper South, 1861–1865* (Norman: University of Oklahoma Press, 2004), 5–11. For more on defining irregular combatants and the problematic nature of doing so, see Daniel E. Sutherland, *A Savage Conflict: The Decisive Role of Guerrillas in the American Civil War* (Chapel Hill: University of North Carolina Press, 2009), xi–xii.

5. John C. Inscoe, *Mountain Masters, Slavery, and the Sectional Crisis in Western North Carolina* (Knoxville: University of Tennessee Press, 1989), 40–58.

6. Victoria E. Bynum, *The Long Shadow of the Civil War: Southern Dissent and Its Legacies* (Chapel Hill: University of North Carolina Press, 2010), 23.

7. Daniel E. Sutherland, "Introduction: The Desperate Side of War," in *Guerrillas, Unionists, and Violence on the Confederate Home Front,* ed. Daniel E. Sutherland (Fayetteville: University of Arkansas Press, 1999), 7–8.

8. Bynum, *Long Shadow of the Civil War,* 23.

9. The best account of this process, and indeed of the antebellum South Carolina upcountry, remains Lacy K. Ford Jr., *Origins of Southern Radicalism: The South Carolina Upcountry, 1800–1860* (New York: Oxford University Press, 1988). See pp. 244–51 in particular on the cotton boom of the late 1840s.

10. South Carolinian districts would not officially become counties until 1868.

11. The reason for looking at Spartanburg is that, in 1860, the census enumerators separated the district into northern and southern divisions, thus making it ideal for such a comparison. Figures calculated from U.S. Bureau of the Census, Eighth Census, 1860, South Carolina, Spartanburg District, Schedule 4 (Agriculture), South Carolina Department of Archives and History, Columbia.

12. Paul D. Escott, "Yeoman Independence and the Market: Social Status and Economic Development in Antebellum North Carolina," *North Carolina Historical Review* 66 (July 1989): 275–300; Allen Tullos, *Habits of Industry: White Culture and the Transformation of the Carolina Piedmont* (Chapel Hill: University of North Carolina Press, 1989), 77–82; Bess Beatty, *Alamance: The Holt Family and Industrialization in a North Carolina County, 1837–1900* (Baton Rouge: Louisiana State University Press, 1999), 15–29, 53–71.

13. The anomalous position of the central Piedmont counties in North Carolina is emphasized by Peter Kolchin's estimate that perhaps as many as 50 percent of all white southerners held "an economic stake in slavery" through family ties or connections to the plantation economy, even if they did not own slaves. Peter Kolchin, *American Slavery, 1619–1877* (New York: Hill and Wang, 1993), 181.

14. David Brown, *Southern Outcast: Hinton Rowan Helper and the Impending Crisis of the South* (Baton Rouge: Louisiana State University Press, 2006), 80–87.

15. Slaveholding levels in Pickens District were anomalous enough that they require mention, with just 18 percent of white families being slaveholders in 1860. This is more than 10 percentage points less than the next-lowest district, Spartanburg, where just under 30 percent of white families owned slaves. South Carolina slaveholding figures were calculated from the data regarding the number of slave owners and free families contained in U.S. Census Office, *Eighth Census of the United States, 1860: Agriculture* (Washington, D.C.: Government Printing Office, 1864), 237; and U.S. Census Office, *Statistics of the United States (Including Mortality, Property, &c), in 1860* (Washington, D.C.: Government Printing Office, 1866), 348, respectively. Southern average figure taken from Mark M. Smith, *Debating Slavery: Economy and Society in the Antebellum American South* (New York: Cambridge University Press, 1998), 16.

16. *Walhalla Keowee Courier,* September 1, 1860.

17. *Spartanburg Carolina Spartan,* December 6, 1860.

18. *Spartanburg Express,* November 28, 1860.

19. John Gilmer, "Application for a Pardon," 1865, cited in Charles C. Bolton, *Poor Whites of the Antebellum South: Tenants and Laborers in Central North Carolina and Northeast Mississippi* (Durham, NC: Duke University Press, 1994), 144–

45. Marc W. Kruman, *Parties and Politics in North Carolina, 1836–1865* (Baton Rouge: Louisiana State University Press, 1983), 213–21, provides a lucid analysis of the abrupt switch of support within North Carolina in April 1861.

20. H. C. Wilson to Governor Ellis, April 22, 1861, in *Papers of John Willis Ellis,* vol. 2, *1860–1861,* ed. Noble J. Tolbert (Raleigh, NC: Department of Archives and History, 1964), 662. Bohanan owned twelve slaves in 1860.

21. W. R. Denny, Joel Shotton, and A. E. Ennis to Thomas Ruffin, March 30, 1861, in *The Papers of Thomas Ruffin,* ed. J. G. de Roulhac Hamilton, ed. (Raleigh, NC: Edwards and Broughton, 1920), 3:142.

22. William K. Ruffin to Thomas Ruffin, February 14, 1862, in Hamilton, *Papers of Thomas Ruffin,* 3:215–16. Paul D. Escott, *Many Excellent People: Power and Privilege in North Carolina, 1850–1890* (Chapel Hill: University of North Carolina Press 1985), 60; Scott Reynolds Nelson, "Red Strings and Half Brothers: Civil Wars in Alamance County, North Carolina, 1861–1871," in *Enemies of the Country: New Perspectives on Unionists in the Civil War South,* ed. John C. Inscoe and Robert C. Kenzer (Athens: University of Georgia Press, 2001), 37–53.

23. Marc Kruman, in *Parties and Politics in North Carolina,* 273–78, argues that it was not the vote for or against the secession convention, held across the state on February 28, 1861, that best demonstrates the depth of support for the Union or the Confederacy (the motion for a session convention was narrowly defeated), but the vote for delegates to the convention. On this basis, voting in the central Piedmont counties heavily favored the Union: Alamance, 967–480; Chatham, 1,854–175; Davie, 718–269; Davidson, 1,726–382; Forsyth, 1,409–286; Guildford, 2,771–113; Iredell, 1,823–176; Moore, 1,257–135; Montgomery, 807–81; Orange, 1,537–356; Rowan, 1,218–837; Stanly, 763–85; Yadkin, 1,490–34. In Piedmont counties bordering Virginia, results were not dissimilar: Caswell, 821–269; Rockingham, 852–685; Stokes, 915–151; Surry, 1,085–218. However, three Piedmont counties bordering South Carolina voted for secession delegates, while the result was very close in another: Anson, 613–449; Mecklenburg, 306–1,318; Richmond, 307–321; Union, 483–548.

24. Robin E. Baker, "Class Conflict and Political Upheaval: The Transformation of North Carolina Politics during the Civil War," *North Carolina Historical Review* 69 (April 1992): 159.

25. Piedmont representatives continued to oppose secession even after the opening shots of the Civil War, something underappreciated in most accounts. As Charles Bolton notes, three senators from the central Piedmont—Josiah Turner, representing Orange County, and L.Q. Sharpe, representing Iredell, Wilkes, and Alexander (combined), as well as Worth—were the only dissenters in the North Carolina Senate voting against holding a secession convention, something which had become inevitable by May 1861. Bolton, *Poor Whites,* 147–48.

26. Emsley Beckerdite to Marmaduke Robins, January 21, 1865, cited in Escott, *Many Excellent People,* 82.

27. Claim 2114, John Julian, Rowan County, March 19, 1876, Settled Case Files for Claims Approved by the Southern Claims Commission, 1871–1880, Record Group 217, National Archives, Washington, D.C.

28. Jonathan Dean Sarris, for instance, notes that initial opposition to the war in Lumpkin County, Georgia, stemmed from an idea that secession was unconstitutional, as it had not been referred back to the people. Jonathan Dean Sarris, "'Shot for Being Bushwhackers': Guerrilla War and Extralegal Violence in a North Georgia Community," in Sutherland, *Guerrillas, Unionists, and Violence,* 34. A similar point is made by Noel C. Fisher regarding eastern Tennessee. Fisher states that loyalists believed disunion to be "a conspiracy, developed in the 1850s by Southern radicals and imposed on the Southern states through fraud, manipulation, and intimidation." Fisher, *War at Every Door,* 4.

29. This interpretation of the secession movement in South Carolina is articulated most coherently in Manisha Sinha, *The Counter-Revolution of Slavery: Politics and Ideology in Antebellum South Carolina* (Chapel Hill: University of North Carolina, 2000); and Stephen A. West, *From Yeoman to Redneck in the South Carolina Upcountry, 1850–1915* (Charlottesville: University of Virginia Press, 2008).

30. The request by Davis is referenced in Francis W. Pickens to Leroy P. Walker, June 30, 1861, in U.S. War Department, *The War of the Rebellion: A Compilation of the Official Records of the Union and Confederate Armies* (Washington, D.C.: Government Printing Office, 1880–1901), ser. 4, vol. 1, pp. 413–14 (hereafter cited as *OR*).

31. Wade Hampton III to Leroy P. Walker, May 27, 1861, in *OR,* ser. 4, vol. 1, p. 296. The following companies were drawn from the Piedmont portion of the state: Infantry Co. B (Edgefield), Infantry Co. D (Anderson), Infantry Co. E (Greenville), Infantry Co. F (Greenville), Cavalry Co. A (Edgefield), and Cavalry Co. B (Greenville).

32. F. M. Goodlett to "Father," April 30, 1861, William H. Goodlett Papers, David M. Rubenstein Library, Duke University, Durham, NC.

33. Charles Edward Cauthen, *South Carolina Goes to War, 1860–1865* (Chapel Hill: University of North Carolina Press, 1950), 135.

34. Bolton, *Poor Whites,* 157. For more on the reasons why so many from the Piedmont stayed at home, see David Brown, "North Carolinian Ambivalence: Rethinking Loyalty and Disaffection in the Civil War Piedmont," in *North Carolinians in the Era of the Civil War and Reconstruction,* ed. Paul D. Escott (Chapel Hill: University of North Carolina Press, 2008), 7–36.

35. David Golightly Harris, journal entries for January 5 and January 9, 1861, in *Piedmont Farmer: The Journals of David Golightly Harris, 1855–1870,* ed. Philip N. Racine (Knoxville: University of Tennessee Press, 1997), 173–74.

36. *Walhalla Keowee Courier,* June 1, 1861.

37. B. M. Edney to John W. Ellis, May 20, 1861, Governor's Papers, Box 151, North Carolina Division of Archives and History, Raleigh (hereafter cited as GP and box number); John C. Inscoe and Gordon B. McKinney, *The Heart of Confed-*

erate Appalachia: Western North Carolina in the Civil War (Chapel Hill: University of North Carolina Press, 2000), 74.

38. For more on the Heroes of America, see William T. Auman and David D. Scarboro, "The Heroes of America in Civil War North Carolina," *North Carolina Historical Review* 58 (October 1981): 327–63; and Nelson, "Red Strings and Half Brothers," 37–53. Auman and Scarboro, 327n3, provide the figure of ten thousand members, basing that estimate on the claim of William W. Holden in the *North Carolina Weekly Standard,* October 24, 1866.

39. Jas. H. Moore to Henry T. Clark, July 18, 1861, GP 152.

40. William Elliott Jr. to Mary Elliott Johnstone, April 12, 1863, Elliott and Gonzales Family Papers, Southern Historical Collection, University of North Carolina, Chapel Hill.

41. Margaret M. Storey, in her study of Alabama Unionists, similarly notes that conscription created an immediate dilemma for all those not committed to the Confederate cause. Margaret M. Storey, *Loyalty and Loss: Alabama's Unionists in the Civil War and Reconstruction* (Baton Rouge: Louisiana State University Press, 2004), 57, 66.

42. R. F. Armfield to Zebulon Vance, February 19, 1863, GP 162; William T. Auman, in "Neighbor against Neighbor: The Inner Civil War in the Randolph County Area of Confederate North Carolina," *North Carolina Historical Review* 61 (January 1984): 69, estimates that 42 percent of the total number of deserters from Randolph County chose to leave in 1862 (more than one in five absconded over the course of the war).

43. Brian Tyson, *A Ray of Light; or, A Treatise on the Sectional Troubles Religiously and Morally Considered* (Raleigh, 1862); Larry E. Tise, "Bryan Tyson," in *Dictionary of North Carolina Biography,* ed. William S. Powell (Chapel Hill: University of North Carolina Press, 1996), 6:71.

44. The most detailed study remains William T. Auman, "Bryan Tyson: Southern Unionist and American Patriot," *North Carolina Historical Review* 62 (July 1985): 257–92.

45. While the summer of 1863 saw this matter worsen considerably, Alfred Ward Grayson Davis, a Confederate quartermaster stationed in Greenville, noted a "a hundred or more" deserters lurking around the district as early as January 1863. Alfred Ward Grayson Davis to General P. G. T. Beauregard, January 17, 1863, *Letterbook* 1, 35, Alfred Ward Grayson Davis Papers, SCL.

46. C. D. Melton to John S. Preston, August 26, 1863, in *OR,* ser. 4, vol. 2, pp. 769–70. For a more detailed account of this instance of desertion, see James T. Otten, "Disloyalty in the Upper Districts of South Carolina during the Civil War," *South Carolina Historical Magazine* 75 (April 1974): 100–101.

47. John D. Ashmore to C. D. Melton, August 7, 1863, in *OR,* ser. 4, vol. 2, p. 771.

48. C. D. Melton to John S. Preston, August 26, 1863, in ibid., pp. 769–70.

49. John D. Ashmore to C. D. Melton, August 7, 1863, in ibid., pp. 771–72.

50. John D. Ashmore to C. D. Melton, August 17, 1863, in ibid., p. 774.

51. John D. Ashmore to C. D. Melton, August 7, 1863, in ibid., p. 773.

52. C. D. Melton to John S. Preston, August 26, 1863, in ibid., p. 770.

53. Geo. W. Lay to John S. Preston, September 2, 1863, in ibid., p. 783.

54. A full account of the antideserter campaign is found in William T. Auman, "Neighbor against Neighbor: The Inner Civil War in the Central Counties of Confederate North Carolina" (PhD diss., University of North Carolina at Chapel Hill, 1988); but see also Barton A. Myers, "Dissecting the Torture of Mrs. Owens: The Story of the Civil War Atrocity," in *Wierding the War: Stories from the Civil War's Ragged Edges,* ed. Stephen Berry (Athens: University of Georgia Press, 2011), 141–59. William T. Auman, *Civil War in the North Carolina Quaker Belt: The Confederate Campaign against Peace Agitators, Deserters and Draft Dodgers* (Jefferson, NC: McFarland, 2014) was unfortunately published too late for consideration here.

55. A. K. Pearce to Bryan Tyson, November 25, 1863, Bryan Tyson Papers, David M. Rubenstein Library, Duke University, Durham, NC . Gordon McKinney notes that restoring law and order was a thankless task: "When Zeb ordered militia officers in the Piedmont counties to suppress open dissent, they found it impossible." Gordon B. McKinney, *Zeb Vance: North Carolina's Civil War Governor and Gilded Age Political Leader* (Chapel Hill: University of North Carolina Press, 2004), 158.

56. McKinney, *Zeb Vance,* 160.

57. J. H. Foust to John W. Ellis, June 10, 1861, GP 151. The distinction between these two groups is clearly made in Bolton, *Poor Whites,* 155–56, but is blurred in other accounts.

58. Myers, "Dissecting the Torture," 144–45. Bynum, *Long Shadow of the Civil War,* provides the most deeply researched examination of Owens and his use of violence, placing it in comparative perspective with Newt Knight of Mississippi and Warren Collins of Texas.

59. John A. Craven to Henry T. Clark, October 21, 1862, GP 160; emphasis in the original.

60. Jason S. Dunn to E. J. Hale and sons, January 8, 1863, GP 161.

61. J. P. Aldridge to John W. Ellis, June 22, 1861, GP 151. There is important work to be done in connecting these criminal gangs that operated during the Civil War to their antebellum settings. On vagabonds in the 1850s, see David Brown, "A Vagabond's Tale: Poor Whites, Herrenvolk Democracy, and the Value of Whiteness in the Late Antebellum South," *Journal of Southern History* 79 (November 2013): 799–840.

62. Fisher, *War at Every Door,* 63.

63. *Fayetteville Observer,* April 28, 1864; Myers, "Dissecting the Torture," 150.

64. C. D. Melton to John S. Preston, August 26, 1863, in *OR,* ser. 4, vol. 2, p. 770.

65. John J. Maguire to Colonel Hugh K. Aiken, August 17, 1863, in Captain

John. J. Maguire, Company H, Sixth South Carolina Cavalry, Compiled Service Records of Confederate Soldiers Who Served in Organizations from the State of South Carolina, 1861–1865, National Archives, Washington D.C.

66. "Cousin Eliza" to Wm. P. Neves, September 3, 1863, Neves Family Papers, SCL.

67. Alsey Albert Neves to Wm. P. Neves, September 11, 1863, Neves Family Papers, SCL.

68. Rubin Hyman III, *South Carolina Scalawags* (Columbia: University of South Carolina Press, 2006), 24–25, 120. For more on the interplay between socioeconomic and political motivations for some South Carolina deserters, see Patrick J. Doyle, "Understanding the Desertions of South Carolinian Soldiers during the Final Years of the Confederacy," *Historical Journal* 56 (September 2013): 657–79.

69. Alsey Albert Neves to Wm. P. Neves, October 11, 1863, Neves Family Papers, SCL.

70. Alsey Albert Neves to Wm. P. Neves, John P. Neves, and George Washington Neves, October 18, 1863, Neves Family Papers, SCL.

71. Milledge Luke Bonham to James A. Seddon, April 22, 1864, James Chesnut to James A. Seddon, June 18, 1864, and James Chesnut to Samuel Cooper, July 5, 1864, in *OR*, ser. 1, vol. 53, pp. 327, 342, 360.

72. Archie Vernon Huff Jr., *Greenville: The History of the City and County in the South Carolina Piedmont* (Columbia: University of South Carolina Press, 1995), 142.

73. Greenville District, Court of General Sessions, Indictments 1865–1890, Indictment No. 2517, *State vs. John Payne,* South Carolina Department of Archives and History, Columbia.

74. *Charleston Courier,* March 23, 1864, cited in Cauthen, *South Carolina Goes to War,* 176.

75. *Charleston Courier,* June 22, 1864, cited in ibid.

76. Sutherland emphasises the fact that virtually all of these raiders were not South Carolinians, but, as the above evidence has shown, natives of the Palmetto State were surely involved, even if the guerrilla problem was considerably more acute in North Carolina and Tennessee. Sutherland, *Savage Conflict,* 254–56.

77. J. C. Burgess to James A. Seddon, ca. July 15, 1864, cited in Sutherland, *Savage Conflict,* 256.

78. Angus M. Brown to James Earle Hagood, June 11, 1864, James Earle Hagood Papers, SCL.

79. Sutherland, *Savage Conflict,* 124. Contemporary sources do not name Bill Owens's wife directly, but Bynum provides the most convincing case that she was called Adeline, not Mary, as cited by some historians. Bynum, *Long Shadow of the Civil War,* 30, 153n3.

80. Thomas Settle to Governor Vance, October 4, 1864, in W. Buck Yearns and John G. Barrett, eds., *North Carolina Civil War Documentary* (Chapel Hill:

University of North Carolina Press, 1980), 103–5. Caroline Hulin and Sarah Moore, from Montgomery County, were both tortured in the same fashion. See Victoria E. Bynum, *Unruly Women: The Politics of Social and Sexual Control in the Old South* (Chapel Hill: University of North Carolina Press, 1992), 143.

81. Michael Fellman has dealt with such issues most articulately. In particular, see Michael Fellman, "Inside Wars: The Cultural Crisis of Warfare and the Values of Ordinary People," in Sutherland, *Guerrillas, Unionists, and Violence,* 187–200.

82. Paul D. Escott and Jeffrey J. Crow, "The Social Order and Violent Disorder: An Analysis of North Carolina in the Revolution and the Civil War," *Journal of Southern History* 52 (August 1986): 393.

83. Bynum, *Long Shadow of the Civil War,* 46.

84. *Edgefield Advertiser,* February 14, 1865.

85. Ash, *When the Yankees Came,* 99–105.

86. Holden was leader of a political movement advocating a negotiated peace and potential withdrawal from the Confederacy, and he unsuccessfully challenged Vance in the 1864 gubernatorial election. As Auman notes, two-thirds of peace movement meetings took place in the central Piedmont. He further comments that "armed rebellion against Confederate authority was inspired in great part by the success and popularity of" peace meetings, although surely his logic needs reversing: the volatile political and social climate caused by guerrilla violence most likely encouraged law-abiding Piedmont folks to seek alternative, peaceful solutions to the problems they faced, such as that offered by Holden's peace movement. Auman, "Neighbor against Neighbor" (PhD diss.), 235.

Indians Make the Best Guerrillas

Native Americans and the War for the Desert Southwest, 1861–1862

Megan Kate Nelson

Felix Collard was exhausted but he could not fall asleep. The march that day had been long and hot; he and his compatriots in Company G, Seventh Texas Mounted Rifles had collapsed on the banks of Limpia Creek as soon as they arrived. The air had cooled considerably, as they were camped along the floor of a high desert canyon. But there was a full moon, and his horse, Pete, was restless. Collard had let him loose to graze on the riverbank and he paced nervously, dragging his rope behind him through the scrub brush. Collard fancied he could hear the horse's heart beating, "thump thump, thump as if he were nearly scared to death." Suddenly, a deafening noise, sounding like "a half-dozen gongs, or two skillet lids rubbed together, or tin pans beaten" began "echoing and reverberating around the rocks and cliffs" that loomed above them. What came next, Collard remembered, was pandemonium. The horses were lunging through the camp, frantic. The Texans were in pursuit, trying to drive them back to the riverbank. And along the undulating ridge of volcanic spires, Indians "darted from rock to rock, lassos in hand." The Texans fired wildly at moving shadows, and when they stopped to reload, there was nothing but silence. Collard and his comrades sat up half the night, nervously watching the canyon walls, but the Indians—probably Mescalero Apaches led by chief Nicolás—had gone.[1]

This was not the first time that Indian raiders had set upon the Texans. From the moment Confederates began to make their way to El Paso and then into New Mexico Territory in the summer of 1861 they fell victim to frequent Apache and Comanche attacks on their column. The Indians ambushed their flanks, often at night, stampeding horses, draft animals, and beef cattle and driving them through the desert to their own camps. The Confederates were not the only Native targets; in northern New Mexico, Navajos and Utes raided wagon trains on their way to supply Union troops in Fort Union and Santa Fe and ambushed small groups of civilians and soldiers traveling to presumed safety at Federal forts. But Confederates suffered more acutely from Native guerrilla raids during their campaign for the territories of New Mexico and Arizona in 1861–1862; as an invading army they were more vulnerable targets, and Native Americans used a range of guerrilla tactics against them. In doing so Native groups—especially the Apaches—influenced the outcome of the war in this region. For them, the white man's war was an opportunity; Federals abandoned forts and concentrated supplies at specific locations, creating sites of vulnerability. The war also put large groups of people and animals on long and winding desert roads, where they were exposed to attacks by small groups of mounted raiders. But guerrilla warfare in the desert Southwest was also part of a long history of Native raiding practices, which were an integral part of their economic and political lives.

Attention to Native raiding in this region during the 1860s reveals that there are, as Elliott West has put it, "dense connections between Indian and white histories" in the West, especially during the American Civil War, which most historians have treated as a war solely between whites over the issues of black freedom and states' rights.[2] It also illuminates the ways that the Anglo-American dream of empire in the West—which both Union and Confederate soldiers believed themselves to be pursuing in 1861–1862—stalled when it ran up against communities long established and sustained through trade relationships, kinship networks, and guerrilla warfare.

The Manifest Destinies of the Civil War

Civil War historians have not paid much attention to war actions in the southwestern theater. This is mostly due to the fact that the clashes there between Union and Confederate forces were short lived, "officially" ending with the Union defeat of the Sibley Brigade at Glorieta Pass in late March

1862. Additionally, the troops in the desert Southwest were few in number compared to the massive armies operating in Virginia and the trans-Mississippi West. There were no long-term campaigns or high body counts, and all of the action occurred almost nineteen hundred miles from Washington, D.C., and Richmond—technically outside of the United States, as the region was organized into territories that were not yet states. But the western territories were at the center of political debates over slavery and secession in the antebellum period, and it was the centerpiece of sectional dreams of empire during the war itself.[3]

One of the loudest voices for the vision of southern Manifest Destiny was Jefferson Davis. As William Cooper has argued, while Davis led the War Department during the Pierce administration (1853–1857), he "made his chief concern the great American West, for in it so many of his interests overlapped and intersected." In Davis's view, it was imperative that Americans cross its vast distances, high mountain ranges, and desert basins, for these topographical obstacles threatened the nation's possession of the Pacific states.[4] He therefore championed a transcontinental railroad along the thirty-second parallel (known as the Southern Route), which would take travelers through Texas and New Mexico (and what would become Arizona, a territory carved out of the western lands of New Mexico) on the way to California. Most Americans, like Davis, believed that the mountain West could be traversed and that its settlement and cultivation were vital to the nation's future. However, by 1861 many proslavery southerners had come to believe that they were the sole inheritors not only of the revolutionary right of rebellion but also of Manifest Destiny. They resented federal attempts to prevent slavery's expansion in the West and "used the liberating mechanism of secession" to claim what they believed was rightfully their own. "Building a Confederate Empire from the rubble of the Union," historian Donald Frazier has argued, "was a basic goal of Southern independence, not an afterthought."[5]

When Fort Sumter fell in April 1861, a significant number of U.S. Army officers resigned their commissions and declared their loyalty to the Confederacy. Most left their posts in Texas and the southwestern territories and went east to lead brigades and corps in the trans-Mississippi West or Virginia. Henry H. Sibley, a career army officer who was posted at Fort Burgwin outside Taos when the first shots of the war were fired, was one of these men. But unlike the others, Sibley planned to return to New Mexico Territory with an army of his own. In a meeting with Jefferson Davis in the spring of 1861, he informed the Confederate president of his plan: he would recruit Texans, arm them with rifles and artillery, and feed them with provisions taken from abandoned Federal arsenals and forts. Once New Mexico was theirs the Confederates would vanquish California, using its Pacific ports to reestablish international trade and subvert the Union blockade. The silver deposits buried deep in New Mexico's Piños Altos mines and the gold extracted from the mountains of Colorado Territory and California's Sierras would fund the Confederate government and its war effort. Through the instruments of empire honed by American expansionist efforts in the previous decades—military presence, government structure, and extractive industry—southerners following Sibley's track would prove that the Confederacy could act as a nation on the world stage and maintain its own independence. Given Davis's emotional and political investments in the West, he was not difficult to convince. Sibley began recruiting Texans to the Confederate cause in the summer of 1861.[6]

By that time, another Confederate officer was already encamped along the Rio Grande. John R. Baylor was a Texas Secession Convention delegate, former Comanche Indian agent, and a commissioned lieutenant colonel who had mustered more than seven hundred men into the Second Texas Mounted Rifles after Sumter fell. While Sibley was assembling his brigade to invade New Mexico, Baylor and the Second Texas marched to the Rio Grande and then up to Fort Bliss, fought a skirmish with Union troops at Mesilla, New Mexico Territory, in late July, and forced the surrender of more than four hundred Union regulars after catching them on their retreat from Fort Fillmore. Baylor subsequently appointed himself provisional governor of the Confederate Territory of Arizona and stationed himself at Mesilla, its newly declared capital.[7] For the Confederates, from the very beginning of the war the desert Southwest was a vital theater of conflict. It was a place in which the new nation would establish its dominion over the Union and over the region's Native Americans. And Baylor and Sibley were there to make it happen.

Stealthy and Sly: Raiding Warfare

Native Americans had been living, trading, raiding, and engaging in guerrilla warfare in the desert Southwest for hundreds of years; they saw these developments in the 1850s and 1860s as merely another chapter in the long histories of their peoples. Civil War guerrilla warfare scholars have rarely included these Native groups in their studies. They have usually examined the tactics of small groups of white, rural elites operating in the border regions (Missouri and Kansas or western Virginia), almost always on behalf of the Confederacy. These white American men had a variety of motives—patriotism, honor, greed, control over women and slaves, home-front defense, revenge—and they launched surprise attacks on Union positions in order to destabilize and undermine the enemy. They operated on horseback, using their knowledge of "difficult" terrain (swamplands, tangled forests) to evade pursuit. The women they left at home controlled their supply lines, producing clothes and food to sustain their men in the brush. Guerrilla activities were part of a larger Confederate military strategy, but they were also considered culturally and militarily "irregular"; guerrillas' tactics were unusual and sometimes unsavory, but they were a wartime necessity. Guerrillas could not win the war, but they could prolong it.[8]

As Daniel Sutherland has argued, not only did Americans associate this style of fighting with Indians—seeing mounted surprise attacks as "stealthy, sly, and cunning"—but direct experience in the Indian wars of the antebellum period had also "taught whites many practical lessons." White guerrillas perceived themselves to be "noble savages," sometimes naming their bands after Native tribes and scalping their enemies as a form of both trophy taking and psychological warfare. Such cultural and tactical appropriations also provoked "savage" responses from Union troops. As Kenneth Noe has discovered, in western Virginia Federals "felt free to confront pro-Confederate mountaineers with tactics usually reserved for Native American populations: the destruction of food resources, the burning of settlements, and a war waged against all elements of the society rather than just warriors."[9] The use of traditionally "savage" tactics in these contexts made everyone guerrillas.

But Native American men were not just reference points or metaphors in Civil War campaigns. They served as soldiers on both sides of the conflict; more than twenty thousand of them volunteered or were pressed into service in all theaters of the war. Almost immediately, Indian Territory became the focus of alliance building; both the Union and the Confederacy were interested in winning the territory's estimated one hundred thousand inhabitants (at least four thousand of them slaves) to their side.[10] The tribes in this region were aware of developments outside their borders, and after the formation of the Confederate States of America in February 1861, the Cherokees, Choctaws, Creeks, Chickasaws, and Seminoles sent delegates to meet with representatives of the Plains tribes at Antelope Hills, in the far western reaches of Indian Territory. Some chiefs argued for neutrality, others for joining the Union, and still others for the protection of slavery and an alliance with the Confederacy. And they waited in vain for the Federals to make their move.

Union officials, while they recognized the significance of this area and the benefits of alliances with its Native populations, made no special efforts to win their loyalty in the first two years of the war. The reasons for this inattention—and restrictions of annuities at federal Indian agencies throughout the West beginning in 1861—are somewhat befuddling. Most historians argue that this inept diplomatic strategy resulted from a conviction that Natives were the least of the Union government's worries and that the most damage they could do would actually work to restrict Confederate access to the Pacific coast.[11] Ultimately, Union indifference did indeed make a difference: four tribes of Indian Territory and half of the Cherokee nation signed treaties with the Confederacy. In return, the Confederacy promised that they would not lose their homelands and that Natives could fight only to protect their land and their people.[12]

These troops fought mostly in the trans-Mississippi West, in and around their own communities in Indian Territory. As Confederate colonel and former Oklahoma Indian agent Douglas H. Cooper reported from Arkansas in May 1862, the Natives in this area were "eminently suitable" to operate as guerrilla bands, given their knowledge of the country. "Indians," he wrote, "will make the very best guerrillas." Other Confederates believed that these Indian Territory guerrillas would be useful as part of an invading force in the western territories. "One regiment of Cherokees or Choctaws, well mounted," wrote one Arizonan, "would inspire more wholesome terror in the minds of our refractory Mexican population than a vast army of Americans from the States."[13] As John Baylor and Henry Sibley entered New Mexico Territory in the summer and fall of 1861, they did not bring any Cherokee or Choctaw soldiers with them, but they were most certainly interested in securing alliances with the region's most powerful tribes: Comanches, Apaches, Pueblos, Kiowas, Utes, Navajos, Pimas, and Papagos (see the chapter map).[14] They were sometimes successful in making temporary agreements with members of these tribes, but for the most part, these Native groups had no fealty to either the Confederacy or the Union. Unlike the tribes of Indian Territory, they were neither invested in black slavery nor linked to the United States through political or economic structures. For

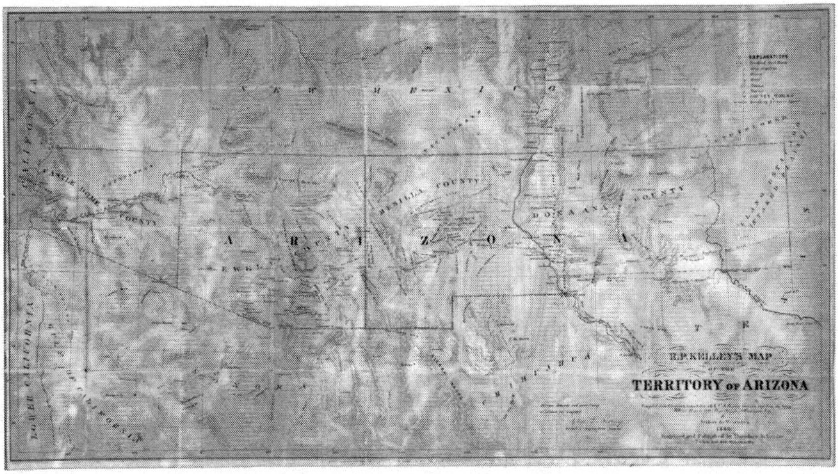

The southwestern territories in 1860, from *R.P. Kelley's Map of the Territory of Arizona.* (Library of Congress, Geography and Map Division)

them, the Civil War was a continuation of imperial conflict but with different players; it was a time of instability and therefore, opportunity.

For Native tribes, warfare tactics that Anglo-Americans perceived to be "irregular" or temporary were long-standing practices that they used to advance their political and economic goals. They used a combination of techniques, moving between them rapidly and fluidly in campaigns against other Natives as well as Spanish, Mexican, and American soldiers and civilians. Sometimes the intent was to inflict as much damage as possible on the enemy, killing men, women, and children and destroying their towns, fields, and camps. At other times they made quick strikes, targeting horses, cattle, and sheep or taking human captives in order to trade them at regional rendezvous and fairs. These attacks were often acts of conquest or vengeance, occasions to establish masculinity and leadership. They focused on male warriors or soldiers but often targeted women and children as well. They were acts of raiding warfare, a cultural practice similar in motivation and strategy to that of white southern guerrillas and bushwhackers operating elsewhere during the Civil War.[15]

Like their white counterparts, Native guerrillas launched surprise raids on horseback from protected positions at sites of vulnerability. In the desert Southwest, this meant roadside campsites, ranchos, military forts, waterholes, mountain passes, and canyon floors.[16] They cut the enemy off from their herds or initiated stampedes, taking as many animals as they could and driving them toward their own camps. Should the enemy give chase Native raiders would scatter, using their intimate knowledge of the terrain to lose their pursuers and then regroup at predetermined sites, where they had cached supplies in advance. Sometimes they would deliberately allow the enemy to catch up and then lead them on long, looping chases through the high desert mountains, crippling their horses and mules and stranding them far from home. Successful acts of raiding warfare necessitated a combination of discipline and flexibility, skills taught to young men as they grew up in Native villages. But raiding warfare was not solely a male activity; Native women, much like white women in guerrilla communities elsewhere, created and maintained supply lines in addition to managing and guarding camps, helping to carry off spoils, and in some cases, acting as decoys.[17]

Native raiding warfare was a form of conquest that was hundreds of years old by the 1860s. Natives used these strategies of ambush, attack, and evasion against enemy tribes; the arrival of Spanish explorers and missionaries in the northern reaches of the Chihuahuan desert in the late sixteenth century rendered raiding warfare even more vital to sustaining Native communities. Spanish horses—small, bred to live off grass and cover great distances between water sources—were uniquely suited to the environmental conditions in the desert Southwest. Most Native peoples in the region quickly integrated these animals into their cultures; the Comanches and Utes in particular were liberated and empowered by horses, building huge herds and, as historian Pekka Hämäläinen has argued, "an advanced equestrian war machine."[18] This dramatic increase in Native dependence on animals—mules, cattle, and sheep, too, but mostly horses—amplified the frequency and range of Native raiding warfare. It also served to create a "dynamic of simultaneous exchange and exploitation," as raids and attacks supplied Native economies with plunder and stimulated demand for exports in Anglo and Mexican communities. Native guerrillas therefore created and cornered their own markets. As a result, the southwestern borderlands became, in Hämäläinen's words, a "zone of blended violence and trade."[19]

In the century before the outbreak of the American Civil War, Comanches, Apaches, and Navajos built large communities and extensive trade networks in the Southwest through raiding warfare. By destroying Mexican and Anglo settlements and draining the region of resources between

1820 and 1845, as Brian DeLay has argued, Natives created man-made deserts within natural desert ecosystems. In these places there was "emptiness, silence, fruitlessness, desolation . . . the absence of industry and improvement, and of human mastery over nature."[20] These ruined landscapes, in turn, stoked the flames of American imperial desire; the purported emptiness of the region—and Mexicans' inability to defend their northern lands—invited American conquest. In the wake of the Mexican-American War, the U.S. Army constructed adobe and wooden forts within the boundaries of Native homelands; these structures symbolized Americans' conviction that they could do what Mexicans could not: "redeem the desert, defeat the Indians, and provide security to the long-suffering people" of the region.[21] So it was Native raiding warfare that brought Federal soldiers to the forts along the Rio Grande and the Santa Fe Trail in the decade before the fall of Fort Sumter, and it was Native raiding warfare that brought the Confederates to New Mexico in the summer and fall of 1861. And it was Native raiding warfare that shaped the campaigns to come.

Making Every Road a Desert: Native Raiders and the White Man's War

As secession conventions met across the Deep South in the winter of 1860–1861, U.S. Army officials stationed in the desert Southwest took the same haphazard approach as the Union government did in Indian Territory: they made treaties with some Native groups and launched campaigns against others. After the Navajo Expedition of 1858–1859, described by Colonel Thomas T. Fauntleroy as "the most distressing Campaign which has ever been inflicted on them," U.S. commanders turned their attention to other tribes that had been attacking soldiers and civilians throughout the 1850s. Fauntleroy deemed a winter campaign against the Kiowas and Comanches a success; it "appears to have caused those Indians to remove from the borders of this Department," he reported, "and to be anxious for peace." Fauntleroy also initiated two campaigns against the Apaches, one targeting those groups raiding west of the Rio Grande and the other moving against the Mescaleros and other Apaches "actively hostile around Forts Stanton and Fillmore" to the south and east.[22] When Fort Sumter fell, Fauntleroy—a Virginian—resigned his commission and left for the East; Lieutenant Colonel Edward R. S. Canby, who had commanded the Navajo Expedition and negotiated the subsequent peace with Navajo chiefs, replaced him as the commander of Union's Department of the West.

By mid-June 1861 Canby had heard creditable rumors that Confederate troops under John Baylor were amassing near Fort Bliss. In order to defend the territories of New Mexico and Colorado from this Texan invasion, Canby began to concentrate his men and supplies at forts along the Rio Grande (see the chapter map). This meant abandoning some installations and combining regiments at Forts Fillmore and Craig.[23] In early summer U.S. regulars vacated Forts McLane and Buchanan in southwestern New Mexico Territory (later Arizona Territory), which protected silver miners and other civilians living and working around Piños Altos (northwest of Mesilla) and Tubac (south of Tucson). Isaac Lynde, a major in command of the Federal Seventh Infantry, had established Fort McLane in September 1860; it was later named after a member of the Mounted Rifles who died in a campaign against Navajos. Canby ordered Lynde to abandon Fort McLane in mid-June 1861, and he did so in early July, bringing all of his men (and their wives and children) with him to Fort Fillmore; there he welcomed additional troops from Fort Buchanan.[24] It did not take long for civilians in the vicinity of Fort McLane to panic, and for Apache raiders to take note.

In mid-July 1861, an eight-wagon train on its way from the mines of western New Mexico to Mesilla neared the abandoned buildings of Fort McLane; as they slowed, seventy-five Apaches descended on the wagons and laid siege to them for two days. When a group of New Mexico farmers and "minutemen" from Piños Altos arrived, the Apaches set fire to the fort (unlike other forts in the region, which were made of adobe, McLane was constructed of wood) and scattered into the mountains.[25] One month later, miners and ranchers living around Fort Buchanan near Tubac decided to leave and formed a refugee column heading toward Mesilla on the Butterfield Overland Mail route. The thirty-one men and women set out on the road with sixteen children, six slaves, and hundreds of beef cattle and sheep. They were tempting and extremely vulnerable targets.

As they entered Cookes Canyon, a four-mile stretch of winding road through increasingly steep hills and rocky outcroppings, the Chiricahua Apache chief Cochise and two hundred guerrillas ambushed the wagon train. "Without no warning at all, the Indians came hellity-larrup, just swarming outen the rocks," remembered Jeff Ake, whose family had relocated from Tennessee to Tubac after the Mexican-American War. "There was a whole cloud of them."[26] The refugees abandoned several wagons, most of their stock, and ten of their neighbors who lay dead in the hot summer sun, making a run for it out of the canyon. "The Indians didn't foller," according to Ake. "I reckon the plunder was more interesting to them."[27]

This upsurge in Apache raiding on the roads of western New Mexico prompted Union commander Edward Canby to report to his superiors that "our Indian relations are still unsatisfactory. The Apaches of Arizona are still actively hostile and have committed many depredations during the past month."[28] For his part, Isaac Lynde thought that these developments might be helpful in combatting the Confederates. Anglos living in this area were known to be secessionist in their leanings, and he believed that by the summer of 1861 "there are not inhabitants enough in Arizona west of Mesilla to be feared at all, as the Indians have driven most of them from the mines."[29] But while the abandonment of Federal forts created opportunities for Native guerrillas, it also cleared the path westward for John Baylor and his Texans, who found almost no opposition to their march to Tucson in the fall of 1861. Except, of course, for the Apaches.

The son of a regimental surgeon, John Baylor had grown up on the outskirts of Fort Gibson in Indian Territory. After trying various professions—schoolteacher, Texas freedom fighter, state legislator, lawyer—Baylor moved with his wife and children to the banks of the Brazos River in Texas in September 1855, to work as Indian agent for the Comanches. There he became convinced that reservation Comanches were conspiring with their kin off reservation to raid local ranches and towns; after his dismissal from the post in 1857 he traveled widely through Texas, whipping up fears of Comanche raids and publishing an anti-Indian newspaper, *White Man.* Baylor later contended that these early experiences with Comanches—and other Native tribes living in Indian Territory—shaped his military vision for New Mexico. "It was with sentiments toward the Indians, the natural growth of years of such acquaintance with them and their deeds," he wrote in 1862, "that at the head of the Second Texas Mounted Rifles I marched into Arizona in 1861 to drive out the Federal troops." For Baylor, the Confederate war in the desert Southwest was both a civil war *and* an Indian war, simultaneously. After capturing the Fort Fillmore garrison (with Isaac Lynde in command) in July 1861—and knowing that Sibley was preparing for a campaign to take the Union's forts in central and northern New Mexico—Baylor shifted his attention westward to the "rich and beautiful country" of Arizona, scarred by the "constant Indian depredations worse even than those inflicted on Texas and executed on a much larger scale."[30]

With a huge territory to cover and only three hundred men to patrol it, Baylor had a difficult time preventing the raids that Apache chiefs launched from their camps in the southern Arizona mountains. He did manage to recruit local miners and ranchers to join small militia companies calling themselves the Arizona Guards. They were charged with local defense, protecting the road to Tucson and the mines at Piños Altos.[31] But the Apaches had a stronghold, and they knew the country. The chiefs Cochise and Mangas Coloradas and three hundred of their Chiricahua and Mimbreño warriors established their headquarters on Cookes Peak in the summer of 1861, and from there they launched raids and attacks in all directions. The peak rises more than eighty-four hundred feet in elevation above undulating sands of the upper Chihuahuan desert; its slopes gave the Apaches prospects from which to spot wagon trains moving along all roads in the area, many miles away.

After his successful raid on the Tubac wagon train in Cookes Canyon, Cochise evaded pursuit by dividing his band; he sent eighty men southward to trade some of the livestock with Mexicans and took the rest back with him to Cookes Peak. The Apaches heading south were subsequently ambushed by a detachment of the Arizona Guards in the Florida Mountains; the Apaches lost eight men killed and abandoned their stolen herd, retreating into the hills. To avenge this defeat Cochise and Mangas Coloradas gathered their warriors and attacked the mining camps around Piños Altos on September 27, 1861. They set fire to buildings and, as Arizona Guard Henry Clay Smith remembered, "Most of the fighting was done from behind pine trees and log cabins on our part, the Indians dodging from place to place."[32] Cochise and Mangas Coloradas eventually withdrew and parted ways, moving farther south into Mexico and west into central Arizona, respectively.

To New Mexican and Arizonan civilians, the intensification of Apache raiding wars in the summer and fall of 1861 provoked fear and paranoia. "The Apaches seem to have united," the editors of the *Mesilla Times* wrote frantically in October, "and their tribes have gathered in hosts and commenced a war of extermination against the whites, in earnest." The Indians, it seemed, were acting with more boldness and daring than ever before, desolating towns and making roads impassable. "We have Indians all around us," the editors cried.[33] Henry Jenkins, a Union-leaning adventurer who was trapped in Mesilla after the fall of Fort Fillmore and Baylor's establishment of a Confederate capital there, saw the impact of these raids in the landscape. The Apaches had created an "Indian Wild" to the west of the town. Along the roads "the rude graves and grim Skeletons of my Early friends from the Rio Grande to the Colorado are finger-posts to mark the track of their Savage ferocity and worse than Savage cruelty."[34] By April 1862, a Confederate soldier accompanying Sherrod Hunter's diplomatic mission to Tucson and Sonora reported that "the Apaches have made and kept the road [between Mesilla and Tucson] a desert. We made the first tracks that have been made on the road for months."[35]

Civilians living in the southern reaches of New Mexico and Arizona Territories lamented their "homes deserted, friends fallen victims to the savage foe." And to make matters worse for those who espoused the Confederate cause, there was "the scourge of war" against the Federals. Like Baylor, southwestern civilians understood that the Confederates were fighting two enemies on multiple fronts.[36] In late September, in response to orders that his men attack Union troops on the Rio Grande, Baylor requested "that some other force be sent to operate against the Indians."[37] Once Sibley joined him in New Mexico in December 1861 and took command of the fight against Union troops along the Rio Grande, Baylor could focus more attention on the Native threat to the west. He sent detachments of his Second Texas Mounted Rifles into the mountains in search of raiders and, in March 1862, ordered two hundred soldiers and one hundred volunteers to cross into the town of Corralitos, Mexico, "on the pretext of pursuing some Apache Indians," nearly provoking an international incident. His men killed several Apaches (who were "at peace with that community"), broke into houses, and, according to the enraged governor of Chihuahua, Luis Terrazas, committed "excesses and outrages that are improper for the subjects of a civilized nation friendly with the Republic of Mexico."[38] "I thought myself justifiable in killing the Indians and recovering the animals," Baylor protested in his report of the invasion, "the Mexican alcalde acknowledging that the Apaches habitually stole property from the whites in Arizona and run it into Mexico."[39] This particular diplomatic storm blew over, and Baylor maintained control of the Confederate territory of Arizona, but due to frequent Apache raids that control was tenuous.

Frustrating Confederate Designs: Native Guerrillas and the Sibley Brigade

The challenges of waging a two-front war against Federals and Natives undermined the Confederate attempt to conquer the desert Southwest in 1861–1862. Baylor was distracted, and his men were scattered over large areas; they could not act as reinforcements for Henry Sibley, who was retreating from Santa Fe down the Rio Grande while Baylor was launching raids into Mexico. This river and its valley—so central to sustaining life in the region—had long been a thoroughfare for imperialists and those who resisted them. Natives attacked northern Mexican towns almost as soon as they were established in the eighteenth century; the presence of U.S. military personnel and the construction of forts along the *el camino real de tierra adentro* in the 1850s did not deter them (see the chapter map). Instead, the increased travel along American military roads and mail routes, in addition to the caching of supplies at U.S. Army forts, offered additional opportunities for raiding. In February 1861 New Mexican civilians living in Doña Ana County requested that the U.S. Army send additional troops to Fort Fillmore for local defense. Descending from camps in the Organ, Magdalena, and San Mateo Mountains, Native guerrillas had stepped up their attacks on towns, ranches, and both civilian and military wagon trains. "Within the last *thirty* days," the New Mexicans wrote, "not less than ten persons have been killed & some children taken prisoners; and sheep mules & other animals to the number of at least six thousand have been stolen by Indians (Navajos & Apaches)."[40]

Between the time of Baylor's arrival at Fort Bliss (July 1861) and Sibley's (December), Apaches "stole from [Sibley's] troops 100 head of horses and mules." After camouflaging themselves with oil, dirt, and grass, they waited for Confederate pickets to pass and then slipped into corrals, cut ropes, and stole away with the animals. It was in retaliation for these thefts, Baylor argued, that he pursued the Apaches into Mexico and attacked the town of Corralitos.[41] As Baylor's—and later, Sibley's—men began to move northward along the Rio Grande, they encountered the Jornada del Muerto (path of the dead man). This huge stretch of desert, sitting east of a bend in the Rio Grande, was a favorite Apache raiding spot. William Anderson Thornton, a U.S. soldier taking part in a military expedition into New Mexico in 1855, noted, "This Hornada is 90 miles across and on account of the Indians who live in the adjoining mountains, and the extreme cold and sand storms, and the great want of water, it is very dangerous to cross." Mail companies used the road that traversed it because it was shorter and "better traveling," but it was "exposed to great privations and danger." Hence Thornton and his comrades "kept down the river route as we have done." Either way, groups on the move in the Jornada and its hinterlands were vulnerable to Apache attack; the desert road was open and exposed, but the river route—the *el camino real*—was equally vulnerable: a fixed, narrow track of sand hewing close to winding riverbanks.[42] In August 1861 Apaches set upon some of Baylor's men as they crossed the Jornada. New Mexican scouts working for Kit Carson later found the wreckage of that attack, letters and other packages lying partially covered by blowing sand.[43]

Apache guerrillas galloped through the Jornada, assaulted wagon trains and troops, and then returned to camps in the mountains looming above the Rio Grande Valley, almost always eluding their pursuers. In September 1861 Confederates under the command of Captain Pete Hardeman chased Mimbreño Apache raiders driving a large flock of stolen sheep into the Black Range of the San Mateo Mountains. Ultimately, their horses gave out and they ran out of food; they had never even caught sight of the Apaches, or their sheep.[44] This experience was repeated on the east side of the river in January 1862, as the Sibley Brigade moved toward Fort Craig and a fight with Union troops there. Apaches descended on the Confederates' camp at Willow Bar and took eighty mules and about the same number of horses. Hardeman, in command of Company A, Fourth Texas, gave chase, riding fifty miles southward and into the Organ Mountains east of Las Cruces. Texas private Theophilus Noel, who participated in this pursuit, remembered that "a grander and a more lovely sight or picturesque landscape view never met the eyes," than from the summits of those mountains. He could see far off to the southeast and to the northwest, all of the desert looking like "a trackless ocean." And as they gazed westward across the Rio Grande Valley to the Black Range, the peaks "looked like the foaming billows of a raging sea as viewed from a ship as the storm approaches." The view was all they managed to capture, however; the track they followed disappeared and "here the chase was given up, and we commenced to beat a retreat."[45]

By one Union scout's count, the Confederates had lost more than two hundred horses by late January, as they concentrated their men and herds at Fort Thorn to launch their attack against the Federals gathered at Fort Craig. Even as they negotiated with some tribes and hired some Apaches (Cadete and Manuelito) as guides, the Sibley Brigade continued to lose horses, mules, cattle, and sheep all along their march.[46] This put considerable strain on the brigade; when Sibley dispatched Hardeman's company to chase down Native guerrillas he lost available manpower, and these pursuits produced nothing but exhausted men and horses. The raiding—and constant fear of it—became so bad that one Confederate soldier reported, "The mountains here are full of Indians and we dread them worse than we do the Lincolnites, by odds."[47] The brigade failed to recover most of their animals, creating a provisions crisis that became life threatening, especially after they were turned back at the Battle of Glorieta Pass in late March 1862 and began their retreat back the way they came.

After taking a disastrous route through the San Mateo Mountains in order to shake their Union army pursuers, the Sibley Brigade staggered back into Mesilla on April 26, 1862. They camped there for three weeks to recover from the effects of near starvation and thirst, and then they departed for Fort Bliss, where they also laid over. In early June they set out for San Antonio, one regiment at a time. Sibley staggered his men on the retreat—as he had in the march out—because desert springs and water holes along the road were small and thus slow to replenish. Water had to be rationed in order to sustain the Texans and the few animals that remained. When Theophilus Noel and the men of the Fourth Texas finally reached Eagle Springs after a long march across the desert highlands from Fort Quitman, they found the forty-foot-deep water hole, sixty feet in diameter, with a "live subterranean stream of pure water flow[ing] through a cavernous rock." Unfortunately, they also found a pile of dead sheep and "the carcasses of some of the oxen of the detachment ahead of us" at the bottom, bathed in its waters. They had no water kegs so they had to move on to Van Horn's Wells, which was similarly contaminated, with dirt and the bodies of sheep and wolves. Noel figured that it was Edward Canby who had ordered these acts of biological warfare (to use the modern term for it) and his chief scout, Kit Carson—"the terror of the plains"—who had helped to carry them out.[48] It is unlikely, though, that Canby was engaged in such plotting from his headquarters in Santa Fe, and at that time Carson was operating in northern New Mexico, in campaigns against the Kiowas. It is much more likely that Comanches or Apaches were responsible. Here again, the vulnerabilities of a fixed route through a vast landscape became apparent. Water sources like this one—and Cookes Springs in Arizona Territory—were "convening" locations, exposed sites at which Native guerrillas asserted their control over desert resources and weakened their enemies.

As Noel and the Fourth Texas limped along the San Antonio–El Paso road in the desert heat (in this area of western Texas, temperatures in June and July often reached 95 degrees), their comrades in Colonel William Steele's Seventh remained in southern New Mexico, as a rear guard. Steele knew by then that the Confederate cause in New Mexico was lost; in late May he had sent a detachment of men on one final raid of their own in order to secure Federal horses for their retreat. He dispatched one hundred men, including the eighteen-year-old private Felix Collard, to capture a Union horse herd corralled at Paraje, a town just north of the Jornada del Muerto. The Confederates rode through the night through the desert and arrived at the Union camp to find all the Federals asleep and the horses free for the taking. But the leader of the expedition, Lieutenant Isaac Bowman, decided to demand the surrender of the garrison; this decision cost the Confederate raiders the advantage of surprise, and the Union troops came out firing—with two mountain howitzers. The Confederates beat a hasty retreat, but this was just the beginning of their troubles.[49]

As they rode back through the Jornada under a blazing sun, the hard overnight riding and lack of water began to take a toll on the Confederates. Collard's horse gave out, and his comrades rode ahead to the Rio Grande, promising to bring back full canteens. "I felt kinder lonesome when the last man rode out of sight," he remembered. "My father owned slaves, and I was a soft 'feather-bed' kind of boy, unused to hardship. Now I was catching it in the neck."[50] His friends did not return that night, and so the next morning Collard left his exhausted, whinnying horse and "walked on, looking back for the enemy, looking forward, looking to the right, looking to the left expecting Indians." He walked all day and then found a concealed position, fell asleep, and dreamed of lying down on the banks of Blue Branch, near his father's plantation, and "drinking like a fish." The next day he continued his walk and soon found a cluster of dead horses, stripped of blankets and saddles. This was ominous. "Indians," he wrote, "like sleuth hounds, had followed the trail in the dark." Half dead, he stumbled into camp that evening.[51] The Paraje raid in May 1862 was one of the final clashes between Union and Confederate troops in the desert Southwest, and it was a fitting end: a Confederate guerrilla raid through the desert in which no one benefited but the Apaches.

Steele's men continued to endure attacks from all sides as they moved slowly out of New Mexico Territory and into western Texas. They were set upon by Apaches and Pueblos but also by New Mexicans, determined to "[run] off what little stock [the company] has left."[52] By the time they reached Fort Bliss, Confederate private Joseph Kirgan reported that the Seventh Texas had "nothing to eat but bread" and "no transportation of any kind." Some had horses—like Collard, who had Pete—but several of these were taken in the Indian raid on Limpia Creek. As they trudged along the road to San Antonio, they left behind them a road filled with debris:

broken-down wagons and dead horses, sheep, and cattle. "Everything betokens," as one Texan put it, "a godforsaken country."[53]

In his report of his brigade's campaign to capture the West for the Confederacy, Henry Sibley later argued that Native raiding had contributed to its failure. Native guerrillas had effectively undermined the Confederate effort to take and hold towns and territories by creating "deserts" empty of provisions. "The indispensible element, food, cannot be relied upon," he reported in May 1862. "During the last year, and pending recent operations, hundreds of thousands of sheep have been driven off by the Navajoes." These losses—both military and civilian—were so disruptive to Sibley's plans that he "determined, as good policy, to encourage private enterprises against that tribe and the Apaches, and to legalize the enslaving of them."[54] Baylor had suggested a similarly "savage" response to Native raiding; in the wake of the Corralitos attack, Baylor authorized his officers to invite Apaches to peace parlays and then to murder them in surprise attacks. "I had just read an article published in the Charleston Courier or Mercury," he explained, "which stated that our Congress had declared a war of extermination against all those wild and hostile Indian tribes who had shown an utter disregard for all treaty stipulations." In Baylor's view, extermination of adults and assimilation (through enslavement) of Native children was the only Indian policy that would make sense in the new Confederate States of America.[55]

It took some time for the news of Sibley's and Baylor's "savage" measures against Native guerrillas to make its way east; by the time it did, the Sibley Brigade had returned to San Antonio, dogged along the way by Apaches raiding what few animals they had left. In November 1862 Baylor was already recruiting soldiers for a second invasion of New Mexico Territory, to be undertaken along the Santa Fe Trail rather than the San Antonio–El Paso road. But when Confederate secretary of war G. W. Randolph heard about Baylor's extermination order, he revoked the Texan's authority to raise troops for this campaign (effectively removing him from command) and demanded that Baylor write a report to Jefferson Davis, outlining his reasoning for such extreme measures. Baylor defended himself by citing his many years of experience with the "savage visitations" of the western tribes upon Texan ranches and towns and their many depredations in the New Mexico and Arizona Territories during the Confederate invasion of New Mexico. He also noted the expectation among those living in frontier counties in the desert Southwest that the Confederate government would protect them from Indian guerrilla attacks in exchange for their loyalty to the new nation.[56] Baylor saw no reason why he should be deprived of the "command of the brave men, most of them my old frontier comrades whom I was prepared to lead to battle against both Abolition and savage foe." There would come a time when Union forces would invade Texas, he warned Davis, and he relished the opportunity to "meet and exterminate a foe hardly less cruel and remorseless than the Comanche or the Apache."[57]

The ruins of Sibley's New Mexico campaign joined abandoned Native pueblos, Spanish missions, and New Mexican towns; destroyed copper and silver mines; and the wreckage of Anglo migrants' wagons as symbols of what historian Sam Truett has called the "fugitive landscape" of the Southwest. It was a space "characterized by mobility and flexibility" and favoring those who could move quickly through vast deserts and mountain passes, raiding and evading and trading their way across the region.[58] It was a land in which Native and Anglo fighters clashed and in which Natives, whose tactics and knowledge were deeply imbedded in the desert landscape, integrated Anglos into their own long history of guerrilla warfare. The Natives took advantage of the exigencies of war—large numbers of men and animals amassing, wagon trains and soldiers on the move—to undermine both Union and Confederate attempts to establish dominion over the region. They attacked soldiers in blue and gray with equal ferocity and civilians of all loyalties. But their raids had a more disastrous effect on Confederates, who relied solely on their animal herds to sustain their campaign for New Mexico and to establish a foothold in Arizona. Raiding warfare, a methodology of violence involving ambushes, attacks, and evasions through which the Native groups of the Southwest created vast networks of influence in the desert Southwest, undermined the Confederacy's imperial aims in 1861–1862.

But by driving the Texans back to San Antonio, Native guerrillas had effectively turned a two-front war into a one-front conflict for the Union army. After the summer of 1862 Federals focused their attention on Apaches, Comanches, and Navajos in a new Civil War campaign to eradicate the "savage foe" or confine them to reservations. In this they would be more successful than the Confederates, using guerrilla tactics in running battles, continuing to fight a war for the West in the midst of the American Civil War.

Notes

The author would like to thank Matt Hulbert, Joe Beilein Jr., and the two peer reviewers of this manuscript for their insightful comments and editing suggestions.

1. Felix R. Collard, "Reminiscences of a Private, Company 'G,' 7th Texas Cavalry, Sibley Brigade, C.S.A.," in possession of Robert F. Collard, Silver City, NM, as quoted in Donald S. Frazier, *Blood and Treasure: Confederate Empire in the Southwest* (College Station: Texas A&M University Press, 1995), 284–85.

2. Elliott West, *The Contested Plains: Indians, Goldseekers, and the Rush to Colorado* (Lawrence: University Press of Kansas, 1998), xviii.

3. The desert Southwest has garnered attention mostly from western historians working in this period, and until recently, these historians have rarely brought Civil War and Native American histories together. See Ray C. Colton, *The Civil War in the Western Territories: Arizona, Colorado, New Mexico, and Utah* (Norman: University of Oklahoma Press, 1984); and Alvin M. Josephy Jr., *The Civil War in the American West* (New York: Vintage, 1993). Donald Frazier was the first historian to argue for the Civil War as a war for empire in the West (in *Blood and Treasure*), an argument more fully developed and refined (and positioned within Native American history) in Ari Kelman, *A Misplaced Massacre: Struggling over the Memory of Sand Creek* (Cambridge, MA: Harvard University Press, 2013).

4. William J. Cooper Jr., *Jefferson Davis, American* (New York: Vintage, 2001), 274–75; Jefferson Davis (1859), as quoted in Thomas L. Connelly, "The American Camel Experiment: A Reappraisal," *Southwestern Historical Quarterly* 69, no. 4 (April 1966): 444.

5. Frazier, *Blood and Treasure,* 4, 5.

6. Martin Hardwick Hall, *Sibley's New Mexico Campaign* (1960; reprint, Albuquerque: University of New Mexico Press, 2000), 21–22; Jerry Thompson, introduction to *Civil War in the Southwest: Recollections of the Sibley Brigade,* ed. Thompson (College Station: Texas A&M University Press, 2001), xiv; Frazier, *Blood and Treasure,* 75; Trevanion T. Teel, "Sibley's New Mexican Campaign—Its Objects and the Causes of its Failure," in *Battles and Leaders of the Civil War,* ed. Robert Underwood Johnson and Clarence Clough Buel (New York: Century, 1887), 2:700.

7. Duane Shaw, *Civil War West* (Bloomington, IN: Authorhouse, 2011), 5–6; Megan Kate Nelson, "Dying in the Desert," *Civil War Monitor* 2, no. 1 (Spring 2012): 48–53, 71–73.

8. Michael Fellman, *Inside War: The Guerrilla Conflict in Missouri during the American Civil War* (New York: Oxford University Press, 1989); Fellman, "Inside Wars: The Cultural Crisis of Warfare and the Values of Ordinary People," in *Guerrillas, Unionists, and Violence on the Confederate Home Front,* ed. Daniel Sutherland (Fayetteville: University of Arkansas Press, 1999); Daniel E. Sutherland, *A Savage Conflict: The Decisive Role of Guerrillas in the American Civil War* (Chapel Hill: University of North Carolina Press, 2009); Victoria E. Bynum, *The Long*

Shadow of the Civil War: Southern Dissent and Its Legacies (Chapel Hill: University of North Carolina Press, 2010); Thomas Goodrich, *Black Flag: Guerrilla Warfare on the Western Border, 1861–1865* (Bloomington: Indiana University Press, 1995); Robert R. Mackey, *The Uncivil War: Irregular Warfare in the Upper South, 1861–1865* (Norman: University of Oklahoma Press, 2004); Kenneth W. Noe, "Who Were the Bushwhackers? Class, Kin, and Western Virginia's Confederate Guerrillas, 1861–1862," *Civil War History* 49 no. 1 (March 2003): 5–31; Mark W. Geiger, *Financial Fraud and Guerrilla Violence in Missouri's Civil War, 1861–1865* (New Haven, CT: Yale University Press, 2010); Don R. Bowen, "Guerrilla War in Western Missouri, 1862–1865: Historical Extensions of the Relative Deprivation Hypothesis," *Comparative Studies in Society and History* 19, no. 1 (January 1977): 30–51; Phillip Shaw Paludan, *Victims: A True Story of the Civil War* (1981; reprint, Knoxville: University of Tennessee Press, 2004); Barton A. Myers, *Executing Daniel Bright: Race, Loyalty, and Guerrilla Violence in a Coastal Carolina Community, 1861–1865* (Baton Rouge: Louisiana State University Press, 2009); Joseph Beilein Jr., "The Guerrilla Shirt: A Labor of Love and the Style of Rebellion in Civil War Missouri," *Civil War History* 58, no. 2 (June 2012): 151–79; LeeAnn Whites, "Forty Shirts and a Wagonload of Wheat: Women, the Domestic Supply Line, and the Civil War on the Western Border," *Journal of the Civil War Era* 1, no. 1 (March 2011): 56–78; Matthew C. Hulbert, "Constructing Guerrilla Memory: John Newman Edwards and Missouri's Irregular Lost Cause," *Journal of the Civil War Era* 2, no. 1 (March 2012): 58–81.

9. Sutherland, *Savage Conflict,* 10, 28, 29, 31, 114; Beilein, "Guerrilla Shirt," 174, 176–77; Noe, "Who Were the Bushwhackers?," 10.

10. Anne Bailey, *Invisible Southerners: Ethnicity in the Civil War* (Athens: University of Georgia Press, 2006), 29.

11. Annie Heloise Abel, *The American Indian in the Civil War, 1862–1865* (Cleveland: A.H. Clark, 1919; reprint, Lincoln: University of Nebraska Press, 1992), 61–62; Clarissa W. Confer, *The Cherokee Nation in the Civil War* (Norman: University of Oklahoma Press, 2007), 46.

12. Laurence M. Hauptman, *Between Two Fires: American Indians in the Civil War* (New York: Free Press, 1995), 18, 25, 65–66; William McKee Evans, "Native Americans in the Civil War," in *Civil War Citizens: Race, Ethnicity, and Identity in America's Bloodiest Conflict,* ed. Susannah Ural (New York: New York University Press, 2010), 192; Bailey, *Invisible Southerners,* 30, 34–35; Craig W. Gaines, *The Confederate Cherokees: John Drew's Regiment of Mounted Rifles* (Baton Rouge: Louisiana State University Press, 1989), 7, 20; Confer, *Cherokee Nation in the Civil War,* 45; Sutherland, *Savage Conflict,* 49; Megan Kate Nelson, "Indian America," in *Blackwell Companion to the U.S. Civil War,* vol. 1, ed. Aaron Sheehan-Dean (Oxford: Blackwell, 2014).

13. Douglas H. Cooper to General Earl Van Dorn, from Skullyville, near Fort Smith, Arkansas, May 6, 1862, in U.S. War Department, *The War of the Rebellion: A Compilation of the Official Records of the Union and Confederate Armies* (Wash-

ington, D.C.: Government Printing Office, 1880–1901), ser. 1, vol. 13, p. 824 (hereafter *OR*); Owen Davis, as quoted in Sutherland, *Savage Conflict,* 49.

14. "The Southwestern Defense System before the Civil War," map showing Federal forts and Native territories, in Robert M. Utley, *Fort Union National Monument New Mexico,* Historical Handbook Series no. 35 (Washington, D.C.: National Park Service: 1962), http://www.nps.gov/history/history/online_books/hh/35/hh35l.htm.

15. Native raiders did not act as partisans in Sutherland's terms, for they did not act in conjunction with a larger army in the field. Instead, they were loyal only to their own tribes and acted to fulfill their own desires and secure their own survival. Sutherland, *Savage Conflict,* xi; Robert Wyatt, "Victorio's Military and Political Leadership of the Warm Springs Apaches," *War in History* 18, no. 4 (November 2011): 460; West, *Contested Plains,* 77, 83.

16. Native tribes did not think of the region as the "desert Southwest" or the "Southwest," of course. They had many names for lands in this region, most related to tribal histories and identities. I use "desert Southwest" and its variations in this discussion of Native warfare traditions only to prevent any confusion within the essay, and to distinguish this theater of war from what Civil War historians usually term "the West" (the trans-Mississippi West).

17. Wyatt, "Victorio's Military and Political Leadership," 460, 471, 476, 484, 494; Brian DeLay, *War of a Thousand Deserts: Indian Raids and the U.S.-Mexican War* (New Haven, CT: Yale University Press, 2008), 121; Whites, "Forty Shirts"; Beilein, "Guerrilla Shirt."

18. Pekka Hämäläinen, *The Comanche Empire* (New Haven, CT: Yale University Press, 2008), 25, 27, 29, 40.

19. Ibid., 81, 85, 99.

20. Ibid., 5; DeLay, *War of a Thousand Deserts,* xv–xvi.

21. DeLay, *War of a Thousand Deserts,* xxi, 287, 291, 293.

22. T. T. Fauntleroy to Colonel L. Thomas (AAG, U.S. Army), from Santa Fe, March 1, 1861, folder 1171, box 10787, subseries 7.1, Albert H. Schroeder Collection, New Mexico State Records Center and Archives (hereafter NMSRCA).

23. Colton, *Civil War in the Western Territories,* 13.

24. Ibid., 14; George H. Pettis, "The Confederate Invasion of New Mexico and Arizona," in Johnson and Buel, *Battles and Leaders of the Civil War,* 2:103–11.

25. Frazier, *Blood and Treasure,* 56.

26. Ibid., 62.

27. Jeff Ake quoted in ibid., 65–66, citing James B. O'Neil, *They Die But Once: The Story of a Tejano,* 41–42.

28. Edward R. S. Canby to AAG, June 23, 1861, folder 1171, box 10787, subseries 7.1, Schroeder Collection, NMSRCA.

29. Isaac Lynde to Colonel E. R. S. Canby, from Fort McLane, June 24, 1861, in *When the Texans Came: Missing Records from the Civil War in the Southwest, 1861–1862,* ed. John Wilson (Albuquerque: University of New Mexico Press, 2001), 29.

30. John R. Baylor to General J. B. Magruder, December 29, 1862, in *OR,* ser. 1, vol. 15, p. 916; Jerry Thompson, "John Robert Baylor," *Handbook of Texas Online* (Texas Historical Association), http://www.tshaonline.org/handbook/online/articles/fbaat, accessed December 31, 2013.

31. Frazer, *Blood and Treasure,* 56–57.

32. Smith as quoted in Frazier, *Blood and Treasure,* 109, citing Curry, *Sun Rising on the West,* 52.

33. "Attack on Pino Alto by the Indians," *Mesilla Times,* October 3, 1861, in Wilson, *When the Texans Came,* 150.

34. Henry Jenkins to George R. Babcock, Esq., from Mesilla, September 16, 1863, folder 13, box 15817, New Mexico Letters and Diaries Collection, NMSRCA.

35. "One of the Escort" to E. H. Cushing, from Mesilla, April 17, 1862, in Wilson, *When the Texans Came,* 186–87.

36. "Attack on Pino Alto by the Indians," *Mesilla Times,* October 3, 1861, in ibid., 150.

37. John Baylor to Captain D. C. Stith (AAG, San Antonio), from Doña Ana, September 28, 1861, in ibid., 150.

38. Luis Terrazas, governor of Chihuahua, to Henry Sibley, "wherever he may be," from Chihuahua, March 17, 1862, in ibid., 231–32. See also Edward H. Jordan to Colonel J. A. Quintero (Monterey), from Chihuahua, March 18, 1862, and Juan B. Méndez, Civil Political Chief, District of Bravos, to Secretary of State, Chihuahua, March 26, 1862, both in ibid., 233–34.

39. John R. Baylor to General J. B. Magruder, December 29, 1862, in *OR,* ser. 1, vol. 15, p. 916.

40. Petition of the citizens of Doña Ana County to Colonel T. T. Fauntleroy, February 13, 1861, folder 1171, box 10787, subseries 7.1, Schroeder Collection, NMSRCA; James A. Lucas to Colonel Fauntleroy, from Mesilla, February 18, 1861, folder 1171, box 10787, subseries 7.1, Schroeder Collection, NMSRCA.

41. John R. Baylor to General John B. Magruder, December 29, 1862, in *OR,* ser. 1, vol. 15, p. 916; Frazier, *Blood and Treasure,* 133–34.

42. William Anderson Thornton, diary, "Military Expedition to New Mexico, 1855–1856," p. 28, folder 12, box 15817, New Mexico Letters and Diaries Collection, NMSRCA.

43. B. S. Roberts to A. L. Anderson, from Fort Craig, August 21, 1861, and John Baylor to Captain T. A. Washington, San Antonio, from Doña Ana, September 26, 1861, in Wilson, *When the Texans Came,* 120–21, 149.

44. Frazier, *Blood and Treasure,* 110.

45. Entry for January 16, 1862, in Theophilus Noel, *A Campaign from Santa Fe to the Mississippi, Being a History of the Old Sibley Brigade* (Shreveport, LA: Shreveport News Printing, 1865), 12.

46. Captain Saturnino Barriento to Canby, from Gallinas Mountains, August 24, 1861, in Wilson, *When the Texans Came,* 163.

47. William J. L. Nicodemus to Major Donaldson, from Belen, January 24, 1862, in ibid., 219; *Austin State Gazette,* February 15, 1862, as quoted in Hall, *Sibley's New Mexico Campaign,* 40. Soldiers in the Sibley Brigade became increasingly anxious about the desert and its threatening Native guerrillas during these marches, just as soldiers became progressively paranoid and fearful of the Eastern Theater's dark and tangled forests in 1863 and 1864. On the latter, see Kathryn Shively Meier, "Fighting in 'Dante's Inferno': Changing Perceptions of Civil War Combat in the Spotsylvania Wilderness from 1863 to 1864," in *Militarized Landscapes: From Gettysburg to Salisbury Plain,* ed. Peter Coates, Tim Cole, and C. J. Pearson (London: Continuum, 2010), 39–56.

48. Theophilus Noel, *Autobiography and Reminiscences of Theophilus Noel* (Chicago: Theo. Noel Co., 1904), 64–65; Noel, *Campaign from Santa Fe to the Mississippi,* 35.

49. Collard, "Reminiscences of a Private," as quoted in Frazier, *Blood and Treasure,* 269–70.

50. Ibid., 270.

51. Ibid., 270–71.

52. E. E. Eyre, lieutenant colonel, First Cavalry California Volunteers, to John Chivington, from Fort Thorn, Arizona Territory, July 10, 1862, in Wilson, *When the Texans Came,* 287–88.

53. J[oseph] A. K[irgan]. to the *Houston Tri-Weekly Telegraph,* from Fort Bliss, July 8, 1862, published August 18, 1862, p. 2 col. 3, as quoted in ibid., 311–12; Robb quoted in Frazier, *Blood and Treasure,* 29.

54. Henry H. Sibley, report from Fort Bliss, May 4, 1862, in *OR,* ser. 1, vol. 9, p. 512.

55. John R. Baylor to General John B. Magruder, December 29, 1862, in *OR,* ser. 1, vol. 15, pp. 914, 915, 916–17.

56. Brigadier General James Carleton (commander of the Department of New Mexico) to Colonel Joseph West (commander of the District of Arizona), November 18, 1862, in *OR,* ser. 1, vol. 15, pp. 599–602; G. W. Randolph (CSA secretary of war) to Major General John B. Magruder, from Richmond, November 7, 1862, in ibid., p. 857.

57. John R. Baylor to General J. B. Magruder, December 29, 1862, in ibid., p. 917–18.

58. Samuel Truett, *Fugitive Landscapes: The Forgotten History of the U.S.-Mexico Borderlands* (New Haven, CT: Yale University Press, 2006), 15.

The Business of Guerrilla Memory

Selling Massacres and the Captivity Narrative of Sergeant Thomas M. Goodman

Matthew C. Hulbert

On September 27, 1864, Confederate guerrillas under the command of William "Bloody Bill" Anderson intercepted a train as it approached the previously unrenowned village of Centralia, Missouri. One among the caravan of passenger cars harbored twenty-five furloughed Union soldiers. They were, by virtually all accounts, unarmed. Nevertheless, Anderson's men de-trained the Federals at gunpoint, lined them up alongside the hijacked locomotive, and unceremoniously forced them to their knees. With his new prisoners at bay, Anderson himself appeared and sought out a sergeant from their ranks. One man, unaware of the guerrilla chieftain's intentions (though likely assuming the worst—they called him "Bloody Bill" for a reason, after all), stepped forward and was culled from his fellow captives. Seconds later, at point-blank range, the guerrillas let loose a devastating volley. To a man, the rest of the Union troopers were felled in cold blood.[1]

Later that day, Anderson and a significantly larger throng of guerrillas lured the Thirty-Ninth Missouri Infantry (Mounted) and its commander, Major A. V. E. Johnston, to the scene of yet another gory encounter. Enraged by the incident at the rail depot, Johnston and his troops rode determinedly into an open field just a short gallop from the heart of Centralia. On all but one side, this space was hemmed in by dense trees and underbrush. Just beyond the tree line, veiled by foliage and shadow, deep

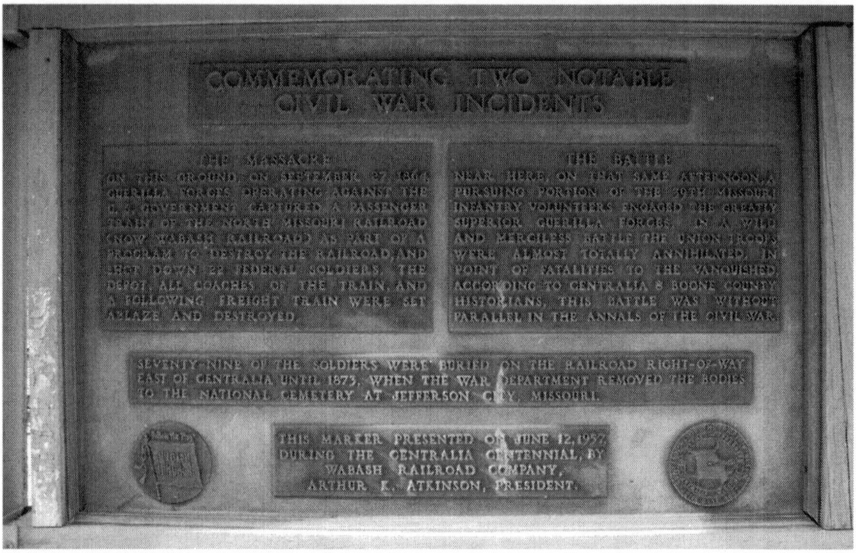

The monument commemorating the morning massacre at the Centralia Rail Depot. (Matthew C. Hulbert)

trenches—deep enough, as the Thirty-Ninth would soon discover, to conceal hundreds of men on horseback—snaked through the woodlands surrounding the meadow. When Johnston drew his regiment to a halt, the whole of Anderson's force lurched forward to meet the unsuspecting Federals from three directions. Then Johnston did something quite odd given the circumstances: he ordered his men to dismount and form a skirmish line. Meanwhile, with revolvers in hand, hundreds of guerrillas led by the likes of Anderson, George Todd, Clifton Holtzclaw, and John Thrailkill thundered down on Johnston and caught the Thirty-Ninth in a lethal crossfire. Already outnumbered and now on foot, the Federal line quickly dissolved. Johnston didn't live to defend his decision to alight—and upward of 125 Union soldiers fell in the slaughter. Afterward the guerrillas mutilated numerous corpses, relieving more than a few of their scalps.[2]

For a brief moment in 1864, news of the unthinkable slaughters spread rapidly across the nation. On September 28, in nearby St. Louis, Missouri, under the headline "Horrible Affair at Centralia," the *Daily Missouri Democrat* reported that "the North Missouri railroad train, which left St. Louis early yesterday morning was captured by guerrillas, Bill Anderson's, at Centralia, on its arrival there. Twenty-one soldiers were taken out of the

A lone monument standing watch over the afternoon massacre site. (Matthew C. Hulbert)

cars, and *shot dead!*" By September 29, word had traveled as far as Boston. There the *Boston Daily Advertiser* informed readers that "the passenger train which left here [St. Louis] yesterday morning on the Northern Missouri railroad was captured at Centralia by Bill Anderson's bushwhackers, and 21 soldiers taken out and murdered." Other papers, such as the *Daily*

Sentinel of Milwaukee, Wisconsin, focused on the details of the Thirty-Ninth Missouri's crushing defeat. On October 6, it ran a story that offered that the Thirty-Ninth was "overwhelmed by superior forces" and "could make no resistance, and the butchery commended." "Major Johnston," the article continued, "was murdered and scalped; and 130 of his officers and men shared the same fate. Most of them were shot through the head, then scalped, bayonets thrust through each of them, their ears and noses cut off and thrust into their mouths." "Such heartless and barbarous acts of atrocity," the paper concluded, "by any but Sepoy savages, are almost too horrible for belief."[3] Despite the sensational nature of the reports emanating from Missouri, other events, such as Sherman's March to the Sea, major battles at Nashville, Franklin, and Cedar Creek, and the election of 1864 soon replaced them; almost as quickly as Centralia had become infamous on a national scale, it was relegated to obscurity.

Four years later, the author of a slim volume published by Mills and Company's Steam Book & Job Printing House of Des Moines, Iowa, boldly claimed to have witnessed the massacres at Centralia. *Both of them.* Considering the necessary logistics involved and the gruesomely lopsided nature of Anderson's victories, this was no small feat. The man's name was Thomas M. Goodman—a resident of Hawleyville, Iowa—and, as it turned out, he did have a miraculous story to tell. Goodman was quite literally the only nonguerrilla who could have seen and survived the pair of run-ins with Bloody Bill and his band of bushwhackers: he was the sergeant whom Anderson had inexplicably spared that morning at the rail station. And now, in 1868, for the mere sum of fifty cents, readers could learn the details of Goodman's ordeal and gain unprecedented knowledge of the late guerrilla commander and the "peculiarities of guerrilla life in the bush."[4]

On the face of it, the publication of Goodman's account doesn't seem especially out of the ordinary. A public demand existed, Goodman had the opportunity to meet it, and he could gain financially in the process. Therein, its title—*A Thrilling Record: Founded on Facts and Observations Obtained during Ten Days' Experience with Col. Wm. T. Anderson, the Notorious Guerrilla Chieftain*—is unquestionably designed to draw attention and foment commercial appeal. As well, the cover of the book touted a "liberal discount made to Booksellers and Agents," while its lengthy subtitle, which describes Goodman as "the only survivor of the inhuman massacre at Centralia, Missouri, September 27, 1864, and an eye-witness of the brutal and barbarous treatment by the guerrillas of the dead, wounded, and captured of Major Johnson's [*sic*] command" reads more like a tabloid headline than an official history of the war. And if this preview alone did not generate excitement enough, advertisements also assured readers that the book wasn't simply an academic rehashing of details; rather, it was action-packed from start to finish: "Read it! It is replete with thrilling interest. Read it!"

Upon closer inspection, however, there is much more to the "business" of Goodman's narrative than a cut-and-dried market transaction. By 1868, when *A Thrilling Record* was released, pundits in both the North and the South had already begun the work of designating how the Civil War should and would be remembered. In addition to a seemingly endless stream of memoirs and diaries published in the years and decades immediately following the war, larger histories, historical sketches, and compendiums were also being churned out at a prolific rate. All told, these accounts were intended to establish and document a factual understanding of the war and, in many ways, to determine who and what were relevant in the memorial equation. As we shall see, from the outset of his own memoir, Goodman was greatly concerned with how Union soldiers caught up in the irregular violence of the Kansas-Missouri borderlands—in this case, the victims of massacres—would be remembered and whether or not their own blood sacrifices, spilled far from the best-known battlefields of Virginia, Tennessee, and Pennsylvania, would be included in dominant, eastern-centric versions of the war.[5]

To be clear, Thomas Goodman did attempt to sell (and in a very loose way to exploit) the guerrilla massacres to which he bore witness in the traditional sense of the word. It is an undeniable fact that acquiring his book (legally, anyhow) required readers to part with fifty cents. On the other hand, though, Goodman had something else entirely on his mind. As the following dissection of his captivity narrative will chronicle, Goodman's spiel was not, at its core, one devised solely for monetary or commercial purposes. Instead, Goodman's true pitch—delivered in the most formative period of Civil War legacy building—was designed to market himself and other Federal victims of the irregular war in the West as worthy of mainstream remembrance and commemorative attention.[6]

Concerning that formative period of legacy building, it may seem odd to think that in the aftermath of untold physical destruction, unhealed emotional scars, and 750,000 men dead, Americans would support a robust market for all manner of war-related literature—but they did exactly that. So with this in mind, despite its unquestionably unique story, *A Thrilling*

Record was actually not unusual in terms of its function; it was part of a much broader pattern of attempts to influence and codify remembrance through published texts. In simpler terms, Goodman took advantage of the fact that the public wanted to hear from veterans—but he didn't say what everyone is accustomed hearing. Goodman had seen something of the "real" face of the war and had a very different sort of celebration in mind.

While exact figures remain elusive, based on modern catalogs and bibliographies, Civil War veterans published hundreds—and more likely thousands—of firsthand accounts of the war.[7] As an example of the sheer volume of diaries, memoirs, and collections of letters published in the 1860s, 1870s, and 1880s, the Main Library at the University of Georgia alone holds several dozen such accounts, hailing from Boston, Detroit, New York, and locales all over the United States (and the former Confederacy). Equally vast—and often more vast—are the quantities of personal narratives offered by libraries at the University of North Carolina at Chapel Hill, the University of Virginia, Penn State University, and Harvard University. Therefore it is a safe bet that virtually every major research university library and many state historical societies in the United States can boast similar holdings—and that these seemingly impressive collections are dwarfed by those of the New York Public Library and the Library of Congress. Furthermore, these tallies do not even begin to take into account the number of reminiscences and soldiers' stories published piecemeal in newspapers, periodicals, and magazines, of which the total was even more plentiful. All of this is to say that in the years following the war, veterans produced a momentous wave of commemorative literature—so much, in fact, that we cannot calculate *how* momentous it actually was.

With titles like *Mr. Dunn Browne's Experiences in the Army* (1866), *Sketches of the War: A Series of Letters to the North Street School of New York* (1865), *Our Boys: The Personal Experiences of a Soldier in the Army of the Potomac* (1865), or *The Yankee Conscript; or, Eighteen Months in Dixie* (1865), these published reminiscences served a dual function for former soldiers. They provided men reassurances that their own experiences and memories would be preserved for posterity (regardless of whether posterity chose to actually read them), which, in turn, served as a coping or venting mechanism. More critically for our purposes—because at the same time elite officers such as Jubal A. Early or Henry Kyd Douglas began to pen their well-known accounts of the war, thus influencing how it ought to be remembered—regular veterans' accounts also allowed men from the rank and file to contribute in small ways to the overall constitution of the war's historical legacy by appealing directly to the public at the state and regional levels.

And adding one's proverbial two cents was especially important for veterans in the period immediately following the war. Because in addition to the *Official Records of the War of the Rebellion* (commissioned in 1866 by a joint resolution of Congress), publishers began releasing one allegedly "factual" history of the Civil War after another. These volumes—such as *Lloyd's Battle History of the Great Rebellion* (1866), which alone included 268 battle descriptions, thirty-nine biographical sketches, and seventeen battlefield maps in addition to a separate, concise history of the entire war—claimed to cover all of the most important armies, battles, leaders, and events. Systemization of the war's history proceeded swiftly as both sides rushed to declare as definitive a version that suited postwar political, economic, and social interests. As such, failure to be deemed a useful component of these renditions and subsequent failure to be included in the numerous "all-encompassing" histories came at a steep price for those involved in a counter-narrative experience such as the western atrocities Goodman witnessed or his ten-day stint with Anderson's guerrilla band: perpetual anonymity.

And yet Goodman and his slain comrades were not the only group in danger of being written out of the war's most popular histories. As argued by historian David W. Blight, in the aftermath of the Civil War, ideological camps formed at the national level, each determined to carve out a lasting legacy for the conflict that best suited its own social and political purposes. Within this arrangement, Blight pits an alliance of "White Supremacists" and "Reconciliatonists"—those looking to mend the bonds between North and South as quickly and seamlessly as possible—against proponents of an "Emancipationist" legacy of the war that highlighted the eradication of the peculiar institution as the seminal achievement of more than 750,000 fallen soldiers. In the end, according to Blight, the emancipationist legacy of the war was by and large defeated; the issues of slavery and race were not only swept over by a tide of mutual valor, shared sacrifice, and reconciliatory feelings—but white supremacy even acted as a catalyst for white-to-white reunification across the Mason-Dixon. Admittedly, the scale and scope of Blight's thesis leaves significant tracts of "gray space" unexplored and without account—in particular, the "guerrilla experience" of the Border West. That said, its basic premise has resulted in nearly *all* of our scholarly attention being focused on one group of the "commemoratively endangered" demographic, even though others, such as Goodman, struggled simultaneously to establish durable memorial footholds.[8]

In addition to these already considerable obstacles, Goodman also had to work in direct opposition to another man with firsthand knowledge of the most notorious guerrillas Missouri had to offer. Major John Newman Edwards, an ex-Confederate cavalry officer turned newspaper pundit, spent much of the late 1860s and 1870s devising and constructing an "irregular Lost Cause" for Missouri. Edwards feared that the state's failure to secede from the Union would isolate it from the rest of the pro-Democrat South after the war. In this way, he had the exact opposite of the problem that Goodman had; Edwards *wanted* to ensure that a lack of Confederate—rather than Unionist—credentials would not preclude Missouri from postwar southern identity and recognition. This being the case, Edwards pitched Confederate credentials, much like Goodman had, and used the state's best-known wartime export, the Missouri bushwhacker, as his propagandistic muse. Beginning with a series of popular newspaper editorials, Edwards laid the foundation of a mythological narrative that would tout Missouri's guerrillas as the most diehard of all Confederate warriors and simultaneously detach them from the regular war and the failed Confederate government. Through a model of guerrilla honor based on killing efficiency and justified homicide, Edwards sought (with much success, it is worth noting) to transform the likes of William C. Quantrill, William "Bloody Bill" Anderson, George Todd, and Jesse James into wartime folk heroes and postwar Robin Hoods.[9]

So it was with these fears and opponents and in this cultural environment that Thomas M. Goodman composed and released *A Thrilling Record*. In this context, the extent to which Goodman and his publishers attempted to verify the authenticity of the account for audiences and for posterity is not at all surprising. According to testimonials included with the book, the "facts and incidents related in this volume are from unquestioned authority—the lips of a participant, and eye-witness to all its horrors, and the *only survivor* of the occasion." And the endorsement of veracity continued by stating that Goodman's story "was simple, concise, yet particular" and "can not fail to leave a conviction of *truth* upon the mind of the reader." New purchases of the book even included a certificate of authenticity signed by three men—G. H. Rumbaugh, William L. Stone, and Captain John Whitcomb—further guaranteeing the details of Goodman's account.

The narrative itself begins a little more than a week after the fall of Atlanta to Union forces in September 1864. Along with twenty or so other veterans of that campaign, Goodman received a "long-promised" and "eagerly-expected" furlough. Goodman himself hailed from Iowa; many of the rest were from various parts of Missouri. Typically, the homeward-bound soldiers would have gone their separate ways. But as all were headed in more or less the same direction, Goodman noted, they "agreed upon the North Missouri R. R. as the nearest and speediest route for all." The decision to travel as a large, uniformed group seemed pragmatic—strength by virtue of number—and all arrived safely together in St. Louis, Missouri, on September 26. Anxious to complete their respective journeys home, many of the native Missourians departed St. Louis that very night. Goodman and what remained of the original group stayed in the city to catch a train for St. Joseph in the morning.[10]

On the evening of the twenty-sixth, Goodman recalled chatting with a stranger in the St. Louis rail terminal. The unnamed man advised Goodman that it would be unwise to travel by rail through Missouri without an armed escort. The area, and therefore the route of the train, was "soon to be infested and controlled by guerrillas." Moreover, "large bodies of them had been observed for a few days past near Sturgeon, Centralia, and other points." According to Goodman, the man "felt confident they [the guerrillas] contemplated an attack soon." The report certainly worried Goodman—but he took solace in the notion that the guerrillas would be much more likely to attack under cover of darkness than in broad daylight. "In this," Goodman offered sadly in hindsight, "subsequent events proved me mistaken."[11]

Early the next morning, Goodman and his travel companions "took seat aboard the mail train for St. Joseph, Missouri" and left St. Louis "in the gray mist of morn." Moving rapidly, the train crossed the Missouri River near St. Charles before setting a course for Macon. During their changeover in the St. Charles depot, however, Goodman's party stumbled upon the Missourians who had departed their company in St. Louis the night before. An explanation was short in coming: "A question or so, soon satisfied us that *they* had heard the same intelligence report which reached us at St. Louis, and they *felt* a good deal better and *braver* at the sight of so many boys in blue." So now, when the conductor's bell "rang its parting clang of warning," the reunited party of furloughed Federals—feeling a bit braver and safe again in their swollen ranks—continued on from St.

Charles. None of the men, including Goodman, had any idea what the consequences of their recombination would entail.[12]

The train thundered into Mexico, Missouri. Here Goodman and company again received reports that guerrillas were out and about along the road—and the conductor, Goodman alleged, ignored a telegram from up the track in Centralia warning that passage would be especially dangerous without armed guards. As the train drew nearer to Centralia, Goodman momentarily paused his narrative to brace readers for "a description of the final horrors of the massacre." On arrival, the Federals came face-to-face with a large company of guerrillas. "In a moment," Goodman recounted, "the door of the car in which our squad, or a larger number of them sat, was burst open, and in crowded our grim, fierce captors, shouting 'Surrender! Surrender!'"[13]

Minus firearms, the Union soldiers were in no position to resist guerrilla demands. "We can only surrender," one of them suggested, "as we are totally unarmed." Upon learning that the Federals were essentially helpless, Goodman contended, the guerrillas withdrew all promises of humane treatment and became "the lawless free-booters, the inhuman monsters, Rumor had always designated them." The guerrillas systematically relieved the soldiers of any valuables they possessed and then ordered them into line. Each Union soldier was commanded to remove his uniform—the guerrillas coveted these as the costumes of espionage and ambush—and the men were then "arraigned before this tribunal of demons to expiate a crime no worse than loyalty to their native land!" According to Goodman, as death became more and more likely, the Union men remained brave. "No emotion, no faltering, no entreaty," he remembered, "only the fixed determination to meet cruelty by sublimity, and in the presence of devils, to die like gods!"[14]

Goodman and his fellow captives were prodded by pistol-wielding guerrillas to exit the train. Then Anderson, whom Goodman labeled the "chief of the guerrillas," came forward and inspected the line of "doomed men." Anderson addressed his prisoners: "Boys, have you a sergeant in your ranks?" Goodman, assuming that Anderson wished to make "some special example in his punishment" of an officer, hesitantly answered. He was immediately secured by two guerrilla guards and pulled away from the other Federals. "I had scarcely stopped at the position assigned me," Goodman reminisced somberly, "when a volley from the revolvers of the guerrillas in front, a demoniac yell from those surrounding, mingled with cries and moans of pain and distress from my comrades smote upon my ear."[15]

The line, as Goodman put it, "had disappeared." Most men fell dead where they knelt; others rolled in agony and tried in vain to shield themselves from death blows. "The work of death went on," Goodman continued, "and one by one my brave comrades met their fate—brutally, inhumanly murdered." Anderson's guerrillas, "with horrid oaths and wild, fierce looks, gloated over the bodies of the slain"—and turned their attention back to the train itself. They set the engine ablaze, and as flames engulfed it, "the fiends had now reached a state of excitement bordering on insanity." Then, approximately one hour after Goodman's train had arrived in Centralia, "the Carnival of Blood" was over.[16]

Following the massacre, Goodman became the personal prisoner of William "Bloody Bill" Anderson. Alone among the guerrillas, Goodman recalled being subjected to constant threats against his life: "I would like to kill the damn Yankee"; "Hell-fire is too good for you, you son of a bitch!"; and "hundreds of such expressions, too obscene and infamous to bear the honor of being printed." Twice in the first few moments of his captivity, as Goodman told it, his pair of bodyguards had to impede "drunken squads" of guerrillas from dispatching him on the spot. Only their fear of crossing Anderson, Goodman implied, kept the other guerrillas at bay and preserved his life. As Anderson's band left the rail depot in Centralia, with a distraught Goodman in tow, the "maimed bodies of the Union boys lay where they had fallen."[17]

At this point in his narrative, Goodman paused again to provide readers with a brief description of his captor. "William T. Anderson, the leader of the most blood-thirsty and inhuman gang of wretches that ever infested Missouri," he began, "was a man of about five feet, ten inches in height; round and compact in form, slender in person, quick and lithe in action as a tiger—whose nature he at times possessed." According to Goodman, Anderson's "great pride and care" was "to be never called 'unarmed.'" "His eye—said to be the index to the character," Goodman went on, "portrayed not his." Anderson's character was altogether "unfathomable" to Goodman. As he put it, Anderson's eyes revealed "a strange mixture of blue and gray, the opposing colors sustained by opposing forces, in the war he waged." Like Anderson, "they were cold, unsympathizing [*sic*] and expressionless, never firing in anger or lighting with enthusiasm in battle."[18]

As far as Goodman could ascertain, the majority of Anderson's men were deserters from the army of Confederate general Sterling Price or "renegades from the Paw-Paw militia." The rest, he believed, were men who, "through some act of violence committed by them," could no longer return to their homes. Soon after, an intelligence report informed Anderson that a group of mounted Federal troops was in the area—hunting the guerrillas responsible for the massacre at the train depot. The guerrillas would lay in wait for the Union patrol around "an old field, skirted by brush and scattered timber." According to Goodman, Anderson divided his force among three sides of the field. Upon catching sight of the Federal force, the guerrillas with Anderson "dashed forward at the full run upon the little line of dismounted Federals in the field" while men under the direction of Anderson's lieutenants, George Todd and John Thrailkill, burst forth on both flanks, "yelling like so many fiends."

"I saw at a glance," Goodman remarked, "that the battle was already won by the guerrillas." The Federals, outnumbered and swarmed by charging guerrillas, hardly had time to fire a volley before being overrun and slaughtered. Anderson's men ordered the soldiers to surrender—and many of them did. However, as had been the case at the train depot earlier in the day, taking "prisoners of war" (with the obvious exception of Goodman himself) was not high on the guerrillas' list of priorities. The remaining Federals were disarmed, and "no sooner was this accomplished than Hell was suddenly transferred to earth, and all the fiends of darkness summoned to join the carnival of blood." "No treatment was too brutal," Goodman offered, "no treatment too cruel to satisfy the greed of that hellish crew; and were it possible for human souls to grow drunk on blood, I trust the idea may offer some palliation for the scenes enacted there—for the bloody, dastardly, cowardly, wanton acts committed upon the living and dead persons of those brave Union boys!" In the aftermath of the second massacre at Centralia, corpses were decapitated, heads shuffled among bodies, "labeled with rough and obscene epitaphs and inscriptions," and tied to saddles, or even arranged on the tops of fence posts.[19]

Following the day's bloodletting, Anderson and his men returned to Centralia and again became "brutally intoxicated." Incidents between residents of the small village and guerrillas were plenty. In one case, when a woman protested a lewd comment offered by a guerrilla, "the inhuman wretches felled her to the ground, like a beast of slaughter, and otherwise maltreated her person." Finally, Goodman noted, the guerrillas returned to camp and were given three hours to rest. Unable to sleep, Goodman reflected on the day's events: "I lay and watched the silent stars; and watching, and thinking of all that had passed that bloody day, I wept."[20]

For the next nine days, the guerrillas held Goodman hostage—and Goodman thought desperately, night and day, of ways to escape. Through conversations with his bodyguards and other guerrillas, Goodman tried frequently to discover the whereabouts of Union patrols or to work out the location of Anderson's camp relative to the nearest Federal garrison. On the second morning of his captivity, Goodman came face-to-face with Anderson. His encounter with the guerrilla chieftain was brief but polite—Anderson did not (and never did, in fact) reveal why he decided to keep the Union sergeant alive. As the days passed, other guerrillas became more and more used to Goodman's presence, and his pair of guards grew relatively friendly. One day, after several hard miles in the saddle, the guerrillas stumbled into a Federal cavalry unit and narrowly avoided an ambush. Assuming his usefulness had all but run out, Goodman was stunned when Anderson turned to him and bellowed, "Prisoner, you must *now ride for your life! Boys, we all must!*"[21]

Goodman did as he was told—and hours later found himself again in camp with most of Anderson's reassembled band. "They seemed to possess some sort of a depository or commissary establishment here," Goodman wrote, "and both 'grub and whisky' were dispensed, with a very liberal hand." By nightfall, Goodman offered, nearly the entire command, including Anderson, had become drunk. "God help me," he confessed, "I never witnessed so much profanity in the same space of time before, nor since." According to Goodman, the guerrillas "whooped, ran, jumped and yelled like so many savages." At one point during the evening, Anderson leapt onto a horse and "rode wildly through the crowd; firing his revolvers indiscriminately, and yelling like one possessed."[22]

The next morning, Anderson and his lieutenants held what Goodman believed was a "council of war"; the guerrillas decided, in a bid to avoid Federal detection, to separate into smaller groups and to reunite on the banks of the Missouri River. After stopping at the house of a woman sympathetic to Goodman's plight (she fed him heartily), Anderson, Goodman, and all camped in the neighborhood. Goodman, by then used to the comings and goings of the bushwhacker lifestyle, recorded a good night's sleep: "I slept tolerably comfortably, as I had on Anderson's old coat, which he gave me when he adopted the federal officer's uniform."[23] The guerrilla company traveled for two more days before pitching camp within earshot of the Missouri River. Goodman had "fully determined to risk attempting an escape so soon as they undertook the passage of that river."[24]

Goodman presented his last days with the guerrillas as bittersweet. On the one hand, he witnessed "some really laughable and ludicrous scenes" that occurred "between parties of the guerrillas at this camp." But on the other, "it was at times the scene of sore trial and suffering to me." "Our squad," Goodman explained, "and so many of the returning guerrillas, wore—either in full or in part—the federal uniform; while others, especially recruits coming in to join the band, were always attired in butternut, or the confederate grey." On the final evening of Goodman's captivity, Anderson and his men at last set out to cross the Missouri River in a series of small skiffs. Each of the boats could carry only half a dozen or so men at once, while the horses swam alongside. For Goodman, this represented his best chance for escape yet. In the confusion of men gathering and loading boats, Goodman wandered away from his guards. In fact, this wasn't altogether difficult, as many of the guerrillas failed to cast a second glance at Goodman. Slowly but deliberately, Goodman made his way to the tree line and thrashed his way through two hundred yards of dense thicket. "My breath came fast and my heart beat so rapidly," he reported, "it almost made me faint and sick."[25]

Well aware that Anderson intended to strike at Fayette, Goodman broke for the town—or at least in the direction he *thought* the town lay—and walked through the night, despite the onset of exhaustion. Eventually, Goodman encountered a "negro passing near an old field" who directed the escaped prisoner toward Fayette. Soon after, a Federal picket intercepted Goodman. "I cried—cried like a child. Strong man as I thought myself, I felt that, in the hands of the Providence that had so far preserved and guided me, I was but as the merest babe!" Now officially rescued, Goodman alerted the Union garrison in Fayette of Anderson's impending attack, and the troops were evacuated. Thomas M. Goodman traveled back to St. Joseph by train, "at which city I gave the editor of one of the papers, a very brief statement of such facts as I have recorded them here." In the end, he reported, "I reached my home in safety. Of what transpired there, I shall not write. You have many of you felt, perhaps, that such meetings as these are sacred to the participants, and not to be held up for the scrutiny of the world."[26]

In more ways than not, it is only logical to assume that *A Thrilling Record* confirmed what many readers already thought about Missouri bushwhackers and guerrilla warfare—assuming readers thought about these things at all. (The possibility that audiences lacked any knowledge of guerrillas like Anderson was equally problematic for Goodman. Either possibility only made Goodman's task of justifying commemorative attention for himself and others like him all the more pressing.) Throughout the book, Bill Anderson and his ilk are extremely violent, unconscionably brutal, and at times, almost subhuman characters. Goodman's personal sketch of Anderson, in particular, with his expressionless eyes; thick, beast-like hair; and unnatural attachment to his weapons, calls to mind the image of a wild man or a deranged killer, not a gallant soldier. And the bushwhackers of Goodman's tale do not kill simply because it is the unfortunate modus operandi of war; rather, they mutilate corpses and take scalps because they enjoy it. As depicted by Goodman, his captors lack both the discipline and the ideological motives of "genuine" military men: they engage in espionage and deceit, they refuse to take prisoners, and they append no symbolic meaning or sanctity to the uniform, blue or gray, and all it represents. In turn, the guerrillas are not worthy of the personal honor bestowed upon veterans of the regular war. As the antagonists of Goodman's narrative, then, Anderson and company are drunkards and criminals, unfit to be cast alongside men who had served with discipline and honor in histories of the Civil War.

Based solely on the narrative of events provided by *A Thrilling Record,* Goodman seemed to be working against his own intended purposes—that is, by discounting the personal honor and commemorative credentials of his primary antagonists, Goodman appeared to be confirming that the guerrilla theater of the western borderlands had no place within histories of the "real" Civil War. However, Goodman frequently interrupted his story to interject commemorative commentary. These annotations force an immediate reconsideration of Goodman's intent and literary effectiveness.

"It is somewhat remarkable," Goodman argued in his introduction, "that an event should have transpired during the late rebellion, so replete with horror and atrocious deeds as the massacre of Centralia, and at this late day still have failed to secure a place in history." The unthinkable carnage witnessed at Centralia, he continued, had "tended to *silence in awe* the pen of the historian; else, the doubt and uncertainty attached to the written and oral statements made heretofore concerning it, have induced fear on their part, that its introduction into their written histories might affect the authenticity of the whole." In plainer language, Goodman understood that the introduction of guerrilla warfare and men like Anderson—wholly at odds with idealized concepts of the Civil War soldier or proper notions of Victorian battle and the "good death"—threatened to infect and corrupt everything honorable and redeeming that Americans wished to salvage from their bloodiest national hour. As such, Goodman asserted in 1868 that "there exists to-day no published history of the affair, and it is partly to supply this deficiency, and to fulfill a promise made in years by-gone, that this little volume is given to the world."[27]

What Goodman actually gave to the world was a surprisingly powerful statement concerning the geographic parameters of remembrance. He began this message with a salesman's touch, beseeching audiences not to accuse him of doing precisely what he really *was* doing: "Kind readers, I hope no one who peruses this narrative will impute other than the best motives to me, nor accuse me of seeking vain glory for name or deeds in inditing [*sic*] this simple record for posterity." Playing this hand for all it was worth, Goodman established early in the minds of readers that the service of Federal soldiers in Missouri's guerrilla war was every bit as valid and valuable to the Union cause as service elsewhere. "To my children, then, if none other," Goodman waxed, "this record will prove of value, inasmuch as its perusal will ever prove a reminder to them of what their father suffered in securing to them a continuance of the great blessings of civil and religious liberty, either of which were incompatible with the purposes and designs of traitors." Before delving into his narrative, Goodman concluded the opening phase of his sales pitch by arguing, "These *are* and of a *right* should ever continue the birth-right of every child born on American soil, and we again bequeath them to posterity, re-baptized in the sufferings and blood of every soldier who fell a martyr in the Union cause." *Every* soldier killed in the service of the Union—regardless of geographic locale, status as regular or irregular foe, or manner of death.[28]

Later in *A Thrilling Record,* immediately following the massacre of Goodman's comrades at the rail station, he again halted his narrative to reflect on the service and commemorative credentials of the slaughtered Federals. "I will die as I live," he wrote, "bearing with me the remembrance of all your fortitude, all your sufferings!" "Ere I leave you there, where bloody and impious deeds were done," he continued, "where hands of strangers laid the sod above your hearts, I would ask in your name, and in the name of the great army of the republic, of which you formed a part, some fitting testimonial to be placed above your graves by the noble State in whose soil your bodies lie entombed—and whose sons you were." Finally, Goodman contended, "Spartan lore offers no heroism excelling thine. Her heroes were the defenders of her honor and her soil. Heroes, then, were you in the resolve that separated you from home and all you held dear, to battle for your native land in the hour-of-her need; heroes again, in the spirit and fortitude displayed in the campaigns of 1862–1863; and heroes for all time to come, in the memory and hearts of your comrades in arms, who have read or will read the story of your fall." "Comrades," Goodman concluded, "though cold in death, to your need shall be our greatest need; and memory shall brighten at the thought of you, so long as life shall last."[29]

This passage is quite telling. It underscores the three fundamental and interconnected tenets of Goodman's argument. First, despite the fact that Goodman and many of his ill-fated travel companions had served under William Tecumseh Sherman during the March to the Sea, the events of September 27, 1864, became the defining moment of Goodman's and his companions' Civil War experiences. As such, Goodman recalled, "It is no vivid play of my imagination called up for present purposes. No! It is indellibly [*sic*] traced upon my brain. It is one episode in my life past, never, never to be forgotten!"

Second, Goodman equated sacrifices made by Union soldiers in the regular army—in this case, Sherman's army—and sacrifices made by Union soldiers in the guerrilla theater. Therefore, as he noted, the men butchered by Anderson had been heroes for the "spirit and fortitude displayed in the campaigns of 1862–1863" *and* they were heroes "for all time to come" because of how and why they died. In this context, it mattered little to Goodman that Anderson and his men were neither honorable nor disciplined. To some extent, the impact of Goodman's argument in *A Thrilling Record* actually depended on the more loathsome qualities of the guerrilla characters. To narrow the sacrificial gap between dying in combat and falling at the hands of a bloodthirsty bushwhacker, Goodman therein implied that the Centralia dead had been cut down by an even greater threat to the Union cause than Confederate muskets: unadulterated evil. Precedent for this rhetorical strategy actually predated Goodman's use of it; in fact, the memoirs and eyewitness accounts of Federal soldiers imprisoned at Andersonville had wielded it to great effect. And in the face of such unspeakable cruelty and barbarism, like the survivors of Andersonville before them, the heroes of Goodman's tale had performed admirably in the face of imminent doom and upheld the underlying conceptual standards, while slightly modified, of the good death.[30]

Finally, the critical third pillar of Goodman's case directly referenced commemoration. Because Centralia had become the definitive Civil War experience of its victims and because those victims had died bravely in the service of the Union at the hands of "traitors," Goodman called, "in the name of the great republic" of which those victims "formed a part," for a physical memorial in their honor. Goodman pushed for this "fitting testimonial" to mark the graves of the soldiers slain at Centralia to provide *permanent* and visible recognition from the federal government. In short, Goodman wanted to ensure that Centralia and its participants would not be forgotten as the history and legacy of the war took shape.

At the end of his story, Goodman did two things. First, he turned to religion as a way to justify both his purpose and his status as messenger. "To the Almighty Ruler of Heaven and Earth we owe our existence and the blessing of life today; and though it is a seeming mystery to us why His beneficence should single me [Goodman] from the great number slain on that memorable occasion as a living example of the sacredness of His promise in the Word, yet in truth and honor of soul and spirit, to His name and His Providence be all the honor and praise." Therein Goodman assumed it his duty to make good use of the mercy shown to him by the Lord—put another way, Goodman didn't just have a memory narrative to sell readers; he was on a mission from God to do so. Perhaps more important, with his divine endorsement in hand, Goodman iterated the argument presented earlier in the narrative and made one final pitch for memorial credibility:

> To our comrades of the gallant old 25th Regiment, and to the Boys in Blue of the corps to which the First Missouri Engineers were attached, one word more, ere I bid you adieu. I have endeavored in this little volume to as faithfully perform as my abilities would admit, the oft-repeated promises made to you in years bygone. I have written for you the "story" so often told by the camp-fire, on the picket, and yet again and again, whenever the name of a "fallen comrade" reminded us of the "blank" Centralia's Horrible Massacre left in our ranks and upon our muster rolls. Have I performed this "duty" well, or poorly, it rests not with me to say—I have only sought to do it truthfully.
>
> Comrades, wherever you are, if this little volume should meet your eye, I ask you to read it, and having done this pay to the Memory of our dead comrades, the tribute of "A Soldier's Tear."[31]

Thus, while events like the Lawrence Massacre and the bloodletting at Centralia were in danger of being expelled from the pages of mainstream renditions of the war, Goodman waded into the partisan arena of memory to keep from becoming collateral damage in that process of postwar legacy building. In short, the removal of Confederate guerrillas from histories of the war that espoused national reunification and reconciliation was a double-edged sword for Unionists—it cut away the likes of Anderson and Quantrill, but to do so swiftly and effectively, the likes of Goodman had to go with them.

Goodman's efforts, regardless of success—and, incidentally, Goodman is fairly well known to historians of the Civil War in the western borderlands today—illustrated the inner workings of a memory industry in America coming into its own in the late 1860s. But *A Thrilling Record* does something much more important for historians of irregular warfare, especially those interested in how bushwhackers like William "Bloody Bill" Anderson *and* their victims fit within the broader scope of Civil War remembrance. Simply put, the story of Goodman's story underscores a key equivalency: just as the guerrilla war of the West constituted a war unto itself, so too was guerrilla memory a cultural industry unto itself—with business dealings that overlapped with and were influenced by trends in mainstream memory but that were often conducted in guerrilla memory's own marketplaces and by its own set of consumers, salesmen, and producers.

As a result, at the same time that men like John Newman Edwards sought to harness the unique nature of guerrilla warfare in Missouri and Kansas for pro-Confederate, partisan purposes, Goodman's narrative provided a clear counteroffer for Unionists who wanted no part of what Edwards had for sale. But in selling guerrilla massacres, *A Thrilling Record* didn't just refute Edwards—it completely repackaged the atrocities at Centralia, and thereby the guerrilla theater more generally, in a way that linked Goodman's service with prevalent patterns of regular war remembrance and greatly enhanced its prospects for commemoration. Its western origins notwithstanding, the existence of this guerrilla memory industry from which Goodman operated brings us full circle and illuminates as much about the national commemorative scene as that of the irregular theater in Missouri or Kansas. Because while the "romance of reunion" did significant cultural work for men and women on both sides of the Mason-Dixon, we would be remiss to think that *only* African Americans and emancipationists were excluded or even injured by that version of cultural rapprochement. On this, Sergeant Thomas M. Goodman and his dealings in guerrilla memory are a case in point.

Notes

1. "A Raid on Centralia," *Missouri Statesman,* September 30, 1864, and "Guerrilla Attack on North Mo. Railroad," *Missouri Republican,* September 30, 1864, from Howard C. Grisham, *Centralia and Bill Anderson* (Jefferson City, MO: H. C. Grisham, 1964), 2–4, 4–7.

2. For historical accounts of both massacres at Centralia, see Albert Castel and Thomas Goodrich, *Bloody Bill Anderson* (Mechanicsburg, PA: Stackpole Books, 1998), 79–86, 88–92; Richard S. Brownlee, *Gray Ghosts of the Confederacy* (Baton Rouge: Louisiana State University Press, 1958), 216–20; Donald R. Hale, *They Called Him Bloody Bill* (Clinton, MO: The Printery, 1975), 39–57. On guerrilla warfare and the practice of scalping, see Joseph M. Beilein Jr., "Household War: Guerrilla-Men, Rebel Women, and Guerrilla Warfare in Civil War Missouri" (PhD diss., University of Missouri, 2012), 158–62.

3. Thomas D. Thiessen, Douglas D. Scott, and Steven J. Dasovich, *"This Work of Fiends": Historical and Archaeological Perspectives on the Confederate Guerrilla Actions at Centralia, Missouri, September 27, 1864* (Lincoln, NE: Friends of the Centralia Battlefield and Missouri Civil War Heritage Foundation, March 2008), 110, 121, 165.

4. Thomas M. Goodman, *A Thrilling Record: Founded on Facts and Observations Obtained during Ten Days' Experience with Col. Wm. T. Anderson* (Des Moines: Mills & Co.'s Steam Book & Job Printing House, 1868), CW0091, A. S. Williams III Americana Collection, University of Alabama, Tuscaloosa. Anderson was shot dead in the midst of an engagement with Union cavalry on October 26, 1864, in the town of Albany, Missouri. Anderson's death marked a major victory for federal authorities in Missouri. Concerning the particulars of Anderson's demise, see Matthew C. Hulbert, "William 'Bloody Bill' Anderson," *Essential Civil War Curriculum,* June 2012, http://www.essentialcivilwarcurriculum.com/; and Hulbert, "Killing Bloody Bill," *Disunion* (blog), *New York Times,* October 29, 2014, http://opinionator.blogs.nytimes.com/2014/10/29/killing-bloody-bill/.

5. For prominent (and often divergent) accounts of Civil War memory making in the immediate postbellum period, see David W. Blight, *Race and Reunion: The Civil War in American Memory* (Cambridge, MA: Harvard University Press, 2002); Caroline E. Janney, *Remembering the Civil War: Reunion and the Limits of Reconciliation* (Chapel Hill: University of North Carolina Press, 2013); Gaines M. Foster, *Ghosts of the Confederacy: Defeat, the Lost Cause, and the Emergence of the New South, 1865–1913* (New York: Oxford University Press, 1987); Michael Kammen, *Mystic Chords of Memory: The Transformation of Memory in American Culture* (New York: Knopf, 1991). Note that all of these histories deal specifically with remembrance and commemoration of soldiers and events from the regular war—and more often than not from the regular war in the East.

6. On responses from pro-Confederate Missourians concerning the possibility of exclusion from Confederate commemoration and the process of "whitewash-

ing" guerrilla warfare in Missouri-Kansas from mainstream narratives of the Civil War, see Matthew C. Hulbert, "How to Remember 'This Damnable Guerrilla Warfare': Four Vignettes from Civil War Missouri," *Civil War History* 59, no. 2 (June 2013), 142–67; and Matthew C. Hulbert, "The Regularly Irregular War: Domestic Violation, Women, and Remembrance in Missouri's Guerrilla Theater," *Common-Place* 14, no. 2 (Winter 2014).

7. See Garold L. Cole, *Civil War Eyewitnesses: An Annotated Bibliography of Books and Articles, 1955–1986* (Columbia: University of South Carolina Press, 1988); Garold L. Cole, *Civil War Eyewitnesses: An Annotated Bibliography of Books and Articles, 1986–1996* (Columbia: University of South Carolina Press, 2000); Charles E. Dornbusch, *Military Bibliography of the Civil War,* vol. 3 (New York: New York Public Library, 1972).

8. See Blight, *Race and Reunion.*

9. See Matthew C. Hulbert, "Constructing Guerrilla Memory: John Newman Edwards and Missouri's Irregular Lost Cause," *Journal of the Civil War Era* 2, no. 1 (March 2012): 58–81; T. J. Stiles, *Jesse James: Last Rebel of the Civil War* (New York: A. A. Knopf, 2002).

10. Goodman, *Thrilling Record,* 11, 16–17.

11. Ibid., 16–17.

12. Ibid., 18–19.

13. Ibid., 20–21.

14. Ibid., 22–23.

15. Ibid., 23–24.

16. Ibid., 24–25. Seventeen of the murdered Union soldiers have been identified. They are Joseph Comer, Charles Hittebidal, James Holley, James Mobley, Edward Pace, Valentine Peters, Caswell Rose, James Thomas, Martin Trail, William Barnum, Joseph Arnold, Charles Carpenter, George Dilley, Owen Gore, Charles Madera, John Russell, and Oscar Williams. According to the Official War Records in the Adjutant General's Office, Jefferson City, Missouri, these seventeen men are interred at the National Cemetery at Jefferson Barracks, Missouri. Grisham, *Centralia and Bill Anderson,* 15.

17. Goodman, *Thrilling Record,* 27–28.

18. Ibid., 30–31.

19. Ibid., 31–35.

20. Ibid., 36–37.

21. Ibid., 40–41, 43, 44–46.

22. Ibid., 48.

23. Goodman claimed that he still owned Anderson's coat—a novelty item, the ownership of which several of his neighbors could allegedly verify—when *A Thrilling Record* was published in 1868.

24. Goodman, *Thrilling Record,* 49–51.

25. Ibid., 54, 58–59, 60.

26. Ibid., 61, 62–63, 64.

27. Ibid., 64–65. On the concept of the "good death," see Drew Gilpin Faust, *This Republic of Suffering: Death and the American Civil War* (New York: A. A. Knopf, 2008), 6–17.

28. Goodman, *Thrilling Record,* 10–11.

29. Ibid., 26.

30. For examples, see Leon Basile, ed., *The Civil War Diary of Amos E. Stearns, a Prisoner at Andersonville* (Rutherford, N.J.: Fairleigh Dickinson University Press, 1981); Ted Genoways and Hugh H. Genoways, eds., *A Perfect Picture of Hell: Eyewitness Accounts by the Civil War Prisoners from the 12th Iowa* (Iowa City: University of Iowa Press, 2001); Glenn Robins, ed., *They Have Left Us Here to Die: The Civil War Prison Diary of Sgt. Lyle Addair, 111th U.S. Colored Infantry* (Kent, OH: Kent State University Press, 2011).

Specifically on the place of prisons and atrocities in Civil War memory, see Benjamin Cloyd, *Haunted by Atrocity: Civil War Prisons in American Memory* (Baton Rouge: Louisiana State University Press, 2010).

31. Goodman, *Thrilling Record,* 64–65.

Tales of Race, Romance, and Irregular Warfare

Guerrillas Fictionalized, 1862–1866

John C. Inscoe

During Christmas week in 1862, Richmond theatergoers were introduced to a new melodrama called *The Guerrillas.* The three-act play, written by a twenty-year-old Richmond native, John Dabney McCabe Jr., was the first original drama produced in the Confederacy. Its enthusiastic reception that week led McCabe to publish—and apparently widely circulate—the script early in 1863, which led to productions on stages elsewhere in the South over the next two years, including Wilmington, North Carolina; Macon, Georgia; and Mobile, Alabama, as well as two encore stagings in the Confederate capital.[1] In an introduction to the published play, McCabe explained that his intent was "to show, in its true light, the condition of affairs in the Western portion of Virginia . . . where the war has been conducted principally by Guerrillas, and has been productive of many dark and terrible tragedies." He went on to say that "our enemies have discarded every feeling of pity and humanity, and have carried death and desolation wherever they have been. Neither age nor sex has been regarded." Curiously though, such descriptors applied not to the tactics of guerrilla warriors but rather to those of Union army forces and their brutal assaults on civilians in the region. "Dark and fearful," McCabe reiterated, "are the tales of woe that are brought across the mountains by those who have fled from the fierce hordes of the North."[2] The guerrillas represented the localized grassroots efforts by those civilians to defend their homes and families from such abuse.

It is noteworthy that the first and arguably the most widely performed original drama produced in the Confederacy dealt with guerrilla warfare in Southern Appalachia; and it is perhaps ironic as well, given what a long latency period that aspect of the conflict underwent in terms of how that war was remembered and chronicled in the late nineteenth and much of the twentieth centuries.[3] But McCabe's was not the only popular treatment of irregular warfare in the region during and just after the war. Two novels by northern writers also enjoyed considerable success. Early in 1864, John Townsend Trowbridge, an antislavery advocate based in Boston, published *Cudjo's Cave,* set in the Cumberland Mountains of Tennessee, which proved to be one of the best-selling novels produced during the war. In 1866 another Bostonian, one of the war years' most prolific writers, James Roberts Gilmore, under the pseudonym Edmund Kirke, published his first postwar novel, *Among the Guerillas,* which was set, like McCabe's play, in the highlands of western Virginia.[4]

Both Trowbridge and Kirke confirmed McCabe's general description of this irregular war in the mountains, and yet they defined "our enemies" and "the fierce hordes" far differently than did the young Richmond playwright. Kirke, in effect, demonized the very forces that were cheered as valiant heroes by southern theater audiences, while Trowbridge celebrated the guerrillas in his story—but made them Unionists rather than Confederates. Thus two of the three depicted their irregular warriors in sympathetic and even ennobling terms, while the third condemned them and instead made their victims his heroic protagonists. Despite their differences in perspective, the three narratives share certain commonalities: all three feature romantic entanglements that draw women into the thick of localized conflicts either as active agents or as victims; all three writers present sympathetic portrayals of benevolent southern mountain people; and most strikingly, all assign central roles to slaves, who, in very different respects, serve as major catalysts and collaborators in the inner civil war as it played out in the southern highlands.

For many northern readers and southern playgoers, these fictionalized treatments of guerrilla warfare would likely have been their first and most substantive exposure to a reality that otherwise received far less attention than the more traditional battles and campaigns. On the other hand, the very popularity of these particular works suggests that the general public on both sides of the Mason-Dixon Line was not as quick to dismiss these unconventional activities as irrelevant or inconsequential to the course of the larger conflict as we've long assumed. These much romanticized and heavily biased treatments of individuals and families caught up in the brutality of this irregular conflict served as important forms of patriotic propaganda while embracing a wide range of issues related to race, class, and gender, along with astute commentary on civilian and military atrocities, on the nature of Civil War loyalties, and on the larger meanings of the war.

John McCabe was certainly more familiar with western Virginia than the two northern novelists who also chose Southern Appalachia as the settings for their guerrilla sagas (though Edmund Kirke had traveled elsewhere in the South before and during the war). Born to an Episcopal priest who boasted that he was a descendant of the first white settler in Pennsylvania's Cumberland Valley, the junior McCabe moved with his parents to several parishes in Virginia and Maryland. At age fourteen, while living in the mountain resort of Abingdon, he made his first literary contributions to the local newspaper; he spent nearly two years in Lexington, as a student at the Virginia Military Institute, before moving to Vicksburg, Mississippi, to teach school. It was there, in 1860, that he produced his first political writings, including a pamphlet entitled *Fanaticism, and Its Results,* in which he warned that "the demon of abolitionism" would make disunion inevitable unless checked by congressional legislation.[5] At some point after the outbreak of war, he returned to Richmond, where he penned his first play in the fall of 1862, inspired no doubt by the surge in activity in the Virginia highlands (including those counties that would soon become the state of West Virginia) through much of the spring and summer of that year.[6]

The Guerrillas opens in a mountain farmhouse in the spring of 1861, where three generations of the Douglas family discuss a newspaper report of General McClellan advancing with Union troops into western Virginia. Blanton, the head of the household, tells his elderly father, "It seems as if you are destined to pass through a second revolution. The clouds are dark . . . now as I speak, our peaceful mountains echo to the tramp of armed men; and God alone can tell how long it will be before they are drenched with blood." Arthur Douglas, the play's protagonist, enters and reports to his parents and grandparents on the recent clash at nearby Rich Mountain, at which McClellan's Ohio troops forced Confederate defenders to flee, taking many prisoners and leaving the mountain residents "alone in the darkest hour of the Revolution" (an event that actually occurred on July 11). His commentary clearly reflects his and his family's pro-southern sentiments and, by implication, those of fellow mountaineers who seemed at that point so vulnerable to the Ohio forces in their midst.[7]

In a nearby cabin, Arthur's betrothed, Rose, is confronted by one of McClellan's officers, a lecherous Colonel Bradley, as McCabe falls back on one of the melodrama's most familiar tropes—a villain making unwanted advances on the hero's fiancée. Arthur breaks into Rose's house as she's struggling with Bradley and hurls him across the room before whipping him until he issues an apology. As the humiliated colonel exits the stage, he vows vengeance on both Arthur and Rose. This personal affront makes Arthur rethink his intentions of enlisting in a Confederate company; instead he organizes a secret nighttime meeting of fellow southerners in a thick mountain forest, who together form the band of irregulars for whom the play is named. The group disperses quickly when word reaches them that Colonel Bradley, in his quest for what he calls his "deep and dire revenge," has learned of their meeting and is on his way to break them up. Arthur becomes the first to articulate just what the advantage of guerrilla tactics is: "These men are all natives of this country," he tells a fellow combatant. "They know every footpath through these mountains; they are too wise to retreat in a body, and see if they have dispersed, as I think they have, in a dozen different directions, our pursuit will be useless."[8]

And so it proved to be, which leads the villainous Bradley to settle for a more fixed target in what has become a very personal vendetta—the Douglas home, which he orders burned to the ground. Curiously, the audience learns of this act from a distressed slave, who reports to Arthur that his house has been destroyed by "de Abulishnours and de Yankees." Arthur rushes home to find the house in ruins, still smoking, and the bodies of his family—parents, grandfather, aunt, and siblings—all lying among the ashes, with their throats slit. Only Rose has escaped death, thanks to the efforts of Jerry, the faithful Douglas slave, who carried her to safety as the Union marauders approached. Arthur resolves that the men he has gathered must adopt the same ruthless methods employed by Bradley's troops and become true guerrillas. Vowing to take revenge for the massacre of his family, he dips a handkerchief in the blood of each of his family members, then approaches his men and declares, "Had our enemies sought to meet us in the open field, I would have fought them fairly. But they have taught me how to war against them. We will not seek the army. Here in these mountains that have witnessed this horrible tragedy must our vengeance be accomplished. We will know no rest until we have shed the blood of every man in Bradley's band. We will follow their example. We will give no quarter. If we cannot strike at their bosoms, like the serpent, let us strike at their heels."[9]

In short, the vicious tactics that came to define guerrilla warfare were, according to McCabe, inspired by—or modeled after—the Union army's brutal harassment of local civilians, these noble mountaineers. Arthur orders his men to kneel with him and to swear that they "will know neither pity nor human feelings while the foot of a foe pollutes our soil." As he concludes his stirring speech, with Rose weeping bitterly beside him and his men bowed down before him, Arthur raises his bloody handkerchief to heaven, and the curtain falls on act 1.[10]

The play's second act jumps forward to the spring of 1862 and opens on General John C. Frémont's headquarters in western Virginia, where he expects Colonel Bradley "has come, no doubt, to report the success of his expedition against the Guerrillas." At about the time McCabe returned to Virginia that year, Frémont moved into the state as well. He had just been reassigned from his post in combating what he called "bands of murderers and marauders" in Missouri and had arrived to command a newly established Mountain Department whose explicit goal was to do much the same there. By midyear, Frémont's heavy-handed tactics—not unlike those he'd employed in Missouri the previous year—were drawing attention from Confederate authorities in Richmond, and most local playgoers in December would have been well aware of the situation still playing out to their west.[11]

Frémont's troops made considerable inroads into bringing Virginia guerrillas to heel—by arresting them and their accomplices; ordering raids on their strongholds and even burning them out; and authorizing courts-martial that resulted in immediate executions, all of which McCabe dramatized at some point in his play.[12] And yet this introductory scene with Frémont offers a far more crowd-pleasing scenario—an admission of failure by Colonel Bradley and, worse, cowardice on the part of his men. "They were too much for me, Sir," he reports to the general. "My men ran as soon as they saw the black flag. And besides, Douglas's men fight like mad devils." Frémont himself then acknowledges the challenge these mountain irregulars posed, noting that "they have cost me many a brave man. . . . Twelve expeditions have they routed and sent back to me in confusion." Cursing this inability to bring them down, he concludes, "By Heaven, I would rather command this band in the service of the Union, than all the cowardly hounds who call me their General," a line that no doubt brought cheers from Richmond audiences.[13]

Acknowledging that Arthur Douglas "is the life of his band," Frémont declares that he intends not only to capture him but to "hang him as high as Haman." The plot thickens as a spy from Douglas's band leads the Union forces to the guerrillas' fort, a "crude log breastworks"; a series of skirmishes ensues, in which Rose, now Arthur's wife, is taken hostage, despite a heroic effort by the slave Jerry to rescue her; the spy is exposed and captured by Douglas, who orders him hanged; and Colonel Bradley also falls into the hands of the mountain men and faces his own execution at Douglas's order. When the colonel begs for mercy, his Confederate nemesis replies, "You sought my home, laid it in ruins, and murdered my family. I swore to be revenged . . . and bent all my energies to capture you." Pointing to the hanged spy, Arthur asks Bradley, "Do you see where that miserable wretch is now dangling in the air a lifeless corpse? To-morrow at sunrise you shall hang there." Act 2 ends with an ambush by Frémont and his men, which only Arthur and a handful of his men survive, though they're taken prisoner.[14]

The final act consists of melodramatic encounters between the forces of good (Arthur, Rose, and Jerry) and those of evil (Frémont and Bradley), characterized by treachery, physical brawls, and several cliff-hanging moments, all of which culminate in farcical rescues and recriminations in which guerrilla virtue is rewarded and Union villainy punished. With Bradley killed and Frémont on the run, Arthur delivers the play's final speech, telling his victorious comrades, "We must be gone from here. Frémont will not remain here long. He will soon be called east of the mountains. The glorious [Stonewall] Jackson is winning laurels in the Valley. We will join him." At that point, he grasps the black flag and waves it over his head, proclaiming, "This flag shall be our battle-flag; 'Virginia and vengeance' our battle cry; and our foes shall rue the hour they encounter the Guerrillas."[15] All of this met with what one Richmond critic termed "so exuberant an audience that their yelling, whistling, stamping, and shouting, sufficed to astound the actors," especially at this final curtain, when "the stage is filled with the bodies of the Federal troops."[16]

For all of its partisanship in terms of the heroics and nobility with which McCabe endows his title band of brothers, of equal interest is how he brings both women and slaves into that band—or rather one of each. Though the obligatory romantic plotline was perhaps the most basic reason for her inclusion in the play (one reviewer noted with approval "the thread of love running through the recital of blood, and wrong, and outrage"), Rose evolves from victim to active combatant over the course of the play.[17] As the object of both Bradley's and later Frémont's amorous advances (even after she marries Arthur), she is in need of rescue at several points in the play. But as "the rebel Captain's wife," she becomes vulnerable for more strategic reasons. When arrested by Frémont's men and delivered to him, he informs her that she herself is to be charged as a rebel and the wife of an outlaw, and thus subject to the same punishment as her husband unless she reveals his whereabouts—or concealment; he then threatens to torture her in order to make her talk. When she refuses to betray Arthur or to offer "any aid to the enemy of my country," Frémont "in great astonishment" responds, "Can it be possible; even the women and children of this infernal rebel land are mad with treason." At that she rises up in full defiance and offers a speech that must have stirred southern audiences as much as any in the play: "We are proud of that which you call treason. Go back, General Frémont, to those that sent you, and tell them that they can never conquer the South. You may kill every man and boy in our land, but you will then have to meet the women; and woe to you when that day comes. We will conquer—we will drive you from our land."[18]

Rose delivers on her grandiloquent words in the final act, which opens as she bemoans the fact that Frémont has handcuffed her: "Fetters on a woman. Oh! It is a deed worthy of a Yankee!" She asks him how he "can see a woman treated thus," to which he replies, "War is no respecter of persons, lady." As Arthur is brought in as a captive, with Frémont's ruling that he be hanged, Rose attempts to negotiate for his life. When he demands a single condition to her terms—that she "consent to be mine, bless me with your love," she refuses, and he declares that both husband and wife will die at dawn. When Frémont continues his advances on her, she grabs an axe and approaches him with it held high; he scurries off, declaring that "I go to condemn your husband. When he is dead, I shall return."[19]

Rose's attitude and actions reflect what historians have only in recent years recognized as the gendered dimensions of irregular war. Women were indeed the targets of harassment and victims of threats and intimidation either by bushwhackers and renegades or by the authorities combating those forces. And yet, like Rose, many wives and mothers were proactive participants as well, often acting as messengers, informants, protectors, collaborators, accomplices, and coconspirators, and even on occasion as combatants.[20] For these multiple roles played by mountain women to have been so readily recognized, dramatized, and indeed celebrated by McCabe this early in the war suggests either that he was introducing their plight to Richmond residents for the first time or perhaps, given the generalized nature of Rose's grand speech of defiance, that he may have meant it to be a rallying cry for all "true" southern women's fully engaged commitment to the cause.

Even more exceptional is the slave character Jerry and the racial signals McCabe relayed through him to his fellow Virginians. Jerry is as fully committed to the Confederate cause as is Rose and is unwavering in his service to both his master and his new mistress. On no less than three different occasions does he come to Rose's rescue—following Bradley's amorous advances; in moving her to safety when Bradley burns the Douglas house; and most dramatically (and in the only such incident actually played out onstage) in fighting off General Frémont in the play's climactic scene. After Jerry tells his master of his actions in saving Rose from the fire, Arthur expresses his gratitude by granting Jerry his freedom. The latter, perhaps not surprisingly given the play's authorship and the audience for whom he intended it, vehemently declines the offer. "A free nigger? I don't want to be free," Jerry insists. When Arthur tells him he can move to the North and "be as good as the white people there," he asks, "De Norf. Ain't dat whar the Abulishuners live?" When Arthur says it is, his slave draws himself up proudly, states that "I 'siders myself a heap better an any abulishuner dat eber libed," and offers a testimonial to the good life he's enjoyed being owned by the Douglases:

> Marse Arthur, I bin in your family eber since I bin born. Ole Marse and Ole Miss 'fore dey went to glory, treat me jis like white folks. When you was little baby, I carried you in my arms; when you was little boy, I arn you how to swim, how to hunt, how to fish, an how to ride. You neber gib me hard word in your life. I lub you jis like you was my own son. If you'se tired of old Jerry, jis take him out in the field and shoot him, but don't send him away from you; don't set him free.

By this point, he is weeping, and Arthur assures him that he'll never leave them: "When I cease to care for you, may God forget me." With that speech, Jerry finds that he's also earned his place as a fellow guerrilla. His owner asks him to escort Rose to safer surroundings and hands him a sword, saying, "You have won it fairly." Jerry bows and replies, "I'd fight de debbil himself now, Marse Arthur." The latter laughs and responds prophetically, "You may have to meet some of his imps yet, for there are a plenty in these mountains."[21]

True to form, the faithful slave thrusts himself into the family's struggle against its Yankee nemeses, most notably in the play's final scene, where, just as Frémont is about to hang his master, Jerry, improbably disguised as the executioner, mounts the scaffold to place the noose around Arthur's neck and also slips him a pistol. At that moment, Rose, armed with a pistol herself and waving a black flag, rushes onto the scene with her husband's guerrilla band, and hand-to-hand combat ensues. Jerry seizes a sword and attacks Frémont, while passing another on to Arthur, who is quick to take on Bradley with it. Bradley, wounded by Arthur, is ultimately killed by a pistol shot from Rose; as the couple stand over his corpse, Arthur declares, "I had hoped to punish him myself. But you, my noble wife, have saved my life and paid my debt of vengeance." Jerry, last seen in hand-to-hand combat with Frémont, appears triumphantly onstage, dressed in the commander's hat and coat. He informs his new legion of admirers that while he didn't get to kill Frémont, he sent him scurrying off on horseback, with doubts that he'd ever trouble those in the area again. In short, a woman and a slave have entered the fray as full combatants and emerge as the most heroic of the hearty band of guerrillas as the final curtain falls.[22]

Perhaps the most daring feature of this scenario is that McCabe offers a racially inverted variation on the southern code of chivalry. Here a slave not only serves as the valiant defender of a white woman's chastity, but he takes the place of her husband, his owner, in so doing. As tempting as it is to read something more subversive into this, the message conveyed is much simpler and more obvious: it reflects merely the sheer devotion of a slave both to his master and to the value system for which the master is fighting (which, paradoxically, is explicitly defined as a defense of slavery when Jerry—and Jerry alone—refers to the Union commanders as abolitionists). Guerrilla warriors were, for McCabe and his audiences, no less aimed at defending the South and southern values than were enlistees in the Confederate army; in fact, to engage in this irregular warfare offered a purer and more visceral means of defending home, family, and honor—if only because of the extent to which Union forces ruthlessly violated those sacred institutions. (It's worth noting that the title page of the published play defines it as "An Original Domestic Drama.") How better to convey that point than to make both a slave and the fiancée/wife of the guerrilla protagonist such vital allies in his struggle?

The romanticization of guerrillas in Confederate culture came early in the war, perhaps because writers like McCabe could depict them as a force for unity rather than divisiveness, as stalwart wives, loyal slaves, and even the most rustic and remote mountaineers found in this irregular war a means of combating the threat posed by those "fiendish hordes" from the North, all the while embodying the best of southern white society, hierarchy, and ideology.

The novels *Cudjo's Cave* (1864) and *Among the Guerillas* (1866) share much in common. Both were written by Boston-based antislavery adherents, John Townsend Trowbridge and James Roberts Gilmore, respectively. Both authors proved to be prolific propagandists through their literary output—both fictional and nonfictional—much of which proved quite popular with northern readers. Guerrillas were central to both novels, though how they're depicted could hardly differ more. Like McCabe, Trowbridge presented a heroic depiction of guerrillas and their cause (though that cause is the opposite of that embraced by the Richmond playwright); Gilmore (or Edmund Kirke, as he'll be referred to henceforth), on the other hand, while equally committed to the Union cause, saw guerrillas as antithetical to that cause, with his protagonists the victims of their abuse.

Trowbridge had long seen his writings as means toward political ends—claiming that the preeminence of the war's function in ending slavery was the primary message he sought to convey to readers. He was never more effective in doing so than in *Cudjo's Cave,* one of three novels he produced during the war years and by far the most successful, due in no small part to an aggressive marketing campaign by J. E. Tilton, his Boston-based publisher. Although he was the author of more than forty novels and hundreds of short stories, it is *Cudjo's Cave,* along with his 1866 travel account, *The South: A Tour of its Battlefields and Ruined Cities,* for which Trowbridge is most remembered and which has stood the test of time somewhat better than the two other works under consideration here. In 1890 playwright George B. Chase adapted it for the stage as *Penn Hapgood: The Yankee Schoolmaster,* using the protagonist's name as his title.[23] The novel itself was reprinted in the University of Alabama Press's Classics of Civil War Fiction series in 2001.[24]

Trowbridge wrote the book "quite rapidly" in the summer and fall of 1863, and it was in print by December (though it carries an 1864 copyright). He acknowledged that his was "a partisan book, frankly designed to fire the Northern heart." The fact that he included a slave's name in his title signaled his intention of reminding his readers that "the war of secession was a war of emancipation from the start," as he later noted in his memoir, or, as one of the novel's characters puts it, "Slavery and the rebellion are brother and sister—they go together."[25] At the same time, he wrote that he "wished to bring into it some incidents of guerrilla warfare and of the persecutions of the Union men in the border slave states." Perhaps the novel's most unique feature is that he combined both of these themes into a single, fully interracial narrative, in which black and white loyalists joined forces to defend themselves against the ever more virulent harassment inflicted on them by their Confederate neighbors and, in the case of the slaves, their former owners.

It is likely that much of the inspiration for both Trowbridge's setting and the central scenario around which he shaped his novel came from a book-length testimonial written by a Union officer and Kentucky native, Major John A. Brents, who served in the area around the Cumberland Gap and elsewhere in the Tennessee mountains early in the war. Entitled *Patriots and Guerillas of East Tennessee and Kentucky,* it was published in New York late in 1862 and would have been readily available to Trowbridge when he began his new novel. Major Brents made clear his biases from page one, where he characterizes Unionists as "unflinching and unselfish patriots" and notes that the notorious southern partisan Champ Ferguson was a "thief, robber, counterfeiter and murderer, [which made him] eminently qualified for the position of guerrilla chief."[26] In his first chapter, "The Suffering of Loyal Tennesseans and Kentuckians near the Tennessee Line," Brents describes the Unionist refugees and fugitives he'd encountered fleeing into Kentucky: "Many of them had squirrel rifles and shot guns; many others were unarmed. Their clothes were torn in tatters; most of them were barefooted, and their feet bleeding from cuts received on the rocks in the mountains. . . . Some were waving little Union flags, made by the mothers, wives, and sisters, and presented to them before their departure from home. Among them were old gray-haired men, middle-aged men, and little boys, who had traveled several hundred miles over the Cumberland mountains."[27] Although Trowbridge never acknowledged Brents's testimony as an influence on his work, the parallels are too striking not to think that much of *Cudjo's Cave* was built on this and other scenarios so vividly described by the Kentucky major.

Like Trowbridge did in *Cudjo's Cave, Harper's Weekly* highlighted the plight of a biracial group of cave-dwelling refugees in the Tennessee highlands. ("Union Refugees in East Tennessee," *Harper's Weekly,* September 19, 1863)

It should be obvious by now that Trowbridge's guerrillas—the heroes and heroines of his novel—are the opposite of McCabe's in terms of their loyalties and the values they personify. They are Unionists who, through a variety of circumstances, come together in the title setting of the novel, where they have sought refuge from the prosouthern and proslavery advocates who seem to dominate their rural community in the foothills of the Cumberland Mountains in northeastern Tennessee. Set entirely in the winter and spring of 1861, the novel opens as Penn Hapgood, a Quaker teacher from Pennsylvania, is dragged out of his schoolhouse by an angry mob of local ruffians, brutally beaten, and then tarred and feathered due to his Unionist proclivities and abolitionist convictions. Hapgood manages to escape the mob but soon collapses in nearby woods, where he is rescued by two unknown black men; when he regains consciousness, he's lying "deep within a cavernous room with an irregular rocky roof that stretched away into vague and obscure distance."[28]

Trowbridge situated his titular cave on the Tennessee side of the Cumberland Gap. Though he had not yet visited the South when he wrote his novel, he knew of the gap from antebellum travel accounts and from newspaper reports of military forays there. He may well have been familiar with President Lincoln's interest in the region as a Unionist stronghold, thus making it an especially effective and timely locale in which to place his drama. (He visited the area late in 1865, as part of his postwar southern tour, and wrote that the cave there—now known as Cudjo's Cave—was remarkably like his description of it in the novel.)[29]

Hapgood's rescuers, who become his hosts and protectors, are two runaway slaves, Pomp and Cudjo, who have made the cave their long-term hideaway. With the outbreak of war, it also becomes a base of operations from which they offer assistance and protection to a motley group of political fugitives, all either "downtrodden fellows" or "deserving union men." Over the course of the novel, the cave will serve as fortress, battleground, hiding place, trap, and prison, as this band of refugees, or "out-lyers," seek to elude, defeat, or punish their numerous persecutors. The latter self-appointed vigilantes include some three or four fully delineated characters, ranging from a chivalrous slaveholding gentleman (the former owner of the escaped slave Pomp) to belligerent scoundrels and ne'er-do-wells. In the early months of 1861, all of them nurse personal grudges and welcome the prospect of secession and war both due to southern pride and as a chance to avenge perceived wrongs done them. As one young man eluding the law explains to his mother, "As soon as Tennessee secedes, I shall be safe enough. I'm going to have a commission in the Confederate army, and that'll be protection from anything that might happen on account of old scores. I'm going to raise a company in this very place, and let the law touch me if it can."[30] And so it comes to be; it is as newly authorized Confederate soldiers that most of these men will continue their harassment of Penn Hapgood and his Unionist compatriots.

The first third of the five-hundred-page novel consists of a series of hostile encounters between local Confederates and Hapgood and his Unionist allies. The latter are generally benevolent, nonthreatening citizens who oppose secession (and some of whom, but not all, oppose slavery as well). While his group is not necessarily a minority in the midst of the South's staunchest concentration of Unionism, Hapgood acknowledges their beleaguered status on the novel's first page. "There are many loyal men in the neighborhood," he states, "but they are overawed by the reckless violence of the secessionists," a not-inaccurate description of East Tennessee in general in early 1861. After numerous attacks, arrests, and court orders imposed on these "patriots" by vigilante committees, Confederate officials, home guards, and night patrols, a group of them escape—or are forcibly expelled—into the nearby hills, where they eventually take refuge in Cudjo's Cave, thus becoming among the first so-called out-lyers, hundreds of whom would eventually sit out the war in wilderness retreats throughout the southern mountains.[31]

As a Quaker, Penn Hapgood opposes not only slavery but also combat and thus refuses to take up arms or to fight back against the "reign of terror" he is forced to endure. But in joining this band of comrades, he gradually comes to terms with the fact that they must all adopt a more militant stance against continued aggression by those who refuse to let them lie in peace. In this mountain fortress, a fellow refugee points out to the rest, "we are safe. Here we can defend ourselves against a hundred. Other Union men can join us, or bring us supplies. We ought to have made this move before. . . . If every Union man in the South had made a bold stand in the beginning, this cursed rebellion never would have got such a start."[32] Soon thereafter, a full-fledged assault on their mountain hideout compels Penn to take a rifle in hand, and so a pacifist takes the first steps toward becoming a guerrilla warrior. His conversion continues as he and his comrades are forced to defend themselves in this wilderness where they have chosen to make their stand.

Like McCabe, Trowbridge drew strong, determined women and slaves into the fray and made them integral to his plot. Reverend Villars, an elderly Methodist minister and outspoken Unionist, is among those who eventually seek refuge in Cudjo's Cave. A widower and blind, he is cared for by his two daughters, one of whom, Virginia, quickly becomes an object of Hapgood's affections, while the other, Salina, is married to one of the more malicious of his Confederate antagonists. In an echo of McCabe's romantic plotline, Virginia Villars attracts unwelcome attention from not one, but two, of her new lover's nemeses. One of those is Augustus Blythewood, the slaveholder from whom Pomp had escaped, thus adding layers of personal resentment on top of the ideological differences that so divide the "patriot" guerrillas from their oppressors. At one point, Virginia is asked to relay messages from the village to the out-lyers in the cave above (a role often taken by wives and mothers in such cases). In a lengthy damsel-in-distress sequence, covering four chapters, she must battle her way through a massive forest fire set by the Confederates in an attempt to burn their enemies out. In a chapter actually entitled "Beauty and the Beast" she encounters a huge bear on a precipice to which both it and she had retreated to avoid the conflagration. After ultimately overcoming these forces of nature, Virginia joins her father and her betrothed in Cudjo's Cave, where they are soon joined by her sister Salina, who finally denounces her husband's wicked ways and allows herself to be taken in by those he's worked so hard to oppress.

Pomp and Cudjo form the centerpiece of the novel. (Trowbridge later commented that "the hero of it is neither Cudjo . . . nor the young Quaker. The real hero, if the story had one, was the proud and powerful, full-blooded African, Pomp.")[33] Trowbridge draws a sharp distinction between the two: Pomp, "dignified, erect, of noble features" and a leader among men who commanded the respect of his white charges; and Cudjo, whom he somewhat surprisingly reduces to "ugly, deformed, with immensely long arms, short bowed legs . . . and a countenance like an ape." Although Cudjo claimed first jurisdiction over the cave bearing his name, it is Pomp who ultimately turns it into the sanctuary that it becomes for so many Unionists in the area and who overrides his companion's concern for all the trouble they would bring upon themselves in so doing.[34]

As with Hapgood, Trowbridge pinpoints a single incident in which Pomp and Cudjo first embrace their new role as guerrillas. They come to Hapgood's rescue a second time when a pair of "assassins" spring toward the bound and helpless young Quaker. Just as one aims "a deadly bayonet thrust straight at his heart," shots are fired from a distance, and Penn's Confederate attacker falls dead at his feet, while the other scurries away, terror-stricken. As Penn expresses his gratitude to Pomp and Cudjo, he also implores them to hurry on to save Reverend Villars as well. At that point, Pomp shrugs his shoulders and frowns, as he realizes that "the time was at hand when he and Cudjo could no longer enjoy in freedom their wild mountain life; even they must soon be drawn into the great deadly struggle." But even he doesn't capitulate without reservation. "Why should we blacks have anything to do with this quarrel?" he asks Villars. Referring to other vulnerable Unionists still below in the village, he asks, "Your friends down there are all slaveholders or pro-slavery men" (which was, of course, true of many Unionists, as Trowbridge astutely acknowledged here). "Why should we care which side destroys the other?" To which the saintly Villars responds, "There is a God who is not prejudiced against color . . . and who, by means of this war that seems so needless and so cruel, is working out the redemption, not of the misguided white masters only, but also of the slave. Whether you will or not, this war concerns the black man, and he cannot long keep out of it. Then will you side with your avowed enemies, or with those who are already fighting in your cause without knowing it?"[35]

And so Pomp is won over, as "these words probed the deep convictions of his heart." At the same time, of course, Trowbridge sends an important message to his readers, reminding them not only that slavery's demise was central to the war's purpose but also of a fact that northern readers perhaps found even more of a revelation: that slaves themselves were integral to the struggle to make that happen.

As the novel moves toward its climax, the physical struggle between the patriots and rebels intensifies and is marked by captures, executions, ambushes, and betrayals that drive much of the subsequent and ever more convoluted narrative. In a fierce clash between the cave-dwelling forces of good and those of treason, intolerance, and repression, the novel's principals engage in hand-to-hand combat deep within the cave, which leads Hapgood to finally commit fully to the rightness of his choice to fight. As Pomp leads his band of combatants in an assault on the advancing Confederates, "he looked around on his little force and smiled. Instead of eight bayonets, there were now nine. Penn had arrived." As they charge forward to meet their foe, Penn looks at his close comrades on either side of him "and forgot that he had ever been a Quaker, hating strife. Not that he loved it now; but, remembering that these were the deadly foes of his country, and of those he loved, and feeling it a righteous duty to exterminate them, he went to the work, not like an apprentice, but like a master—without fear, self-possessed, impetuous, kindled with fierce excitement."[36] In providing so fervent a description of his Quaker schoolmaster's conversion, Trowbridge fully endorsed the rationale and "righteous duty" of southern Unionists to protect themselves through guerrilla tactics.

The cave's defenders, including the female and African American characters, emerge victorious in killing or driving out their Confederate attackers. Nearly all of the former survive—though significantly, both Cudjo and Salina are among the casualties of the subterranean combat. Augustus Blythewood is captured and confined thanks to the combined efforts of both Pomp, his former slave, and Virginia, the earlier object of his lust. Humiliated by the identity of his captors, he bemoans his circumstances: "What a situation for a son of the chivalrous south! . . . Here he was, the haughty, the proud, the ambitious, overawed by a negro's threats, and carried away captive by a girl."[37] Thus Trowbridge reminds his readers once again of the disparate bedfellows brought together by irregular warfare.

Just as southern troops begin closing in on the cave dwellers late in the novel, one of them lays out the options open to his companions: "It seems your retreat cannot remain long concealed," he warns them. "Make your preparations to disperse at any moment. You may be compelled to hide for months in the mountains and woods, hunted continually, and never permitted to sleep in safety twice in the same place." That, he says, "will be the fate of hundreds. There is but one thing better for you. . . . Force your way over the mountains into Kentucky, join the national army, and hasten its advance." This, in effect, is what they ultimately choose to do. The "patriots" abandon the cave as a group—and at Pomp's direction. Hapgood and "many of his brother refugees" move from irregular into regular service—joining a Pennsylvania regiment that, Trowbridge assures his readers, gave them "the joy of participating in those military movements of last summer [1863], by which East Tennessee was relieved; of beholding the tremendous ruin which the blind pride of their foes had pulled down upon itself; and of witnessing the jubilee of a patriotic people released from a remorseless and unsparing tyranny." Pomp himself "by his intrepidity, intelligence, and wonderful celerity of movement . . . rendered important services to the Army of the Cumberland," thus adapting those traits that served him so well as a guerrilla into an only slightly more conventional form of military service.[38]

Edmund Kirke was fully as prolific a wartime writer as Trowbridge. As much a journalist as a novelist, he drew on his own extensive travel in the slaveholding South in much of his literary output, which served as an exposé of the region's cruelties and abuses in both fictional and nonfictional form. (Much of the latter includes compilations of dispatches he composed for the *New York Tribune*.) In a deft blend of both fact and fiction, in the ironically titled *My Southern Friends* (1863), Kirke quoted a friend who told him just after the fall of Fort Sumter, "If you cannot shoulder a musket, you can blow a bugle." This, he wrote, is what he sought to do through his books, noting that "it is no unimportant part of this great war of freedom to know the social condition of our enemy, and the actual influence of the institution which inspires such hatred for us."[39] In a previous venture, the equally popular *Among the Pines; or, The South in Secession-Time* (1862), he claimed, "Lest someone who has not seen the slave or the poor white man of the South as he actually is should deem my picture as overdrawn, I would say that 'the half has not been told'! . . . If the southern system, in all its naked ugliness, should be fully exposed, the truth would read like fiction."[40]

During the war, Kirke saw much of that ugliness embodied in guerrillas. During a six-week stint in the Border South as a correspondent for the *Tribune* in the summer of 1863, he actually had a fleeting encounter with a menacing band of irregulars. In a compilation of the dispatches from that trip entitled *Down in Tennessee* (1864), the Boston journalist offered a scathing critique of his would-be attackers. When a band of guerrillas forced the train on which he was heading south from Louisville to Nashville to stop, one passenger fretted, "Reckon the Bushwhackers are on us." Though in reality, they had only displaced two or three rails and moved on without assaulting the much-relieved passengers, Kirke commented to his traveling companion, "It is barbarous—this guerrilla system," to which the latter replied, "It is more than that—it's hellish. Jeff Davis should be hanged for inaugurating it," and then launched into a lengthy diatribe that Kirke recorded in full:

> If you imagine all the thieves and cutthroats of New York let loose upon the city, with unlimited license to kill, burn, and destroy, you will have a faint idea of what it is. The lowest dregs of society, our gamblers, horse-thieves, and criminals make up these bands. Now and then a respectable man, too cowardly to go into the regular army, joins them; but he soon becomes as bad as the rest. They submit to no restraint, but range the country, plundering and murdering friend and foe. If a worthless fellow has a grudge against a neighbor, he joins them, denounces his enemy as a Union man, and stealing on him at night, either shoots him down before his wife and children, or burns his house over his head.

After further condemning the guerrillas for their indiscriminate attacks on defenseless women and the elderly, Kirke's companion declared, "Wherever they go terror reigns . . . and more than one-half of this State and Tennessee is under their control." Another passenger confirmed that assessment, stating, "The East Tennesseans have suffered terribly, but the barbarities practiced on them have been committed all over this section. Wherever the guerrillas have gone, they have left a trail of burning houses, and butchered men and women. Some of them are such monsters of crime that one is tempted to believe the Devil has become incarnate in long hair, slouched hat, and butternut trousers."[41]

These characteristics all come fully into play in Kirke's first postwar work of fiction. *Among the Guerillas,* published early in 1866, was no doubt spurred, at least in part, by the animosity engendered by his brief confrontation with these so-called terrorists in Kentucky three years earlier; thus it comes as no surprise that a similar set of southern partisans serve as the villains rather than the heroes of his narrative. His protagonists—a young Union soldier from Ohio and a mixed-race slave boy—are both victims of mountain renegades, though both ultimately triumph over them. The former, named simply James, is wounded in battle near a plantation in Virginia and is taken in by an elderly slave woman, Ole Katy, who nurses him back to health; at the same time, her eighteen-year-old mulatto grandson, named Robby, returns home, and she reveals to him for the first time not only that his master is also his father but that the master sold his slave mother south, where she died at the hands of an abusive owner.[42] When the master, Captain Thompson, returns to the plantation at the head of a roving band of guerrillas, he takes an interest in James and reclaims ownership of his son-slave Robby, forcing both boys to accompany the group as they head back west into the hills, where they continue their mission of harassing Unionist highlanders.

Unlike McCabe and Trowbridge, Kirke based his fictional guerrillas on a very real band of irregular forces, Mosby's Rangers, certainly the most celebrated or notorious such group by war's end. This band of partisan rangers was sanctioned by Confederate secretary of war James A. Seddon in January 1863 and was led by the "Gray Ghost," John Singleton Mosby, who had early proven his prowess as an advance scout and scout for J. E. B. Stuart's cavalry. As the Forty-Third Battalion Virginia Cavalry, Mosby's Rangers were given relative freedom to choose their own targets and wage their own operations through much of northern Virginia—basically the home turf of most of Mosby's men. That campaign proved so effective that local residents hailed them as "our Bushwhackers" and referred to the area over which they fought as "Mosby's Confederacy"; the *Richmond Examiner* once dubbed Mosby himself "our prince of guerrillas."[43] Northern journalists gave considerable coverage to Mosby and his exploits as well, sometimes romanticizing him and sometimes dismissing him as a common criminal. By war's end, the *New York Tribune,* for which Kirke served as correspondent, had become among the most critical of his actions, accusing his band of "using the conflict as a cover for murder and robbery" and of "preying alike upon friend and foe."[44]

It was this latter depiction of Mosby and his men that Kirke chose to convey in *Among the Guerillas.* Though Mosby himself makes only a

Edmund Kirke focused his novel *Among the Guerillas* on the ruthless war John Singleton Mosby and his rangers waged on Virginia civilians, as illustrated in the first postwar account of Mosby's Rangers. ("Fire and Sword in Mosby's Confederacy," in Major John Scott, *Partisan Life with Col. John S. Mosby* [New York: Harper & Bros., 1867])

minor appearance toward the novel's end, Kirke shows his rangers harassing and oppressing loyal Union men and their families. (Mosby himself, when accused of crossing a line in making civilians his primary targets, claimed that his activity was military in nature, insisting that "my attacks on scouts, patrols, & pickets, which have provoked this threat, are sanctioned both by the customs of war & the practice of the enemy.")[45] Perhaps because much of Kirke's purpose was to ennoble poor southern whites, he relocated Mosby's base of operations to Virginia's western highlands and made loyal mountaineers the targets of the rangers' oppression.

Much of the conflict centers on an elderly blacksmith, Miles Holley, and his family, devout Unionists all. When Captain Thompson inquires as to what made Holley a traitor to the Confederacy, given that he owned slaves, his guide responds that the blacksmith did have two or three slaves, " 'fore our folks stole 'em; but he allers hed the notion that the kentry ar' uverythin' and old Virginny nothin'. That's all thar is agin him; for he'm the honestest, biggest-hearted old man ye uever know'd on.' There weren't ten men within ten miles of his farm, he declared, that wouldn't risk their lives 'to save old Miles from a halter, traitor or no traitor.'"[46]

Holley had three sons who enlisted in the Union army, all of whom lost their lives in battle; after the youngest, a mere fifteen-year-old, is killed, the bereft father goes to retrieve his body and bring it home for burial. When warned that he has been targeted by Mosby's men, Holley takes refuge in the woods adjacent to his farm. In so doing, he joins a host of other local out-lyers (not unlike Penn Hapgood and his compatriots in *Cudjo's Cave*). Together they pose a formidable challenge to their would-be captors, who see their task as not only to ferret out deserters and draft dodgers but also to inflict punishment—including execution—on any proactive "traitors" to the southern cause. (In this respect they acted in much the same way as home guard units, state militia, and even, on occasion, regular troops in dealing with dissident civilians elsewhere in Southern Appalachia.)[47]

Mosby's men seem daunted by the task. "Hain't it likely that he's friends lyin' out, as he is axin' ter holp him?" asks one about Holley, to which another responds, "We'd better reconnoiter the roads and beat the bushes opposite the house. A half dozen men in that underbrush could give us a good deal of trouble." He concludes that "we mought as well look for a needle in a hayrick, as for those fellers 'mong the bushes." Again women enter the fray as coconspirators in protecting their menfolk and their hiding places. One bold wife chides Thompson in "a tone of keen, cutting scorn," not only for harassing harmless civilians such as herself but for doing so disguised as Union soldiers (a tactic often employed by Mosby and his troops). "He's nary a traitor, he's a honest man," she declares, "but I reckon them as gits inter a false coat ter trap pore wimmin ter betray thar husbands, are wurs than traitors—they's mean 'nuff ter trade in niggers."[48]

Ultimately, the partisans capture Holley but hold him only briefly; their other captives, James and Robby, contrive to free the blacksmith, and together the three make their escape. In utter frustration, Thompson orders his men to set the blacksmith's house on fire, though he considers himself quite chivalrous in waiting until Mrs. Holley has vacated the premises before doing so (a gesture that sets him apart from McCabe's far more vindictive Union captain Bradley, who burns down the Douglas house with members of the family trapped inside). What follows is a series of cat-and-mouse maneuvers in which all parties seek to attack, entrap, or deter each other as they move steadily westward toward Mosby's headquarters. The blacksmith, slave, and Ohio soldier form a fast alliance and manage to outrun and outwit Captain Thompson and other Mosby forces in several dramatic and increasingly preposterous encounters. The final showdown occurs when all parties converge on what Kirke calls "the camp of the Rebel highwayman," where Robby emerges as the ultimate victor when he kills his father and owner in much-sought revenge for the master's complicity in the death of his slave mother.

While wives and mothers of various guerrilla targets play expected—and in the case of Ole Katy, unexpected—supporting roles in Kirke's saga, romantic attachments are far less in evidence than was the case in *The Guerrillas* or *Cudjo's Cave.* And yet the novel's predominant backstory is that of the once-loving relationship between Captain Thompson and his slave mistress that ends when he recklessly loses her because of a gambling debt, sending her farther south and to her death. Ole Katy, the source of these revelations, was also the elderly slave who rescued James and nursed him back to health. She becomes the novel's most compelling female character and remains in the thick of the action as she decides to seek out Mosby on her own to plead for the release of her grandson after Thompson whisks him away as his captive.

Kirke made fairly explicit the theme he most wanted to impress on his readers: the rigidity of the South's class distinctions and his championing of poor whites—and to only a slightly lesser extent, the newly freed slave populace—as the great hope for the emergence of a new and radically different postwar social order in the region. In a revealing passage, one of Holley's captors tells him that casting his lot with the Confederacy would mean fighting "not fur this cursed Rebellion [but] fur ole Virginny. I couldn't sleep o' nights ef I didn't do all I could fur the old State." "And what has she done for you, or for poor men like you?" Holley responds. "'Nothing,' answered his captor, smiling, 'but guv'n us a chance ter root or die.'" That evokes a tirade from the blacksmith: "She has not. She has taken the bread from your mouths to feed the rich man. She has cursed you with a set of aristocrats who have stolen all the best land, and left you only a sorry patch, just big enough for your graves. That is all she has done for you, and yet you fight for her!"[49] Shortly thereafter, Holley (by then sounding remarkably like Hinton Rowan Helper, whose subversive *The Impending Crisis* Kirke must have read at some point) further explains to James this manipulation of the lower classes by their betters, stating, "That is the way the Rebel leaders brought about Secession, and filled the Southern army—by getting the poor whites down, and holding them down till, all but in name, they were as much slaves as the blacks." He insists that this planter aristocracy "has legislated the poor man out of all his rights—out of schools and churches, and so kept him ignorant and degraded, made him servile and independent, without any ambition or any aspirations for a better future."[50]

Perhaps because Kirke's heavy-handed proselytizing on behalf of both African Americans and southern poor whites held little interest for northern readers in 1866 (he follows the novel with a twenty-page commentary entitled "The Sum of the Whole," explaining what it all meant), *Among the Guerillas* did not enjoy nearly the attention or the success of the other two works under consideration here. A *New York Times* critic condemned the book on just those grounds. "Mr. Gilmore's familiarity with the habits, manners, and peculiarities of the poorer classes living in the Southern States has given us some very graphic pictures of their mode of life, but this last work justifies the assertion that this vein is pretty well worked out." He went on to suggest that if an author has to explain to his readers what classes the different characters are meant to represent, it reflects either a failure of good storytelling or a failure to make any meaningful contribution to the real history of the war.[51]

In February 1862 Union commander James A. Garfield, then stationed in southwestern Virginia, characterized the guerrilla activity he observed there as having turned the region into "a home of fiends, and converted this war into a black hole in which to murder any man that any soldier, from envy, lust, or revenge, hated."[52] While his intent was the denigration of the mountain populace for whom he and other Federal troops invading the region held such disdain, it curiously seems an apt description of the approach of all three of these fictionalized depictions of the inner civil war in the southern highlands. In personifying for dramatic effect the motives and agendas of their characters caught up in this particular form of combat, McCabe, Trowbridge, and Kirke did indeed forefront envy, lust, and revenge, all tried-and-true elements of nineteenth-century melodrama. Yet they did so without demeaning southern highlanders, whether their loyalties lay with the Confederacy or the Union, portraying them instead in far more sensitive and sympathetic terms than did most subsequent chroniclers of the region.

Perhaps most striking about these works is that McCabe, Trowbridge, and Kirke all chose to set their narratives in Appalachia, the one area of the South in which race was so often assumed to be irrelevant and a black presence negligible; yet each made slavery and race integral to both those stories told and the messages imparted. In *Fiction Fights the Civil War,* Robert

Lively observes that "the Negro of the Civil War novel is, on the whole, a personification of each writer's conception of what he ought to have been."[53] Such seems to be the case for the African American characters created by our three writers, from McCabe's valiant but fully subservient slave to the assertive and equally valiant newly freed blacks created by both Trowbridge and Kirke, who fight for their own liberty while protecting white Unionist allies. Even more intriguing, guerrilla warfare serves as the means through which these sympathetic characters—Jerry, Cudjo and Pomp, Robby, and Ole Katy—all prove themselves and advance their cause through their derring-do, thus infusing this "savage conflict" with an additional propagandistic layer rarely seen elsewhere in either fiction on the Civil War or in historical treatments of its irregular war.

In short, three very different writers chose to make this otherwise little recognized element of the war the context through which they made impassioned pleas for the values and ideals that, to them, gave the war its meaning. A range of characters—guerrillas and their victims, men and women, blacks and whites—personify clear-cut moral agendas as to what the war could and should accomplish. Perhaps the greatest deviance from reality in the often-compelling depictions created by McCabe, Trowbridge, and Kirke is that they chose to ignore the considerable extent to which, in actuality, neutrality, ambivalence, or confusion characterized Southern Appalachia's war within a war. Given the intensity of their own ideological commitments and the height of the stakes that each saw in the war's outcome, their messages had to be clear-cut, persuasive, and inspiring. For all the variables of scenario, plot, and characterization embodied in these three works, each served first and foremost as a palatable form of propaganda for one of two competing causes. Anyone with a vested interest in one of those causes would thus identify with—or at least care about—either the perpetrators or targets of guerrilla activity, as prompted by the highly partisan creators of these narratives.

In April 1863, James McCabe proclaimed in his Richmond periodical, the *Magnolia Weekly,* "We must build a popular literature of our own."[54] As Alice Fahs has argued in *The Imagined Civil War,* both northerners and southerners were well into building such a literature by the war's midpoint and would continue to build it for the duration of the conflict and beyond. She insists that for both North and South such politically charged fiction proved vitally important "in shaping a cultural politics of war" and in engaging a broad public in a "cultural conversation concerning the evolving relationships between diverse individuals and the nation in wartime."[55]

Long before historians began to study this irregular version of the Civil War or its own participants began to chronicle their own experiences through memoir and reminiscences, playwrights and novelists recognized the dramatic potential of guerrilla warfare and provided their contemporaries with vivid depictions of what was still ongoing activity. Though somewhat romanticized and heavily weighted with ideological and propagandistic agendas, such accounts were nevertheless often reasonably accurate re-creations of how these grassroots conflicts emerged and how they functioned in much of the mountain South. Two of the three works dealt with here—McCabe's *The Guerrillas* and Trowbridge's *Cudjo's Cave*—were among the more effective efforts at fulfilling the functions of "shaping a cultural politics of war," though for very different constituencies; and if the impact of Kirke's *Among the Guerillas* was somewhat less, it was due as much to its postwar timing as to the agenda he felt he was advancing, which for many northerners felt less relevant or compelling by 1866. Yet all three works remain more valuable as historical documents than as literature, and it is in that mode—as the earliest and most popular treatments of both guerrilla warfare and Appalachia's inner civil war—that they are worthy of our attention and scholarly scrutiny today.

Notes

1. The fullest treatment of McCabe's play is Carla Waal, "The First Original Confederate Drama: *The Guerrillas*," *Virginia Magazine of History and Biography* 70 (October 1962): 459–67; see also Arthur Hobson Quinn, *A History of American Drama from the Civil War to the Present Day* (New York: Appleton-Century-Crofts, 1927), 6–7; Charles S. Watson, *The History of Southern Drama* (Lexington: University Press of Kentucky, 1997), 81–83; and "Civil War Theater," special issue, *Civil War History* 1 (September 1955), esp. Richard B. Harwell, "The Richmond Stage," 295–304. For a somewhat different perspective on the wartime theater scene in Richmond, see Robin O. Warren, "Acting Feminine on the South's Antebellum and Civil War Stages" (PhD diss., University of Georgia, 2005), 56–59.

2. Editor's introduction to James D. McCabe Jr., *The Guerrillas: An Original Domestic Drama in Three Acts* (Richmond: West & Johnston, 1863), 3.

3. On guerrilla warfare in Appalachia and how it was remembered—or forgotten—in the postwar decades, see Kenneth W. Noe, "Toward the Myth of Unionist Appalachia, 1865–1883," *Journal of the Appalachian Studies Association* 6 (1994): 67–84; Richard D. Starnes, "'The Stirring Strains of Dixie': The Civil

War and Southern Identity in Haywood County, North Carolina," *North Carolina Historical Review* 74 (July 1997): 237–59; Jonathan D. Sarris, *A Separate Civil War: Communities in Conflict in the Mountain South* (Charlottesville: University of Virginia Press, 2006), chap. 5; C. Brenden Martin, "To Keep the Spirit of Mountain Culture Alive: Tourism and Historical Memory in the Southern Highlands," in *Where These Memories Grow: History, Memory, and Southern Identity,* ed. W. Fitzhugh Brundage (Chapel Hill: University of North Carolina Press, 2000), 259–62; and John C. Inscoe, *Race, War, and Remembrance in the Appalachian South* (Lexington: University Press of Kentucky, 2008), chaps. 8, 12, 13, 15.

4. J. T. Trowbridge, *Cudjo's Cave* (ca. 1864; reprint, Tuscaloosa: University of Alabama Press, 2001); Edmund Kirke, *Among the Guerillas* (New York: Carlton, 1866). Kirke used the spelling "guerilla" in his title and throughout the text of his novel, as did many other writers during the war years and beyond.

5. The fullest biographical data on McCabe is a three-page sketch in James Wood Davidson's postwar compilation *The Living Writers of the South* (New York, 1869), 345–47; see also Waal, "First Original Confederate Drama," 462.

6. On guerrilla warfare in various parts of western Virginia (including what would become West Virginia), see Kenneth W. Noe, *Southwest Virginia's Railroad: Modernization and the Sectional Crisis* (Urbana: University of Illinois Press, 1994), chaps. 6 and 7; Noe, "Exterminating Savages: The Union Army and Mountain Guerrillas in Southern West Virginia, 1861–1862," in *The Civil War in Appalachia,* ed. Kenneth W. Noe and Shannon H. Wilson (Knoxville: University of Tennessee Press, 1997), 104–30; Ralph Mann, "Family Group, Migration, and the Civil War in the Sandy Basin of Virginia," *Appalachian Journal* 19 (Summer 1992): 374–92; Mann, "Guerrilla Warfare and Gender Roles: Sandy Basin, Virginia as a Test Case," *Journal of the Appalachian Studies Association* 5 (1993): 59–68; Brian D. McKnight, *Contested Borderland: The Civil War in Appalachian Kentucky and Virginia* (Lexington: University Press of Kentucky, 2006); and Sean Michael O'Brien, *Mountain Partisans: Guerrilla Warfare in the Southern Appalachians, 1861–1865* (Westport, CT: Praeger, 1999), chaps. 15, 16.

7. McCabe, *The Guerrillas,* 7–8. On McClellan's campaign in western Virginia, see Richard O. Curry, *A House Divided: A Study of Statewide Politics and the Copperhead Movement in West Virginia* (Pittsburgh: University of Pittsburgh Press, 1964), 55–68; and Noe, "Exterminating Savages," 106–22.

8. McCabe, *The Guerrillas,* 15–16.

9. Ibid., 18–19.

10. Ibid.

11. Richard O. Curry and F. Gerald Ham, eds. "The Bushwhackers' War: Insurgency and Counter-Insurgency in West Virginia," *Civil War History* 10 (December 1964): 427–30; and Daniel E. Sutherland, *A Savage Conflict: The Decisive Role of Guerrillas in the American Civil War* (Chapel Hill: University of North Carolina Press, 2010), 24–25, 96–97.

12. Sutherland, *Savage Conflict,* 96.

13. McCabe, *The Guerrillas,* 19–20.

14. Ibid., 26–33.

15. Ibid., 44.

16. *Daily Richmond Examiner,* December 23, 27, 1862, quoted in Waal, "First Original Confederate Drama," 460–61. For other critical reactions to the play, see Iline Fife, "The Theatre during the Confederacy" (PhD diss., Louisiana State University, 1949), 246–49; and Warren, "Acting Feminine," 59.

17. Quote from the *Richmond Examiner,* December 27, 1862, in Watson, *History of Southern Drama,* 81.

18. McCabe, *The Guerrillas,* 29–30.

19. Ibid., 33–34.

20. On women's involvement in guerrilla activity during the Civil War, see Michael Fellman, "Women and Guerrilla Warfare," in *Divided Houses: Gender and the Civil War,* ed. Catherine Clinton and Nina Silber (New York: Oxford University Press, 1992), 147–65; Mann, "Guerrilla Warfare and Gender Roles"; Gordon B. McKinney, "Women's Role in Civil War Western North Carolina," *North Carolina Historical Review* 69 (January 1992): 69–82; William A. Strasser, "'A Terrible Calamity Has Befallen Us': Unionist Women in Civil War East Tennessee," *Journal of East Tennessee History* 71 (1999): 66–88; John C. Inscoe and Gordon B. McKinney, *The Heart of Confederate Appalachia: The Civil War in Western North Carolina* (Chapel Hill: University of North Carolina Press, 2000), chap. 8; Victoria Bynum, *The Free State of Jones: Mississippi's Longest War* (Chapel Hill: University of North Carolina Press, 2000); LeeAnn Whites, "Forty Shirts and a Wagonload of Wheat: Women, the Domestic Supply Line and the Civil War on the Western Border," *Journal of the Civil War Era* 1 (March 2011): 56–78; and Joseph Beilein Jr., "Household War: Guerrilla-Men, Rebel Women, and Guerrilla Warfare in Civil War Missouri" (PhD diss., University of Missouri, 2012).

For accounts by Appalachian women of being hounded by both Union guerrillas and regular troops, see John N. Fain, ed., *Sanctified Trial: The Diary of Eliza Rhea Anderson Fain, a Confederate Woman in East Tennessee* (Knoxville: University of Tennessee Press, 2004); and Cornelia Peake McDonald, *A Woman's Civil War: A Diary with Reminiscences of the War, from March 1862,* ed. Minrose C. Gwin (New York: Gramercy Books, 2003). McDonald lived in Winchester, Virginia, at the northernmost end of the Shenandoah Valley.

21. McCabe, *The Guerrillas,* 25.

22. Ibid., 43–44. The almost farcical nature of Jerry's heroics in the final scene led one critic to suggest that McCabe modeled it on a similar scenario in Shakespeare's *Measure for Measure.* Quinn, *History of American Drama,* 7.

23. George B. Chase, *Penn Hapgood; or, The Yankee Schoolmaster: A Drama in Three Acts* (Clyde, OH: Ames, 1890), microform copy in the University of Georgia Libraries. Curiously, Chase eliminated both the novel's principal black characters, Cudjo and Pomp, from the play and set only two brief scenes in the cave, which is the centerpiece of the novel. This likely explains the change of title.

24. Dean Rehberger's introduction to the 2001 reprint is the fullest treatment of both the novel and Trowbridge's career. Robert A. Lively includes *Cudjo's Cave* in his list of the thirty best novels about the Civil War. See Lively, *Fiction Fights the Civil War: An Unfinished Chapter in the Literary History of the American People* (Chapel Hill: University of North Carolina Press, 1957), table 1, pp. 12–13.

25. John Townsend Trowbridge, *My Own Story, with Recollections of Noted Persons* (New York: Houghton Mifflin, 1903), 260; Trowbridge, *Cudjo's Cave,* 218.

26. For the fullest treatment of Ferguson, see Brian D. McKnight, *Confederate Outlaw: Champ Ferguson and the Civil War in Appalachia* (Baton Rouge: Louisiana State University Press, 2011).

27. Major J. A. Brents, *The Patriots and Guerillas of East Tennessee and Kentucky* (New York: Henry Dexter, 1862), 11. Brents too used the spelling "guerillas" in his title.

28. Trowbridge, *Cudjo's Cave,* 114.

29. Rehberger, introduction to Trowbridge, *Cudjo's Cave,* xvii–xviii. For the best accounts of military activity in and around the Cumberland Gap early in the war, see McKnight, *Contested Borderland,* chaps. 6, 7, 8; and Noel C. Fisher, *War at Every Door: Partisan Politics and Guerrilla Violence in East Tennessee, 1860–1869* (Chapel Hill: University of North Carolina Press, 1997), chap. 4.

30. Trowbridge, *Cudjo's Cave,* 72.

31. For a treatment of this phenomenon, including a somewhat different take on *Cudjo's Cave,* see John C. Inscoe, "'The Strength of the Hills': Representations of Appalachian Wilderness as Civil War Refuge," in *The Blue, the Gray, and the Green: Toward an Environmental History of the Civil War,* ed. Brian D. Drake (Athens: University of Georgia Press, 2014).

32. Trowbridge, *Cudjo's Cave,* 202.

33. Ibid., 262. The author went on to make Pomp the central character of his third and final war novel, *The Three Scouts* (1865).

34. Ibid., 118. For an astute analysis of the mixed racial messages conveyed through these two characters, see Alice Fahs, *The Imagined Civil War: Popular Literature of the North and South, 1861–1865* (Chapel Hill: University of North Carolina Press, 2001), 178–80.

35. Trowbridge, *Cudjo's Cave,* 208, 210–11.

36. Ibid., 446.

37. Ibid., 471.

38. Ibid., 400–401.

39. Edmund Kirke, *My Southern Friends* (New York: Carlton, 1863), 299–300.

40. Edmund Kirke, *Among the Pines; or, The South in Secession-Time* (New York: Charles T. Evans, 1862), 303–4. See Fahs, *Imagined Civil War,* 159–61, for an extended discussion of *Among the Pines.* The fullest biographical treatment of Gilmore/Kirke is in John A. Garraty and Mark C. Carnes, eds., *American National Biography* (New York: Oxford University Press, 1999), 9:68–69.

41. Edmund Kirke, *Down in Tennessee and Back by Way of Richmond* (New York: Carlton, 1864), 36–37, 42.

42. For an insightful discussion of this scenario in *Among the Guerillas* in terms of interracial family dynamics, see Amy Murrell Taylor, *The Divided Family in Civil War America* (Chapel Hill: University of North Carolina Press, 2005), 202–4.

43. Sutherland, *Savage Conflict,* xi, 165–66; James A. Ramage, *Gray Ghost: The Life of Col. John Singleton Mosby* (Lexington: University Press of Kentucky, 1999), chap. 7; and Paul Ashdown and Edward Caudill, *The Mosby Myth: A Confederate Hero in Life and Legend* (Wilmington, DE.: Scholarly Resources, 2002), quote on 139.

44. Ashdown and Caudill, *Mosby Myth,* 135.

45. Mosby quoted in Sutherland, *Savage Conflict,* 166.

46. Kirke, *Among the Guerillas,* 72–73.

47. See, for example, Noe, *Southwest Virginia's Railroad,* 128–29; Inscoe and McKinney, *Heart of Confederate Appalachia,* chap. 9; McKnight, *Contested Borderland,* esp. chap. 2; and O'Brien, *Mountain Partisans,* esp. chaps. 3, 4, 14. In fictional form, Charles Frazier demonized the home guard for these sorts of activities in western North Carolina in *Cold Mountain* (New York: Atlantic Monthly Press, 1997).

48. Kirke, *Among the Guerillas,* 56, 74. On Mosby's men dressing as Union soldiers, see Ramage, *Gray Ghost,* chap. 9, "Masquerading as the Enemy."

49. Kirke, *Among the Guerillas,* 112.

50. Ibid., 114–16.

51. Review in *New York Times,* April 16, 1866. Curiously, *Among the Guerillas* is the only one of his books not mentioned in the biographical sketch of Gilmore in Garraty and Carnes, *American National Biography;* nor do Ashdown and Caudill make any mention of the novel in their chapter "Mosby in Popular Literature and Biography" in *Mosby Myth.*

52. James A. Garfield to My Dear Harry, February 12, 1862, quoted in Noe, *Southwest Virginia's Railroad,* 118.

53. Lively, *Fiction Fights the Civil War,* 49. For his discussion of black characters in other war-related fiction, see pp. 47–55.

54. *Magnolia Weekly,* April 11, 1863, quoted in Fahs, *Imagined Civil War,* 3.

55. Ibid., 1. For a different take on the wartime literary culture of the South alone, see Coleman Hutchins, *Apples & Ashes: Literature, Nationalism, and the Confederate States of America* (Athens: University of Georgia Press, 2012).

In Search of Manse Jolly

Mythology and Facts in the Hunt for a Post–Civil War Guerrilla

Rod Andrew Jr.

Civil War–era guerrillas, like other outlaws, can be mysterious and elusive figures. Factual records on shadowy figures such as Civil War guerrillas are often sparse, incomplete, and unsatisfying. Myths, on the other hand, claim to tell us more. As thrilling and fascinating tales, they often inspire readers to attempt to learn the truth. They suggest insights into the motivations and personalities of the guerrillas as well. They sometimes even claim to explain the meaning of the Civil War and Reconstruction. The myths, though, while claiming to offer much more than the factual record does, can be misleading and can distort and oversimplify. In the case of the outlaw guerrilla Manse Jolly of South Carolina, neither the myth nor the historical record alone tells us the most about the subject himself and the postwar society in which he lived. Instead, the myth and the history are in constant tension, at various points reinforcing, refuting, or modifying each other. It is actually the combination of the myth and the history that tells us the most about the character and the motivations of Manse Jolly, and together they reveal him to be a far more complex and fascinating figure then either of them alone could manufacture.[1]

Manse Jolly remains ignored and virtually unknown in academic scholarship. His story is a useful case study, however, in the significant body of literature on "social bandits" and "outlaw heroes," as described by historians Eric Hobsbawm, Graham Seal, and others. Building on Hobsbawm's discussion of "social bandits," Seal has described the "cultural tradition" of the "outlaw hero." Seal agrees that "outlaw heroes" share many common characteristics, at least among British, American, and Australian examples. The outlaw hero generally "is driven to outlawry through no fault of his own" but rather because some injustice committed by those in authority forces him into outlaw behavior. He is a trickster who is difficult to catch; he depends on his local village for support and is generally protected from the authorities by his own people; and in the American and Australian traditions he has strong kinship ties that help explain his behavior. According to cultural expectations, the outlaw hero must never harm the poor, the weak, orphans, widows, or women in general; he must have gentlemanly courtesy; he generally kills only for just revenge or in self-defense; he must die bravely against overwhelming odds or express defiance even as he is executed; very often he is ultimately betrayed by a friend; and in many cases he lives on after death—that is, legends circulate that he did not really die.[2]

The mythical Manse Jolly fits most of these criteria of the outlaw hero or the social bandit, but there are two ways in which Seals's description more closely matches the Jolly myth. One of the most important defining elements of Hobsbawm's social bandit is that he is a "Robin Hood" figure who "takes from the rich to give to the poor." Seals agrees but points out that this Robin Hood quality should not necessarily be understood in an economic sense or in a classical Marxian sense. It may be more helpful to define the "rich" as those who have power and authority and the "poor" as those who feel disfranchised and oppressed. The mythical Jolly, and probably the factual one, did redistribute property—he recaptured horses and other valuables taken by Union soldiers from his white neighbors and returned them to their original owners. Similarly, the "class" represented by Jolly generally consisted not of landless peasants but rather white small landowners and former slave owners. Jolly executed their wrath against northern U.S. Army officers and against recently freed slaves, the latter more closely resembling a landless proletariat.[3] Additionally, Hobsbawm and other scholars see social bandits' activities as mostly devoid of political significance and conscious political goals.[4] The factual Manse Jolly's behavior may have been more inspired by personal and family honor and by hatred than by politics, though he did run for sheriff. Both his foes and his supporters, however, clearly understood the political implications of his actions. The myth of Manse Jolly was even more unmistakably political, and it remains so. The claim that Manse was supposedly driven by individual grievances and family honor does not change the fact that his actions were understood as a sharp rebuke to political authority that white southerners deemed tyrannical and illegitimate, whether it was "Yankee rule," "negro rule," or both. His story expressed nostalgia for, and a longing for, the return of native white rule.

The legend of Manse Jolly is generally unknown to those without family roots in Anderson, South Carolina, in the hilly, northwestern corner of the state. To native Andersonians, however, the folklore is fairly well known. Manson Sherrill Jolly was a Confederate soldier who served throughout the war. After the war, whether driven by continued commitment to the Confederate cause, family vengeance, personal honor, racism, community defense, or all of the above, he continued a one-man war against U.S. Army occupation troops in the Anderson area, black and white. He killed a large number of Federal soldiers (twenty-nine, dozens, over one hundred, or over two hundred in different versions of his story) and freedmen (though these alleged victims receive less attention) and goaded and humiliated local garrisons and their commanding officers. He threw many of the bodies down the well in the yard behind his house, and the skeletons, it is said, were discovered many years later. The "Yankees" never caught him, and he eventually moved to Texas, bought a farm, married, and started a family. Only a few years later, though, he drowned while crossing a swollen, fast-running creek. His house still stands on the northern outskirts of Anderson and is said to be haunted by his ghost. These foregoing elements of the Manse Jolly story are well known, but everyone who has heard the story knows that many of the tales about Manse are contradictory, exaggerated, or at least unproven.[5]

Some factual details of Manse Jolly's life can be verified with reasonable certainty. Born in 1840, he was the eighth of eleven children born to Joseph Morehead Jolly and Anna Cole Sherrill Jolly in Anderson District, South Carolina. The Jollys and related families had lived in the upcountry of South Carolina since the days of the Revolution and, in fact, some of their ancestors had participated in the brutal partisan war between Whigs and Tories and Indians on the southern frontier. Joseph, Anna, and their eleven children belonged to the yeoman class. In the 1850 census, the value of their three-hundred-acre farm just outside the town of Anderson was estimated at $1,500. They owned no slaves then, though they had owned two in 1840. Joseph died in 1856.[6]

Manse and all six of his brothers saw Confederate service. There is no

Manson Sherrill Jolly, ca. 1861. (Pendleton District Commission, Pendleton, SC)

reason to doubt the claim of legend and family tradition (most of which can be validated in official military records) that five of Manse's brothers died in the war: four were killed in battle and one died of sickness. When the war ended, the only male survivors of the family were Manse, age twenty-four, and his younger brother Freeman Liberty Jolly, nineteen.[7] After a brief career—perhaps seventeen months—of allegedly robbing, harassing, embarrassing, and killing Union occupation troops and black residents in the area, Manse did leave Anderson with a handful of companions and settled in Milam County, Texas, south of Fort Worth and northwest of Houston. There, in fact, he married, fathered a daughter, and later drowned crossing a swollen creek in 1869 at the age of twenty-nine. His untimely, accidental death far from home underscored the fact that U.S. Army soldiers had never been able to apprehend or kill him despite their many attempts to do so.

When South Carolina made its bid for secession, Manse had been among the first young southerners to enlist. Records show that he volunteered for service with the First South Carolina Infantry (Regulars) on February 5, 1861, over two months before the firing on Fort Sumter, and that he was six feet, four inches tall, with a "ruddy complexion," red hair, and blue eyes. The following month he was promoted to corporal and later to sergeant. This regiment saw little action in the first year of the war; after his twelve-month enlistment expired in March 1862, Manse left the unit and enlisted for the duration of the war in Company F, First South Carolina Cavalry.[8]

What little is known of Manse's service indicates that he was not only an eager volunteer but also a capable and resourceful soldier. Having reenlisted as a private, he soon began rising through the ranks again, earning promotion to corporal by November 1862 and to first sergeant by August 1863. In the cavalry, he became a scout—a mounted man on detached service with the mission of reconnoitering roads and terrain, locating enemy units, and operating between the lines, sometimes in disguise.[9] Colonel John Logan Black, his regimental commander, recalled an incident in which Manse's resourcefulness helped Major General Jeb Stuart extricate his cavalry corps from a dangerous predicament during the Mine Run campaign of late November and early December 1863. Many years after the war, Black recalled that one day Stuart's cavalry had been pursuing Yankee cavalry in a "running fight." As darkness fell, however, Stuart realized that he was caught between two large Union elements. Black called for Jolly and sent him to Stuart. "Poor Jolly was a bad talker," Black remembered, "but a better man or soldier never lived. He did not impress Stuart who . . . told him to go back and get an overcoat (Yankee) and to cover and conceal his uniform. . . . While away, Stuart asked me about him. I told him there was no better man in the corps and Jolly soon came back and departed on his mission & went through to our lines." Disguised as a Union soldier, Manse was liable to be hung as a spy if captured. Before daybreak, however, he had delivered Stuart's column out of its trap and helped reunite it with the main body of Robert E. Lee's army.[10]

After the war, Manse returned to the home of his widowed mother in Anderson and lived briefly with her, his younger brother Freeman, and probably an older sister.[11] Unfortunately, a rogue column of deserters from the U.S. Army cavalry had recently visited Anderson. This band of ruffians rode into town on May 1, 1865. Several residents recorded in their diaries that the soldiers threatened and robbed citizens at gunpoint, stealing horses, liquor, watches, and other valuables. Louise Vandiver remembered that they tied a rope around the neck of Mr. Daniel Brown and threw the other end over a tree, threatening to hang him as his little daughter screamed, "My papa, oh! My papa!"[12] Dr. A. P. Carter was "hung up by his thumbs and when he could make no disclosures [of the location of valuables] he was left hanging that way" until his two aunts and an old black woman cut him down. A white youth was fatally shot in the middle of the street "in cold blood." On May 21 another undisciplined column of U.S. troops made an equally terrifying raid on the village of Pendleton, which was nearly as close to the Jolly farm as Anderson was.[13]

The first group of marauders departed Anderson two days later, upon the arrival of more disciplined troops, but the May 1 incident set the tone for relations between the citizens of the town and U.S. Army garrisons. Anderson was occupied by a succession of U.S. Army units for at least eighteen months. As far as can be gathered from extant army records and reminiscences of Anderson citizens, units that garrisoned or patrolled the area around Anderson during various periods included elements of the Fifteenth Maine; First Battalion, Maine Volunteers; Twenty-Fifth Ohio; Fifth U.S. Cavalry; and Company I, Eighth U.S. Infantry.[14] There was constant tension between the white residents and the troops. Andersonians complained of theft, robbery, and abusive behavior by the soldiers, who in turn reported that they were shot at, sometimes fatally, by bushwhackers, and that the populace shielded and assisted those criminals. The bushwhackers sometimes stole federal property, a crime that white citizens often considered to be justified by the seizure of their property by the troops.

By far the most unpopular unit among white Andersonians, however, was the Thirty-Third U.S. Colored Troops, which garrisoned the town for several months in the summer of 1865. Hatred for the black soldiers was intense, and violent incidents between the soldiers and the white population were frequent. In August a white lieutenant in the regiment, Jerome T. Furman, was murdered in the nearby town of Walhalla. Thirty-nine years later, the commander of the Thirty-Third, Lieutenant Colonel Charles T. Trowbridge, claimed that it was "Mance Jolly" who killed Furman and that Trowbridge had offered a reward of $2,000 for Jolly's body, dead or alive.[15] The citizens of Walhalla passed a resolution honoring Furman and condemning the murder, but it undoubtedly fueled greater mistrust between the troops, their commanders, and the white population. When the First Maine Battalion replaced the black regiment in September, the *Anderson Intelligencer* rejoiced. The Thirty-Third departed Anderson by rail around the middle of the month, only to be fired upon from ambush as the train traveled between Anderson and the smaller community of Belton.[16]

The white people of Anderson preferred the presence of the First Maine Battalion to the black troops, but trouble developed between them and the Maine men as well. On the night of October 8, three young Maine soldiers were guarding some bales of cotton on the bank of the Savannah River thirteen miles from Anderson. They were found dead the next morning, having been shot through the head execution-style. Local citizens passed a resolution condemning the act and expressing sympathy for the families of the deceased soldiers. The army arrested several men, including a fifty-one-year-old planter named Crawford Keys. Keys and two other men were charged with murder, tried by a military commission, and sentenced to hang in April 1866. The trial was very controversial, however, and allegedly included unnecessarily harsh treatment of the defendants and several incidents of the military prosecutors tampering with witnesses to obtain a conviction. The citizens of Anderson sent a petition to President Andrew Johnson with over seven hundred signatures. The president commuted the death sentence and a federal judge ordered the men's release in November 1866. The three men were freed after having endured confinement in several military prisons and in the Dry Tortugas. Later Congress would investigate the reasons for their release.[17]

The murder of the three Maine soldiers brought more notoriety and public attention to Manse Jolly. Folklore surrounding Manse asserts that he began exercising retribution on Federal troops for their behavior soon after his return home to Anderson, and that may be true. However, the first official references to Manse in army records are connected to the Crawford Keys case, which began nearly six months after the end of the war. Though Manse was never arrested for the crime, senior officers suspected him of it. Major General Daniel Sickles would later testify to Congress that there were others who participated in the murder "who were never arrested. I tried very hard . . . to secure one of them—a notorious fellow by the name of Jolly, a very bad man who escaped . . . and . . . has gone into Texas. . . . He was undoubtedly one of the men who fired upon the soldiers."[18]

Only three days before the murders, Manse had put his name forward for the office of sheriff of Anderson District. The election was finally held on January 8, 1866, and Manse finished third out of three candidates in the race, gathering 279 votes to the other candidates' 859 and 416, respectively. Army officers, however, were furious that a known outlaw such as Jolly had received so many votes and considered it further proof of the lawless and defiant attitude of the white population. General Adelbert Ames bitterly resented the "spirit . . . which gave the known outlaw Jollie hundreds of votes for the office of sheriff" and complained that Jolly had long since been declared an outlaw when the election took place.[19] He claimed that the only reason for Manse's defeat was the sympathy he enjoyed among the population, who knew that if he won he would certainly be arrested and punished by "the Yankees."[20]

Manse Jolly was by no means the only "guerrilla" or "bushwhacker" operating in the South Carolina upcountry at this time. Harried army officers were constantly attempting to respond to complaints of robberies, murders, and other "outrages" by "banditti," "guerrillas," and "bands of outlaws." Shadowy figures, some of whose names were known, fired at Federal troops, stole government property, and beat and murdered ex-slaves. Federal troops believed that white citizens colluded in the crimes by refusing to name the perpetrators and even hiding and supporting them. (In the 1930s, eighty-one-year-old George M. Reid gave support to the officers' suspicions when he claimed that, as a boy, he had posted himself as a lookout so that Manse could sleep safely for a few hours in his grandfather's house without being found by the "Yankees." Reid remembered fanning flies from the guerrilla's face as he slept.)[21] Manse's name was not the only one that appeared in the occupiers' correspondence on guerrillas, but their pursuit of him did appear to intensify in early 1866. He was mentioned specifically in a dispatch by Major Alexander Moore, an officer frequently detailed on special missions to hunt bushwhackers by General Sickles. On April 20, 1866, Moore reported to Sickles from Abbeville that he would soon depart for Anderson, "in hopes to secure the notorious Jolly."[22]

Moore's attempt to arrest "the notorious Jolly" led to a confrontation between troopers of the Fifth U.S. Cavalry and two women in the Jolly residence. According to the affidavits of the soldiers involved, when they entered the Jolly house, one of his sisters "attacked one of the men," pointed a revolver at him, and threatened to "blow his brains out." The soldiers stated that First Sergeant Joseph Fought then disarmed the woman and they left. Not long after, however, Manse's younger brother Freeman Jolly complained to the first sergeant that one of the soldiers had stolen a gold watch from his mother, Anna Cole Jolly (or, as later versions of the story asserted, from Manse's sister). The noncommissioned officers conducted an inspection and reported that no watch was found among their men. The issue, however, was not yet closed. Mrs. Jolly wrote to Governor James L. Orr, who happened to be an Anderson native, alleging that she and her daughter had been beaten and robbed. Orr in turn wrote to Sickles to demand punishment of the soldiers for this attack on a "virtuous truthful woman" as well as to complain of other alleged misbehavior of troops in his hometown. Later, exaggerated versions of this encounter would reappear in local folklore and fiction.[23]

There is one more official mention of Manse's criminal activity. In a "Report of Outrages committed by White against Black persons" near Anderson, Jolly was accused of assault and battery on a freedman named Priestly Ware on May 23, 1866. The report stated that Manse gave Ware a "scalp wound" when he "knocked [him] down with a pistol."[24] Around mid-September of that year, Manse concluded that Federal pursuit of him had made the South Carolina upcountry too dangerous for him, and he departed for Texas with a few companions. He settled in Milam County, Texas, bought a farm, and married. On July 8, 1869, he drowned attempting to cross a swollen, raging creek, leaving behind his young widow.[25]

The foregoing is nearly all that is known from official records about Manse Jolly as a guerrilla. He may have killed Lieutenant Jerome Furman, he may have been involved in the Brown's Ferry massacre, Federal troops were certainly looking for him, and he definitely struck one black man over the head with a pistol. The Yankees never caught him, and he died a relatively nonviolent death when one considers all the bloodshed that is associated with his legend. One must admit that the story of the factual Manse Jolly is somewhat anticlimactic after first reading about the mythical one. The mythical Manse killed scores, if not over a hundred, Yankee soldiers, often with a sadistic flair. The factual Manse may indeed have been a bloodthirsty killer, but there is no absolute proof that he killed a single person after the war was over. The mythical Manse terrified Federal troops and "impudent" black civilians; the factual Manse was certainly a target for Federal troops, who found his presence a real threat, but the same was true of other outlaws at the time.

The mythical Manse often appears as a daring, romantic figure capable of taking audacious risks and making miraculous escapes. This part of the myth appears to have some basis in reality, as myths usually do, and the recollections of Federal officers themselves have contributed to it. Sickles and Ames did their part to paint Manse as a particularly desperate character, but no army officer contributed more to the Jolly myth than Lieutenant Colonel Trowbridge, commander of the Thirty-Third U.S. Colored Troops. In a public address thirty-nine years later, Trowbridge identified Manse as the murderer of Lieutenant Furman. After Furman's death, Trowbridge demanded information on the identity of the perpetrator and received a tip that three days later, on a Sunday morning, Manse would be worshipping at a certain church twelve miles outside of Anderson. Trowbridge had the church surrounded in the predawn darkness. That afternoon, as Manse entered the church, some of the soldiers secured his horse while others rushed in the building after him. Manse, however, "being on the alert jumped out of a window and made his escape into the cornfield where all track of him was soon lost."[26]

Over the next week or so, Trowbridge received several warnings that Manse was stalking about and admonitions from friendly blacks or comrades not to pursue him alone. Manse, though, made two dramatic appearances in which he seemed more determined to taunt Trowbridge and his men than to kill them. Just after finishing his breakfast on the Monday morning after the episode at the church, Trowbridge stepped onto the porch of the house where he was residing, having left his pistol inside. Just then Manse rode to the edge of the sidewalk and declared "'My name is Mance Jolly, the man you are looking for, now take me if you can.' Then striking spurs to his horse he rode away."[27] A few days later Manse approached a guard detail just after the morning guard mount. Manse rode up to the group of soldiers and said, "Tell your Colonel that unless he delivers my horse that his men stole from me at the meeting house on Sunday, I will kill him and every man in his regiment before they get out of this country." The sergeant of the guard ordered his men to fire on Manse, but Manse rode away quickly, laying his body over the neck of his horse. The sergeant followed him, "keeping up the fusillade until he was out of town. The horse was wounded and soon died but [Jolly] escaped."[28]

It seems clear, then, that the factual Manse Jolly had a flair for the dramatic gesture and had personal goals beyond simply killing any soldier he could. This, then, is the point from which we can begin to study Manse Jolly as myth. The working definition of "myth" used here is a story with some basis in fact, that serves some social purpose. Its distinguishing characteristic is not that it is mostly fictional, or even mostly factual, but that it serves that function for those who retell it and those who receive it. The Manse Jolly myth has fulfilled several overlapping social purposes for white Andersonians and South Carolinians after the Civil War, and to a lesser extent even into the late twentieth and early twenty-first centuries. First, for a people who felt they were the victims of "Yankee tyranny" and "negro rule" in the period of military occupation and Reconstruction, Jolly's alleged activities and fierce defiance expressed the longing and the promise of deliverance and retribution. Second, in the midst of rapid social change, when black people might successfully defy white authority and black soldiers could wield guns and theoretically, at least, compel white submission, stories of Manse's escapades were told in order to justify and reassert white supremacy. Finally, Manse's alleged ability to kill and elude Yankee pursuers was a reassertion of white southern manhood and fighting skill by a people who sharply felt the humiliation of military defeat.

A few white Andersonians were horrified by tales of Manse's killings, but it seems that many more took grim satisfaction in them. Perceiving themselves as the victims of tyranny and gratuitous insults, they could at least vicariously enjoy a measure of revenge through the violent exploits of one of their own townsmen. The mythical Manse killed in the name of family and community. While various tellings of Manse's life emphasize different events, virtually all of them claim that he killed Yankees to avenge the deaths of his brothers. That indeed has been one of the most fundamental pieces of the Jolly myth from its earliest tellings to the present day. Most accounts claim that Jolly swore to kill five Yankees for each of his dead brothers, while a few claim the number was actually ten. Fiction has embellished the family vengeance theme even further. J. W. Daniel's 1905 novel *Maid of the Foot-Hills; or, Missing Links in the Story of Reconstruction* retells the story of Reconstruction in Anderson District and other parts of the South Carolina upstate from the white southern point of view. The hero of the novel is a local ex-Confederate guerrilla named Mance Holley, obviously based on Manse Jolly. In the novel, Holley's youngest and only surviving brother is murdered by black soldiers with whom he had been drinking whiskey, and the sole reason for his death is that he is Mance's brother. Upon seeing the body of her youngest son, Mance's mother suffers a stroke and dies, and mother and son are buried together. In a scene a few pages later, Mance leaves the cemetery in grief and rage, swearing that "one hundred of them shall pay the penalty."[29] Over the years, Daniel's novel has been influential in shaping the Manse Jolly myth, and several later accounts that are meant to be nonfictional have treated Daniel's story about the alleged death of Jolly's (or Holley's) youngest brother as fact.[30] Actually, Freeman Liberty Jolly lived long after the death of Manse.

One of the few early accounts of Manse that does not mention his brothers does emphasize that Manse killed in defense of his neighbors. An article by Mrs. Olive Cochran Minor published in 1905 claims that Manse killed his victims not because they were Yankees but "for being with a command that robbed and pillaged old and young, white and black, and for committing crimes after the war was over that would make a Comanche Indian hang his head in shame."[31] It seems likely that actual physical violence by renegade Union soldiers against the local population decreased sharply after the initial May 1, 1865, raid, but Anderson residents continued to complain bitterly about the seizure of horses, watches, cotton, and other valuables. The problem was serious enough that General Ames himself acknowledged cases of illegal seizure of horses and mules by Federal troops and issued an order in December 1865 specifically prohibiting the practice.[32] When Manse stole from the Yankees, Andersonians claimed, he was taking what the soldiers had already robbed from his neighbors. Often, like a "brave, avenging Robin Hood," he returned stolen goods to their original owners.[33]

For white citizens of Anderson, the race of some of the Union soldiers made their subjugation even more humiliating. Taught from childhood to regard black threats or even black self-assertion as an intolerable affront, white Andersonians were enraged by the sight of black men wielding rifles and by the necessity of taking orders from them. Embedded in the mythical Manse's (and white southerners') resentment of Union troops in general was a vendetta against "insolent" black soldiers in particular. Several versions of the myth assert that Manse's career of violent retribution began with an encounter with freedmen and black soldiers. The story is that a small group of ex-slaves attacked one of Manse's neighbors and stole money and silver from him. Manse found the main culprit, tied him to a tree, and horsewhipped him until he revealed where the valuables were hidden. After his whipping, the black man reported the incident to the "colonel of the negro regiment," who sent two mounted black soldiers to arrest Manse. The two black men were never seen or heard from again, but the next day Manse "had two horses hitched to the plow . . . working right along as if nothing had happened." The colonel then sent four black soldiers after Manse. They too vanished into "the abyss of mystery," and Manse "confiscated" their horses as well. It was after this episode, these versions claim, that the Federal officer published a reward for Manse's capture or killing, although he dared not send any more of his soldiers after him.[34] Clearly, the stories implied, neither a Yankee colonel nor black men with guns were a match for one fierce Confederate veteran.

Some tales about Manse were meant to be humorous but also to reassure whites of their superiority by portraying black people as simpleminded, superstitious, and easily frightened by whites. In one of the stories, Manse and a friend disrupted a meeting of the Negro League, a wing of the Republican Party designed to organize freed slaves and push for racial equality in the South. The meeting was to take place one evening at the Old Stone Church near Pendleton, a building around which revolved many mysterious and frightening stories. Manse and his companion snuck unobserved into the balcony before the meeting began. Not long after the meeting was underway in the dimly lit ancient church, the two white pranksters made loud, screeching noises, "as a cat makes when in distress," followed ultimately by pistol shots. The black attendees "stampeded" out of the building in terror and the meeting broke up.[35]

A third social purpose of the Manse Jolly myth was to reassert southern white manhood in the wake of Confederate defeat. One core element of the Lost Cause legend that was already taking hold in the white South was the insistence that the "better men"—the most courageous, honorable, and skilled fighters—had lost the war due to the North's overwhelming numbers and resources.[36] Manse Jolly stories frequently mention the hero's marksmanship and horsemanship. Far more common, however, are stories of Manse confronting and humiliating his foes in face-to-face encounters. Lieutenant Colonel Trowbridge himself testified to Manse's challenging him and then several of his soldiers after the death of Lieutenant Furman and the soldiers' seizure of Manse's horse. Dramatic retellings of the meeting between Trowbridge and Jolly are almost universal in Manse Jolly narratives. Usually the name of the Union colonel, however, is "Whitehead" or "Bartow." (There was a Captain Barrows who commanded a detachment of troops in the Anderson area in the early months of 1866.)[37] In several accounts, Manse marches directly into the room where the colonel is sitting, usually drinking beer or cognac. The colonel greets the tall stranger smugly, rudely, or arrogantly, after which Manse holds up the reward poster with his name on it and asks if the colonel is looking for Manse Jolly. When the colonel replies in the affirmative and asks the tall stranger if he knows where he is, Manse replies, "I'm Manse Jolly."[38] The colonel, suddenly "paralyzed with fear," nervously downs another shot of cognac or drops his mug of beer.[39] Then Manse fires his pistol three times, intentionally shooting into the floor or into the wall behind the colonel's head. The colonel either falls backward in his chair—"not a very dignified position for an officer"—or dives out of the nearest window in terror.[40]

In other versions, the officer is Captain, not Colonel, Bartow. One article tells the story of Manse's confrontation with a Colonel Whitehead but also recounts the humiliation of the arrogant Captain Bartow in a separate incident.[41] Another tale has Manse riding up to a Lieutenant Chase of the Twenty-Fifth Michigan in the middle of the Pendleton town square. When Chase attempts to arrest Manse, the latter points "two navy six shooters" in his face. Manse promises not to kill Chase if he buys a round of drinks for Manse's friends and then returns his sister's watch to her. Chase obediently performs both tasks.[42]

Thus there are numerous accounts of Manse confronting and humiliating Federal officers in face-to-face encounters. Equally ubiquitous are Manse Jolly "escape" stories, in which Manse makes a brazen appearance in front of a number of soldiers and then defies their attempts to capture him, through his superior cunning, horsemanship, and ability to intimidate them. As related earlier, Trowbridge himself recounted two of these escape stories, and some of the later ones appear to be more colorful adaptations of his accounts. But by far the most popular Manse Jolly escape story recounts how he eluded a large number of Yankee soldiers on the day he departed Anderson for good.[43]

Despite all the variations of Manse Jolly stories, there is remarkable agreement among them about the date that Manse left Anderson: January 29, 1866. (Ironically, letters written by Manse and made public years later make it clear that he actually departed in mid-September 1866.) Theories on the reasons for his departure abound—local citizens and town leaders encouraged him to leave for the sake of the town's peace and stability; his mother feared for his safety if he stayed; he took advantage of an opportunity to make off with a large amount of cotton stolen by the Federal troops, floating it down to Augusta and making a fortune; or simply that the Anderson area had become "too hot" for him as more and more Federal patrols were dispatched after him. But all the stories emphasize that Manse did not sneak away quietly. A typical version of the story of Manse's "last wild ride" in Anderson appears in a 1975 article by newspaper writer and local amateur historian Frank A. Dickson. According to Dickson, on a Sunday morning, Manse rode his horse, Dixie, to the intersection of East River and Fant Streets. He then "headed straight into the . . . Yankee encampment on Fant Street where McCants Junior High and the cotton platform now stand. He pounded his spurs into Dixie and, with six-shooters blazing in his hands, he sped pell-mell into the enemy territory with yells like Indians on the warpath. Convinced by the sounds that Jolly headed a band of guerrilla raiders, the Yankee soldiers, and a large number of Negro recruits, panicked and fled in all directions."[44]

Other accounts agree that the Federal soldiers were routed in confusion, some of them wounded by Manse's pistol shots. Manse was unhurt and, by a prearranged plan, joined several of his companions who were waiting for him on the other side of town, and from there they began their journey to Texas.[45] The former Confederate may have withdrawn from the field, but even as he did so he proved that the Yankees were no match for southern dash and gallantry.

Another story connected with the Manse Jolly myth revolves around his sister, one of the alleged victims in the watch-stealing episode. An Anderson newspaper article published in 1919 claimed that Manse's sister was "a stout, well-built and healthy woman of about thirty-five summers" when the soldiers came to the Jolly house in search of him. After they failed to find him, "Miss Jolly assisted each one out, officers and all, with a well-planted kick that would have reflected credit on a trick mule in a circus. The men all took their medicine without a murmur, except one little five-foot corporal, who was almost rendered hors du combat and had to be carried back to camp."[46] The message behind the story was clear. Even the South's women possessed more manly honor and fighting spirit than did the craven Yankee soldiers.

One of the most fundamental facts about Manse Jolly the man and Manse Jolly the legend is that he was never captured. In a very real sense, Manse has been just as elusive to his southern white contemporaries and to historians as he was to the U.S. Army. The man inspired the myth. Over the years the myth, in turn, created more interest in the man, while simultaneously making him harder to understand and define. Most people who encounter the Manse Jolly myth soon feel the need to separate the man from the myth and find out how much of the myth is "actually true." Even white southerners who lived in Anderson at the same time as Jolly disagreed on how much credence to give to the stories. James George Harper, who helped hide Jolly in his grandfather's house as a boy, confidently repeated many of the Jolly stories as fact and commented, "How many [Yankees] he killed and helped to kill nobody knows now, but there is no question but what he did kill several."[47] A young Andersonian named Emmala Reed, on the other hand, recorded in her diary entry of January 29, 1866, that "a large reward [has been] offered for 'Jolly' a *reported bushwhacker* &c but I don't know that he had really done much!"[48]

Historians have found Manse just as elusive. While some amateur historians as well as novelists have been led far astray, uncritically accepting and even contributing to the fictional Manse, others have made a serious attempt to separate fact from fiction. Perhaps the most credible attempt was made by Lander University president Elmer Don Herd in the 1980s. Herd theorized that Manse, embittered by Confederate defeat and the death of his brothers, indeed led a gang of outlaws who hid out in the woods and attempted to harass Federal garrisons. Herd correctly points out that there were many bands of outlaws—bushwhackers and former Confederate deserters and draft dodgers—hiding out in the wooded uplands of northwestern South Carolina, and he suggests that Manse's name was often associated with criminal acts committed by others. Manse's gang "usually camped in a heavily wooded area of Anderson District." Herd suggests it was principally involved in stealing cotton, horses, and military equipment from occupation troops and local scalawags, then floating the booty down the Savannah River for sale in Augusta, Georgia. Manse did not deliberately target Federal troops for assassination. However, on one of these raids, Herd believes, Manse ended up killing the three soldiers at Brown's Ferry, the murders for which Crawford Keys and three others were arrested and tried.[49] Herd also throws cold water on the outlandish claims that Manse killed one hundred men or more: "These estimates seem quite unrealistic when one considers the furor that arose over the killing of just three troopers at Brown's Ferry. If . . . anywhere near a hundred soldiers were killed or disappeared, then there would certainly have been massive retaliation by the occupation forces. . . . There are only three references to Jolly's direct connection to the killing of Yankee soldiers, and none of these accounts is contemporary with the actual events."[50]

Herd's theory is plausible enough but leaves plenty of questions unanswered. If Manse was an outlaw hiding in the woods, for example, how does one explain his putting his name on the ballot for sheriff? Was that not a public act that had to be done in broad daylight in the county courthouse? Additionally, U.S. Army records show the signature of "M. S. Jolly" on the petition that Anderson residents sent to President Johnson on behalf of the Brown's Ferry defendants. The handwriting is similar to that found in a handful of Manse's letters written the following year. Did Manse ride into town in broad daylight to sign the petition, or did someone who knew where his hideout was bring it to him? Both scenarios conjure the image not of a bushwhacker in a remote lair but of a guerrilla "hiding in plain sight" among the native white population.

Additionally, if the body count of Manse's victims was very low, why were army officers so obsessed with tracking him down? Military correspondence from the period is full of complaints about how serious the problem of bushwhacker and guerrilla activity was in South Carolina, particularly in the upstate region.[51] According to reports, a large number of Federal troops and officers, as well as inoffensive citizens, were murdered, beaten, and robbed. If Manse was responsible for very little of this, why did General Sickles identify him as "one of the worst" of the bushwhackers?[52] Why did Major Alexander Moore, handpicked to lead armed patrols in search of bushwhackers, report specifically that he was on his way to Anderson from Abbeville for the express purpose of capturing "the notorious Jolly?"[53] Indeed, Lieutenant Colonel Trowbridge himself was confident that it was Manse who killed Lieutenant Furman in Walhalla.[54] It is undoubtedly true that Manse Jolly tales grew taller as the years went by. But his 1869 obituary proves that even his contemporaries in 1865 and 1866 saw him as something of a romantic hero and a real threat to the military garrison. The *Anderson Intelligencer* noted that news of Manse's death would be "received with regret by the many friends of this bold and daring Confederate soldier. . . . The thrilling exploits and adventures of Manson Jolly in this section of the country, immediately after the war closed, are fresh in the recollection of all. His name was a terror for a long time to the garrison of United States soldiers."[55]

Again and again, the diligent researcher finds tantalizing evidence in one place that seems to lead to the "real Manse," only to find a frustrating lack of it or contradictory information somewhere else. Many writers abandon the trail quickly and content themselves with chasing the mythical Manse rather than the strictly factual one. In 1932 journalist Rufus M. Newton wrote a two-part newspaper series on Jolly in which he conceded, "It is not the purpose of the writer to adhere strictly to established facts, since that would be impossible." The Manse Jolly story was better established, he explained, in oral tradition than in written records: "The reader can rest assured that he will in the main be given absolute facts. Most of this information has been handed down from old people, contemporaries of Jolly, by word of mouth."[56] One frustrated pursuer of the factual Manse Jolly is David S. Adams, senior producer and director of South Carolina Educational Television. After producing a documentary on Manse in 2005, Adams tried to explain to a newspaper reporter why he found Manse Jolly so intriguing: "I read about Manse in college, and he was just very mysterious. The more I looked into it, the less I knew."[57]

Manse Jolly chasers have tried to pinpoint not only his location in the realm of fact and fiction but also where he stands on the scales of right and wrong. Even his own southern white contemporaries felt compelled to wrestle with moral judgments on Manse's activities. Olive Cochran Minor was willing to excuse Manse's murders due to the alleged barbarity of the Yankee occupation. She reasoned that "while bushwhacking should be condemned, if there ever was a time when it was justifiable it was when Federal soldiers robbed and murdered a people who, without arms and ammunition, had surrendered."[58] Anderson native Louise Vandiver, another contemporary, was far more critical. Vandiver acknowledged that Manse served "faithfully" during the Civil War and readily understood why her neighbors thrilled at stories of his "daring appearances in the very presence of the Yankees." She insisted, however, that "when one comes to examine the actual record, horror takes the place of admiration."[59]

It is important to note that Vandiver's condemnation rested not on Manse's fight against the army of occupation but on his actions against innocent civilians. She recounted stories of Manse capturing inoffensive Yankee travelers, stealing their valuables, and then shooting them in cold blood.[60] Subsequent writers agreed that Manse crossed the line when he supposedly began killing innocent strangers. The second half of Rufus Newton's two-part newspaper series on Manse included the subtitle "Later Career More Horrible Than Admirable—Extends Vengeance from Federal Soldiers to Yankee Civilians."[61] In the late nineteenth and early twentieth centuries, however, this sympathy for northern civilian visitors did not extend either to southern white "scalawags" or to black southerners who were suspected thieves or informants or who wore Yankee uniforms. Referring to Manse's alleged killing of the black soldiers sent to arrest him, a 1919 article smugly noted, "What became of the coons has never been known."[62]

Louise Vandiver's criticism of Manse's activities shows that contemporaries were at least ambivalent about whether his alleged murders were justified, but it should be kept in mind that Vandiver was writing several decades after the end of the Civil War. As time gradually removed southerners from the horror and hatred of the war years, ironically there may have been a growing awareness of just how grisly and awful some of Manse's alleged activities were. As the legend of the Lost Cause sanitized and glorified other wartime memories, the vicious nature of Manse's alleged crimes made him appear as a figure who was just as sinister as he was heroic. One event that seems to have fed this darker image of him occurred a few decades after his death, probably around the turn of the twentieth century. With the Jolly home in the hands of new owners, someone reported finding human skeletons in a well in the yard near the house. Other accounts said that U.S. Army belt buckles and uniform buttons were also found, leading to the speculation, or rather the popular conviction, that Manse disposed of the bodies of dozens of his victims by throwing them into the well.[63]

Affected perhaps by the increasing moral relativism of the twentieth century, some later writers suggested that perhaps Manse's atrocities should be understood in light of the horror he himself had experienced as a soldier. In 1958 journalist F. C. McConnell III noted that "Manse was a simple farm boy" when he left home and enlisted, "but he learned violence in the war."[64] Wilton Earle Hall Jr., an Andersonian who wrote the 1996 novel *Manse,* has suggested that Manse suffered from "post-traumatic stress disorder."[65] Claiming to have read the diary of Manse's widow, Hall thought he could trace the man's "inexorable path from battlefield horrors to . . . trauma-induced madness."[66]

Even before Americans used the term "post-traumatic stress," however, some observers reflected on the moral landscape on which Manse's guerrilla war was fought. In 1939 Pendleton resident David B. Burress examined the morality of Manse's and others' behavior during the Civil War era. Burress's article, which was otherwise filled with praise of Jolly and bitter condemnation of Union troops, contained one passage that was a thoughtful attempt to assess the moral climate in which Manse and others operated: "Today it is impossible from our present viewpoint to justify Manse Jolly in many things he did. And on the other hand, how utterly impossible is it to condone a single act of the Union Army of Occupation when they knew the cause was lost and all organized resistance had been absolutely crushed. However, it was an epoch in which adversity reigned supreme and the hearts of men were hardened by spilling of much blood."[67] Thus, even some of Manse's most admiring followers have found it difficult to fully endorse all his actions. Overall, though, the Manse-as-victim portrayal has not overcome that of Manse as villain, and certainly not that of Manse as hero. Taken as a whole, moral evaluations of Manse's life have been ambiguous enough to suggest that the "real Manse Jolly" is still at large.

At times Manse's image was so transformed into a frightening one that the Manse Jolly legend became something of a ghost story, a tale that has the power to produce fear and horror.[68] One white account says that black parents would threaten their restless children at night with the warning that if they did not go to sleep, "Manse Jolly would get them." One Anderson resident apparently tried to start a rumor that Manse had not really died in Texas. "One man who knew Jolly well," reported Rufus Newton, "suggested that probably he was not drowned at all, but that he had the story circulated to mislead the government and cause it to stop hunting him."[69]

Maybe, then, Manse never drowned—maybe he did not die but rather vanished, only to return and resume a shadowy existence in his old haunts. Indeed, there are ghost stories of modern origin connected to Manse. The Jolly farmhouse, now restored, still stands on the northern outskirts of Anderson, on a road now officially known as Manse Jolly Road. The owner, Nancy Stein, whose family moved to Anderson from New Jersey before the 1980s, affirms that there are many ghost stories connected with the house. Stein occasionally hears the sound of a mandolin playing in the empty attic above her bedroom; others have heard "the hoofbeats of phantom horses approaching the house, and the footsteps of soldiers pounding up the porch." One visitor to the house "swore he saw Manse Jolly himself peering through a window of the house late one night." Just before this "visitation," Stein reports, "the fire in the fireplace blew out and her visitor said he felt 'an unexplainable dread, a horrible anxiety of impending doom.'" Other tales tell of caves where Manse hid from patrols, which locals say are now covered over by the man-made Lake Hartwell. Others have seen "a man sitting on the porch" of the Jolly house when there was no one there.[70]

As a ghost, Manse still has the power to intrigue but has lost much of his power to frighten. Stein herself says that the strange encounters she has had in the house are with a benign rather than malevolent presence.[71] Indeed, by the late twentieth century, just as many Manse-chasers thought they had finally defined him as a brooding, angry character, Manse turned the tables on his pursuers once again. In 1975, eighty-four-year-old Bessie Casey Hammond, Manse Jolly's grandniece, donated a collection of letters to Anderson College. Most of the letters had been written by Manse to his mother and his sister Mattie in 1866 and 1867 while he was making his escape to Texas and beginning a new life there. The letters were eagerly devoured by a modern generation that was perhaps more capable of accepting someone with complex motivations and less compelled to render a moral judgment than to try to understand what made a person "tick."

When the letters came to public notice, one might have anticipated that Manse's ghost had finally left his pursuers a clue—concrete evidence about his personality and motivations. The letters did reveal a few things about Manse, but they were surprising insights that proved once again how elusive he had always been. First, the letters had a surprisingly literate quality that dispelled any stereotypes of a rough, illiterate character. There were some irregularities in spelling and grammar, but the prose was smooth and articulate, the handwriting fluid and easily legible. Occasionally earlier articles had imagined Manse's speech to be grossly colloquial. Eugene Blake's 1953 article had quoted him telling Captain Bartow, "I'm the man you're so hogwild to get. This here is Manse Jolly, mister—Take a good look. Don't tremble so. I don't enjoy shootin' stray dogs unless I have to."[72] Manse's letters often used the popular dialect of the upland South, frequently informing his sister that he was getting along "finely." Speculating that a former girlfriend might marry and not wait for him to return for her, he wrote, "I guess they are as good fish in the sea as has been caught out of it."[73] At other times, however, he wrote with a playful formality, seemingly mocking a more stilted style with which he was familiar and capable of using. "Dear Sister," he wrote in one letter, "with the utmost facility I avail myself of the present opportunity of acknowledging the receipt of your very kind epistle yesterday."[74] Moreover, readers of Manse's letters found very little angry vituperation and dark hatred; indeed, he seemed to exhibit few antisocial qualities at all. He wrote of pretty women he had met on his journey and social gatherings with kin. There was tender concern for a niece's education, kind greetings to friends in Anderson, and concern for the health of relatives, including his mother. Manse seemed hurt by a comment a female friend made to him shortly before he left South Carolina, when he and friends were discussing their move to Texas. "Miss Alice" told him, "'Yes, Mr. Jolly you are to blame for all this.' Without asking her what I was to blame for, I said, 'Miss Alice, I am really sorry for it.' I expect she thought I persuaded Herb Williams off, whom she loved so devotedly." Manse confessed that he had dwelt "a good deal" on Alice's accusation.[75] Manse also sent a message to a black man he knew. "Tell Burrell Coleman & crowd," he wrote, "to remain in S.C. as I intend to make him an offer to come west, next year, a negro can do better here than he can anywhere else."[76]

Those who imagined Manse to be rough, uncouth, and completely indifferent to violence found passages that seemed to contradict that image. Manse said he was well pleased with Texas and the opportunities it offered, but "dam the people that lives in it. Society is bad, no use for preachers out here."[77] He was disgusted with their habit of using snuff and ironically seemed to disapprove of the culture of violence: "When two men has a little falling out they are very apt to draw their Six Shooters and go to shooting each other. This is the style of Texas."[78]

Manse clearly hoped to leave his outlaw existence behind. He was concerned about the army tracking his whereabouts. He and his companions were cautious in their trek to Texas, warily avoiding U.S. Army units. He sometimes used aliases in signing his letters. He instructed Mattie not to publicize where he was and told her to mail her letters to him from the Pendleton post office to foil those who might note the address she used for him. Once Manse arrived in Texas, he and his friends worked hard to establish themselves as farmers. He was determined to prosper with "honesty, industry, and economy," he wrote, and several times he expressed his desire to find a wife. He did marry, of course, and soon had a baby girl.[79] Above all, Manse appeared to be a man who longed for peace.

Andersonians eagerly grappled with the implications of the letters. A 1976 article in the *Anderson Independent* was headlined "Manse Jolly: Warm-Hearted Warrior." Journalist Joanne Thrift noted that Manse's reputation was that of a "fierce leader of marauding guerillas [*sic*]. . . . But was he also a warm, home-loving person who cared deeply about his family and who was concerned about his own good name?"[80] Robert S. McCully, a faculty member in the psychiatry department of the Medical University of South Carolina, weighed in as well. Speaking to the Anderson County Historical Society, McCully claimed that the letters revealed "distinct personality characteristics" of a man who possessed "insight and a keen sense of humor."[81]

But Manse did not allow his future letter readers to peg him simply as a gentle, harmless man either. He furiously denounced a man in Texas named John Todd who he believed had cheated the Jollys and dishonored the memory of his brother, John A. Jolly. Somehow Todd had become the executor of John's estate and had a trunk full of his possessions. Manse believed that Todd had used some of John's goods, especially clothes, for his own benefit and then lied about it. When a relative named Alfred Sherrill confronted Todd over other dishonest dealings, Todd drew a pistol on him. Manse swore to his mother that "if [Todd] draws a gun on me, I intend to *kill* him if I *can*."[82] In another letter, Manse added a slight humorous touch to his denunciation of an enemy. He had heard that since he left home, Thomas Harper had been calling him "a murder [*sic*] and a highway robber. He would be a little surprised if I was to ride up into Anderson someday and throw a lasset on him and wear him out with a Texas raw hide whip. I don't suppose he ever thinks of this."[83] There is no evidence that Manse followed through with his threats against either John Todd or Thomas Harper, but both of them read as though they were written by a man who was accustomed to committing violence.

One must conclude that the "real" Manse Jolly still refuses to be caught—to be pigeonholed or defined in any simplistic way. He certainly belongs in the academic discussion of "social bandits" and "outlaw heroes." While the personal motivations of the factual Manse Jolly are obscure, contemporaries and later generations have correctly ascribed political and social significance to his activities. He represented the bitterness and the longings of white southerners whose political and social power, at least temporarily, had been overthrown. Thus his story—the myth at least—more closely resembles one of Graham Seal's "outlaw heroes" than Eric Hobsbawm's more apolitical "social bandits."

But positioning Manse within a historiographical discussion does not answer the questions about him that most people want to know. We will probably never know, for example, what crimes or exploits he did or did not commit in the first year and a half after the guns fell silent at Appomattox. And those who are honest and open-minded in their search for him must admit that his true motivations, character, and personality are hard to define as well. The factual records do not give us nearly enough information to do so, and in fact they alternately tease and frustrate us. The myth promises fuller answers but is never fully trustworthy. The known facts and the myth together, working in tandem, probably bring us as close to the "real" Manse Jolly as we can hope to get.

And yet the questions remain. Was Manse Jolly a noble vigilante or a murderous horse thief and bushwhacker? Was he driven by hatred or was he a devoted family man caught in a maelstrom of violence and vengeance he did not create? And what was Manse's war about—racial hatred and white supremacy, personal vindication, family defense, regional and community honor, or a complex mixture of all of the above? Manse's most dedicated pursuers are like students of the Civil War itself. They find themselves unable to answer the questions fully and yet irresistibly drawn to them—mesmerized by a specter that is often dark, perhaps noble, and always fascinating.

Notes

1. Daniel E. Sutherland helpfully differentiates between "guerrillas," "bushwhackers," and similar terms in *A Savage Conflict: The Decisive Role of Guerrillas in the American Civil War* (Chapel Hill: University of North Carolina Press, 2009), xi–xii. I do not attempt to define Jolly as either a guerrilla, bushwhacker, or simple horse thief here because, as will be seen, the exact nature of his activities is not entirely certain. Some of the numerous recent works that have attempted to study guerrillas or irregular warfare through the lens of mythology include Paul Ashdown and Edward Caudill, *The Mosby Myth: A Confederate Hero in Life and Legend* (Wilmington, DE: Scholarly Resources, 2002); Matthew C. Hulbert, "Constructing Guerrilla Memory: John Newman Edwards and Missouri's Irregular Lost Cause," *Journal of the Civil War Era* 2, no. 1 (March 2012): 58–81; Paul Christopher Anderson, *Blood Image: Turner Ashby in the Civil War and the Southern Mind* (Baton Rouge: Louisiana State University Press, 2002); John C. Inscoe, *Race, War, and Remembrance in the Appalachian South* (Lexington: University Press of Kentucky, 2008); T. J. Stiles, *Jesse James: Last Rebel of the Civil War* (New York: Vintage Books, 2002).

2. Eric J. Hobsbawm, *Social Bandits and Primitive Rebels: Studies in Archaic Forms of Social Movements in the 19th and 20th Centuries* (Glencoe, IL: Free Press,

1959), 3–25; Graham Seal, *The Outlaw Legend: A Cultural Tradition in Britain, America, and Australia* (Cambridge: Cambridge University Press, 1996), xii–13.

3. Hobsbawm, *Social Bandits;* Seal, *Outlaw Legend,* 4–6.

4. Those who see outlaw heroes as generally apolitical include Hobsbawm, Michael Fellman, and Richard White. Hobsbawm, *Social Bandits,* 24–25; Michael Fellman, *Inside War: The Guerrilla Conflict in Missouri during the American Civil War* (New York: Oxford University Press, 1989), 254; Richard White, "Outlaw Gangs of the Middle Border: American Social Bandits," *Western Historical Quarterly* 12, no. 4 (October 1981): 395–97, 402, 406–7. T. J. Stiles disagrees, arguing that Jesse James, for example, was a profoundly political figure. Stiles, *Jesse James,* 383–91. Hulbert shows how the memory, or myth, of Jesse James was mobilized for political purposes. Hulbert, "Constructing Guerrilla Memory."

5. The foregoing summary of the Manse Jolly legend is a brief composite constructed from the reminiscences, local newspaper articles, and local histories cited in the remainder of this essay. There is no one source that is more comprehensive or authoritative than all others in recounting the Jolly legend; however, the foregoing summarizes the key elements that people who know the story most commonly recite. This of course suggests that the evolution of the story owes much to oral tradition.

6. E. Don Herd, *The South Carolina Upcountry, 1540–1980: Historical and Biographical Sketches* (Greenwood, SC: Attic Press, 1982), 2:387; U.S. Census, 1840, 1850.

7. "Genealogical Charts Compiled by Tommy Cole," Manse Jolly Collection, Pendleton District Commission, Pendleton, SC (hereafter MJC, PDC). Confederate service records confirm the death of Jesse A. Jolly in a Confederate hospital in Richmond on June 9, 1862, and of James S. Jolly, First South Carolina Regiment, killed at Chancellorsville, May 3, 1863, as well as confirming the Confederate service of all seven of the Jolly brothers. Compiled Service Records, M267, National Archives, Washington, D.C. (hereafter NA).

8. A. S. Salley, *South Carolina Troops in Confederate Service,* 3rd ed. (Columbia, SC: R. L. Bryan, 1913), 2:126; Compiled Service Records, M267, NA; Furlough paper for Sergeant Manson S. Jolley [*sic*], August 4, 1861, Manse Jolly Letters, Anderson University Library, Anderson, SC (hereafter AUL).

9. Herd, *South Carolina Upcountry,* 2:394.

10. John Logan Black, *Crumbling Defenses; or, Memoirs and Reminiscences of John Logan Black, Colonel, C.S.A.,* ed. Eleanor McSwain (Macon, GA.: Eleanor D. McSwain, 1960), 68.

11. Jolly's surviving sisters in 1865 were Martha Ann (or Mattie), age unknown; Mary Jane, about thirty-five; and Ruah, about thirty-one. All three sisters married at some point, but later stories and official reports suggest that one sister lived at the house in the spring of 1866. U.S. Census, 1850; "Genealogical Charts Compiled by Cole," MJC, PDC.

12. Louise Ayer Vandiver, *Traditions and History of Anderson County* (Atlanta: Ruralist Press, 1928), 239.

13. Olive Cochran Minor, "Incidents of the Anderson Raid," in *South Carolina Women in the Confederacy* (Columbia, SC: State Company, 1903–1907), 2:372–76; R. C. Hoyt's account in ibid., 2:369–71; Ernest M. Lander Jr., *The Life and Times of Ella Lorton, a Pendleton, S.C., Confederate* (Clemson, SC: Clemson Printers, 1996), 72–73; Floride Calhoun, *A Rebel Came Home,* ed. Charles M. McGee and Ernest M. Lander Jr. (Columbia: University of South Carolina Press, 1961), 87; John B. Adger, *My Life and Times, 1810–1899* (Richmond, VA: Presbyterian Committee of Publication, 1899), 340–45.

14. Vandiver, *Traditions and History,* 250; Capt. William Stone to Lt. Col. John Devereaux, March 23, 1866, Records of the Field Offices for the State of South Carolina, Bureau of Refugees, Freedmen, and Abandoned Lands, 1865–1872, roll 44, M1910, RG 105, NA; Special Order No. 35, February 26, 1866, Special Orders and Circulars, Western South Carolina, Letters Received, entry 870, part 1, RG 393, NA; Lt. Col. Nat. Staughton's report, April 21, 1866, entry 2404, Letters Sent, Western South Carolina, vol. 220, part 2, RG 393, NA; Lt. James P. Ruggles to Bvt. Lt. Col. Alexander Moore, May 6, 1866, entry 4158, "Reports of Outrages," Department of South Carolina, part 1, RG 393, NA; Brig. Gen. Adelbert Ames to Maj. Gen. Daniel Sickles, April 4, 1866, Letters Received by the Office of the Adjutant General, roll 512, M619, NA; Returns from Anderson, May 1866–December 1867, roll 27, Returns from U.S. Military Posts, 1800–1916, M617, NA.

15. Charles Tyler Trowbridge, "Six Months in the Freedmen's Bureau with a Colored Regiment: Address by Lieut. Col. Charles Tyler Trowbridge," October 11, 1904, in *Glimpses of the Nation's Struggle: Papers Read before the Minnesota Commandery of the Military Order of the Loyal Legion of the United States,* vol. 31 (Minneapolis: Aug. Davis, 1909), Sanders Family Homepage, http://www.sandersweb.net/ed/TrowbridgePaper.htm.

16. *Anderson Intelligencer,* August 31, September 14, 1865; Bvt. Maj. Gen. Davis to Maj. Gen. Adelbert Ames, September 16, 1865, and Ames to Lt. Col. Calvin S. Brown, September 18, 1865, Letters Received, Department of Western South Carolina, entry 870, RG 393, NA.

17. Crawford Keys Case, Records of the Office of the Judge Advocate General, MM3888, RG 153, NA; Thomas B. Keys, *The Army and Crawford Keys: Aftermath of the Brown's Ferry Outrage* (1974). Judge Willard Hall of the U.S. District Court for Delaware ruled that, at the time the military commission was appointed to try the case in December 1865, South Carolina's civil government was legally functioning and that therefore the men should have been tried in a civilian court (Keys, *Army and Crawford Keys,* 70–74). After examining papers surrounding the case and the report of Secretary of War Edwin Stanton, a special committee of the House of Representatives made its report. The majority report, delivered by Congressmen Frederick Pike of Maine and John F. Farnsworth of Illinois (both Repub-

licans) on February 22, 1867, accepted the guilt of the defendants, disapproved of their release, and argued that martial law and the precedence of military courts were still needed in the ex-Confederate states. A minority report by Edmund Cooper, a former Unionist from Tennessee, argued that the defendants' guilt was not absolutely proven, supported the decision by the civilian federal judge to release them, and opposed the continuation of martial law. "House Journal," *Congressional Globe,* December 13, 1867, p. 72, January 9, 1867, p. 140, February 22, 1867, p. 475; *New York Times,* February 23, 1867, p. 5, columns 1–2, February 26, 1867, p. 5, columns 1–2; Keys, *Army and Crawford Keys,* 78–83. More recent research on the Keys case is being done by Professor Bruce Baker of Newcastle University, England.

18. Keys, *Army and Crawford Keys,* 79–80.

19. Ames to Lt. Col. Burger, March 13, 1866, Letters Sent, Department of Western South Carolina, entry 867, part 3, RG 393, NA.

20. Ames to Sickles, April 4, 1866, Letters Received by the Office of the Adjutant General, roll 512, M619, NA.

21. "81-Year Old . . . [remainder of title obscured]," clipping, undated, 1930s, MJC, PDC.

22. Maj. Alexander Moore to Maj. Gen. Daniel Sickles, April 20, 1866, facsimile found in Eugene H. Blake, "The Joke Wasn't So Jolly for the Man Who Found Manse Jolly," *Columbia (SC) State,* June 14, 1953.

23. "Statement of 1st Sergt. Joseph Fought, Apr. 27, 1866"; "Statement of Sergeant T. A. Nixon, May 8, 1866"; James L. Orr to Maj. Gen. D. E. Sickles, April 30, 1866; and Lt. Ruggles to Lt. Col. Alexander Moore, May 6, 1866, all in Reports of Outrages, 1865–1867, entry 4158, RG 393, part 1, NA. The *Anderson Intelligencer* also reported on the alleged robbery of Manse Jolly's mother in its issue of May 3, 1866.

24. "Report of Outrages committed by White against Black persons in the Dist. of Anderson, South Carolina," May 16–31, 1866, Records of the Field Offices for the State of South Carolina, Bureau of Refugees, Freedmen, and Abandoned Lands, 1865–1872, roll 44, RG 105, M1910, NA; see also "Report of Outrages Committed by White against Black persons, Anderson, S.C.," May 13–28, 1866, entry 4158, Reports of Outrages, RG 393, part 1, NA.

25. John M. Jolly to Anna Jolly, July 12, 1869, August 2, 1869, Manse Jolly Letters, AUL.

26. Trowbridge, "Six Months in the Freedmen's Bureau."

27. Ibid.

28. Ibid.

29. J. W. Daniel, *Maid of the Foot-Hills; or, Missing Links in the Story of Reconstruction* (New York: Neale, 1905), 79. Some of the earliest surviving accounts of the Jolly story include "'Manse' Jolly," clipping from Anderson newspaper, n.d. (1890s), MJC, PDC; Letter of James George Harper, Seneca, April 1926, MJC, PDC; Minor, "Incidents of the Anderson Raid," 2:375; "Manse Jolly, Celebrated

Bushwhacker of Anderson County," *Lavonia (GA) Times,* February 15, 1919, MJC, PDC.

30. For example, see "When Jolly Went After a Man He Got Him," *Anderson Independent,* June 10, 1928; F. C. McConnell, "Unsubdued Rebel Jolly Waged Own Bitter War against Yanks," *Columbia State,* December 25, 1958.

31. Minor, "Incidents of the Anderson Raid," 2:375.

32. Circular, December 23, 1865, Special Orders and Circulars, July 1865–April 1866, Department of Western South Carolina, entry 870, part 1, RG 393, NA.

33. "Mance Jolley: A True Story," *Anderson Intelligencer,* August 15, 1894; Kenneth D. Lee, "The Rogue," 5, MJC, PDC; Letter of James George Harper, Seneca, April 1926, MJC, PDC; quote from "Manse Jolly Took Last Ride Here 102 Years Ago," *Anderson Daily Mail,* January 29, 1968.

34. Lee, "The Rogue," 3; Rufus M. Newton, "Manse Jolly, Anderson Guerrilla, Kept Federal Garrison in Terror," part 1, *Columbia State,* August 7, 1932; "Mance Jolley," *Anderson Intelligencer,* August 15, 1894 (quotes are from Newton and "Mance Jolley"). See also McConnell, "Unsubdued Rebel Jolly," *Columbia State,* December 25, 1958; and McConnell, "South Carolina Had Own Jesse James," *Anderson Daily Mail,* December 24, 1958.

35. Rufus M. Newton, "Manse Jolly," part 2, *Columbia State,* August 14, 1932. There is another story about Jolly playfully disrupting a meeting of black people in a church, this one led by a southern white minister in daylight, in Elise Mauldin Paget, "The Paternal Ancestry of Elise Mauldin Paget," South Caroliniana Library, University of South Carolina, Columbia.

36. Thomas L. Connelly and Barbara Bellows use the phrase "better men" in their study of the Lost Cause, *God and General Longstreet: The Lost Cause and the Southern Mind* (Baton Rouge: Louisiana State University Press, 1982). For a perceptive study of how one version of the Lost Cause made room for the romanticized and mythologized bushwhacker, see Hulbert, "Constructing Guerrilla Memory." For further discussion of how events of the Civil War era challenged and then reconstructed southern manhood, see, for example, Lee Ann Whites, *The Civil War as a Crisis in Gender* (Athens: University of Georgia Press, 1995).

37. See correspondence of January 18 and February 13, 1866, Letters Sent, Department of Western South Carolina, entry 867, part 3, RG 393, NA.

38. "Jolly Took Off 92 Years Ago," *Anderson Independent,* January 29, 1958, MJC, PDC.

39. McConnell, "South Carolina Had Own Jesse James," *Anderson Daily Mail,* December 24, 1958.

40. Versions of this story appear in numerous articles and accounts, including "Manse Jolly, Celebrated Bushwhacker," clipping, *Lavonia Times,* February 15, 1919; "When Jolly Went After a Man," *Anderson Independent,* June 10, 1928; "The Joke Wasn't So Jolly," *Columbia State,* June 14, 1953; and "Town of Anderson Thrown into Uproar 64 Years Ago," *McCormick (SC) Messenger,* 1931, all in

MJC, PDC; "Jolly Took Off 92 Years Ago" and "Manse Jolly Took Last Ride Here 102 Years Ago," *Anderson Daily Mail,* January 29, 1968; Frank A. Dickson, "The Yankee Scourge," *Anderson Independent–Daily Mail,* May 25, 1975; Caroline S. Coleman, "Palmetto Robin Hood: How Jolly Avenged His Brothers," *Charleston News & Courier,* June 4, 1939; Newton, "Manse Jolly, Anderson Guerrilla," pt. 2, *Columbia State,* August 14, 1932. Undoubtedly the development of the story, including the character of Captain Bartow, owes much to Daniels's novel, *Maid of the Foot-Hills,* 242–45.

41. "When Jolly Went After a Man He Got Him," *Anderson Independent,* June 10, 1928.

42. "Manse Jolly Homeplace to Be Sold at Auction," *Anderson Independent,* November 13, 1966; Steve Biondo, "The Legend of Manse Jolly," *Anderson Independent,* April 12, 1981.

43. For sample versions of this particular story, not all of which agree on the date of January 29, 1866, see previously cited articles in *Columbia State,* December 25, 1958, August 14, 1932; *Anderson Independent,* November 13, 1966; *Anderson Daily Mail,* December 24, 1958, January 29, 1958, January 29, 1968; Lee, "The Rogue," 6; Frank A. Dickson, *Journeys into the Past: The Anderson Region's Heritage* (Anderson, SC, 1975), 120.

44. Frank A. Dickson, "Stream Claims Jolly—Yankees Couldn't," *Anderson Independent,* June 1, 1975, MJC, PDC. Jolly's letters from 1866 and 1867 indicate that he indeed owned a horse named Dixie that he prized highly and that he owned Dixie while he still lived in Anderson. Manse Jolly Letters, AUL.

45. Thomas E. Turner, "Legendary Rebel Lies in Remote Grave," clipping, *Dallas News,* 1965, MJC, PDC.

46. "Manse Jolly, Celebrated Bushwhacker," clipping, *Lavonia Times,* February 15, 1919, MJC, PDC.

47. Letter of James George Harper, Seneca, April 1926, MJC, PDC.

48. Robert T. Oliver, "A Faithful Heart: The Journals of Emmala Reed, 1866–1867" (MA thesis, Clemson University, 1997), 97.

49. Herd, *South Carolina Upcountry,* 2:399–404.

50. Ibid., 2:408.

51. See Letters Sent, Department of Western South Carolina, entry 867, part 3, RG 393, pp. 128–89, NA; Letters Sent, Department of South Carolina, entry 4088, part 1, vols. 16 and 46, RG 393, NA; correspondence of July 27 and October 2, 1865, vol. 15, pp. 396–401, 1459, Letters Received, Department of Western South Carolina, entry 870, part 1, RG 393, NA; Letters Received, Office of the Adjutant General, roll 512, M619, NA.

52. Keys, *Army and Crawford Keys,* 80; Herd, *South Carolina Upcountry,* 2:407.

53. Moore to Sickles, April 20, 1866, in Blake, "The Joke Wasn't So Jolly," *Columbia State,* June 14, 1953.

54. Trowbridge, "Six Months in the Freedmen's Bureau."

55. "Manson Jolly," *Anderson Intelligencer,* August 5, 1869.

56. Newton, "Manse Jolly, Anderson Guerrilla," pt. 1, *Columbia State,* August 7, 1932.

57. Kelly Davis, "Documentary to Feature Civil War Figure," *Anderson Independent-Mail,* February 27, 2005, p. 1B.

58. Minor, "Incidents of the Anderson Raid," 2:375.

59. Vandiver, *Traditions and History,* 228.

60. Ibid.

61. Newton, "Manse Jolly, Anderson Guerrilla," pt. 2, *Columbia State,* August 14, 1932.

62. "Manse Jolly, Celebrated Bushwhacker," *Lavonia Times,* February 15, 1919, MJC, PDC.

63. Vandiver, *Traditions and History,* 228; Franklin Acker, "The Story of Manse Jolly," *Anderson Independent,* March 4, 1962; "Manse Jolly's Old Home Still Standing," *Anderson Independent,* April 18, 1937; "Manse Jolly Took Last Ride Here," *Anderson Daily Mail,* January 29, 1968.

64. F. C. McConnell III, "South Carolina Had Own Jesse James," *Anderson Daily Mail,* December 24, 1958.

65. Deb Richardson-Moore, "Rebel Hero or Renegade Killer?" *Greenville (SC) News,* September 6, 1996. The novel was published as Wilton Earle, *Manse (One Man's War): A Biography Based on the Life and Legend of Manson Sherrill Jolly* (Atlanta: Adept Books, 1996). Despite the title, the book is actually a novel, not a biography. Other novels on Manse Jolly include Steve Biondo, *The True Story of Manse Jolly,* parts 1 and 2 (New York: iUniverse, 2002, 2004).

66. Joanne Thrift, "When the Novelist Met the Folk Legend," *Anderson Independent,* June 6, 1996, p. 7B. I have found no other evidence of either the location or existence of this diary.

67. David B. Burress, "Manse Jolly and Reconstruction and the Yankee Army of Occupation," 1939, MJC, PDC.

68. For more detailed consideration of a Confederate hero as a "ghost" or "ghost story," see Ashdown and Caudill, *Mosby Myth,* 65–66, 91, 116–19, 134, 137, 206.

69. Newton, "Manse Jolly, Anderson Guerrilla," pt. 2, *Columbia State,* August 14, 1932.

70. Steve Biondo, "Legend Feeds Mystique of Jolly House," *Anderson Independent,* April 19, 1981.

71. Nancy Stein, interview by author, 2005.

72. Blake, "The Joke Wasn't So Jolly," *Columbia State,* June 14, 1953.

73. Manson Jolly to "My Darling Sister," February 24, 1867, Manse Jolly Letters, AUL.

74. Manson Jolly to "Dear Sister," n.d., Cameron, TX, Manse Jolly Letters, AUL.

75. "R.E.D. Horse" (Manson Jolly) to "My Dear Sister," September 27, 1866, Manse Jolly Letters, AUL.

76. Manson Jolly to Mattie A. Jolly, January 28, 1867, Manse Jolly Letters, AUL.

77. Manson Jolly to "My Darling Sister," April 16, 1867, Manse Jolly Letters, AUL.

78. Manson Jolly to "My Darling Sister," February 24, 1867, Manse Jolly Letters, AUL.

79. Manson Jolly to "My Dear Sister," April 16, 1867, Manse Jolly Letters, AUL.

80. Joanne Thrift, "Manse Jolly: Warm-Hearted Warrior," *Anderson Independent,* January 29, 1976.

81. Martha Sheely, "Speaker Says Manse Jolly Man of Insight, Humor," *Anderson Independent,* October 16, 1975.

82. Manson Jolly to Anna Jolly, November 25, 1866, Manse Jolly Letters, AUL.

83. Manson Jolly to "My Darling Sister," February 24, 1867, Manse Jolly Letters, AUL.

“Nothing but Truth Is History”

William E. Connelley, William H. Gregg, and the Pillaging of Guerrilla History

Joseph M. Beilein Jr.

Like so many veterans of the Civil War, William H. Gregg recorded his experiences of the war during the first decade of the twentieth century. Unlike most other veterans of the war, however, Gregg had fought as a southern-sympathizing guerrilla on the Kansas-Missouri border under the leadership of William Clarke Quantrill. Characterized by hit-and-run tactics and waged around the guerrillas' homes and in the presence of women, children, and old men, warfare under Quantrill was a world apart from the conventional warfare that comes to mind when thinking of the Civil War. William E. Connelley, a writer and amateur historian, promised to publish Gregg's unique memoir on the condition that Gregg sold him the exclusive rights to the story. Gregg also promised to help Connelley research his own history of the border war. As Connelley's primary source, Gregg remarked that “nothing but truth is history” but that this essential quality had eluded the narrative of the guerrilla war. With this in mind, the old guerrilla explained that “if I don't tell the truth as far as I know it, then my work will be condemned. . . . The whole truth is going to be told . . . and when it is told, it will open the eyes of some people.” Indeed, “even Quantrill's men will be spoken of more in accord with their just deserts.”[1]

When Connelley published *Quantrill and the Border Wars* (1910), it became clear that he had written a much different history of the war than what Gregg had hoped. Although Gregg was a witness to the inner workings of the guerrilla war effort, many of his insights would be left out of

Connelley's book. Choosing an interesting idiom, Connelley claimed in the introduction of his book that "nothing has been written in a sensational way . . . and the old idea that truth is stranger than fiction is demonstrated." He used his evidence to fit a particular vision of the truth, however—a truth that appeared very strange to those who actually lived through and fought in the guerrilla war. After acquiring documents like the Gregg memoir, Connelley used only the passages that suited his needs and omitted portions that challenged or complicated his stark, two-dimensional image of the guerrilla as a wholly demonic character. Moreover, the publication of *Quantrill and the Border Wars* also revealed to Gregg that Connelley had no intention of publishing his memoir as a stand-alone piece. Without the publication of the memoir, Gregg's perspective on the war and his version of the truth were seemingly pushed out of sight. Through his piratical research tactics, Connelley effectively created a stock historical image of the southern-sympathizing guerrilla as a twisted, murderous, freebooting outlaw that is still an accepted part of mainstream Civil War history.[2]

This essay will investigate the process through which the (shaky) foundation of guerrilla history was constructed. It will look closely at the methods employed by Connelley in writing *Quantrill and the Border Wars.* In particular, I will examine Connelley's relationship with some of his more representative sources—both documentary evidence and the men and women whom he interviewed in the course of his research. His relationship with Gregg is of special interest because of the bond they formed and because of the ample written sources Gregg produced in an effort to help Connelley write his book. From there, I will look at the books produced by modern scholars. The works of these scholars, which are in keeping with the standards of the profession as it has come to exist, nevertheless project an image of the guerrilla that lines up with the contours of the guerrilla as sketched out by Connelley. In the end, this essay will demonstrate how the historical arguments of a long-dead amateur historian continue to dominate the field of guerrilla studies.[3]

Despite the lasting power of the image of the guerrilla that he created, Connelley's biases are easily recognizable. Albert Castel's observations in *William Clarke Quantrill: His Life and Times,* the first and only biography of Quantrill by a professional historian, are representative of those of later guerrilla scholars more generally. He offers heavy criticism of Connelley. *Quantrill and the Border Wars,* Castel observes, "is seriously impaired by Connelley's extreme pro-Union, pro-Kansas, and moralistic bias, which made it impossible for him to deal objectively, accurately, and fairly with so controversial and emotion-charged a subject as Quantrill and the border wars." While few other scholars list the major flaws in Connelley's approach to the history of the guerrilla conflict in such detail, his summation has generally been accepted by subsequent scholars.[4]

The origins of Connelley's perspective on the guerrillas can be traced all the way back to the war itself. Despite Castel's contention that Connelley's feelings on the war were grounded in his identity as a Kansan, they were in fact forged during his childhood in war-torn eastern Kentucky. While Gregg, Quantrill, and their comrades were waging a guerrilla war against Union troopers and the pro-Union populace of Kansas and Missouri, Connelley, who was born in 1855, watched as the war all but destroyed his family. His father left home and fought for the Union army. While Connelley's father was away, his mother died, leaving him orphaned, along with his siblings. When the war ended, his father returned a broken man. Growing up a Unionist in a divided slave state, the young Connelley undoubtedly blamed southern sympathizers for his family's plight. Also, it is likely that his original understanding of guerrilla warfare was derived not from firsthand accounts of the fighting on the Kansas-Missouri border but from what he had witnessed as a child and overheard in stories about the very different internecine conflict that raged in the Appalachian Mountains during the war. Indeed, Connelley's contrived depiction of Quantrill would bear a striking resemblance to the legend created around the antebellum and wartime career of Champ Ferguson—a desperate man with a track record of murder before and during the war.[5]

Whether his bias originated in Kentucky or Kansas, the direct catalyst for Connelley's book was his wish to counter a narrative of the guerrilla war already in existence. The infamous journalist John N. Edwards, in his 1877 publication *Noted Guerrillas,* romanticized the guerrillas' struggle, making them out to be virtuous heroes. Edwards was a Virginian who settled in Missouri in the 1850s and then fought as a Confederate officer under the famous cavalry commander Jo Shelby. He knew many of Quantrill's men personally, and after the war they would come to serve as sources for his "history." Edwards took his unabashed belief in the Confederate cause and combined it with flowery prose to create a heroic presentation of these men. *Noted Guerrillas* is not a true history but political propaganda, a counter-narrative to the wartime and postwar journalism of northern and Republican newspapers that painted the guerrillas as savages. Edwards's openly apologetic stance on the guerrillas contributed to the taint of any subsequent history of the guerrillas that did not castigate them as evil incarnate.[6]

Regardless of his motivations, Connelley did not originally present himself to Gregg as a guerrilla-hating Unionist. His bias was well hidden when the two men were introduced in 1902 and remained under wraps right up until the abrupt end of their eight-year relationship. It helped that Gregg was much too trusting. When he was introduced to Connelley, the old man was vulnerable: deathly ill, impoverished, and depressed. More than anything, he was desperate to tell his story to someone before he died. Harry L. Arnold—a shadowy figure in this story—was a special examiner for the U.S. Bureau of Pensions who introduced Gregg to Connelley. Of course, Connelley was more than willing to listen to Gregg's recollections of the war. As the relationship between the old guerrilla and the amateur historian grew, Arnold would continue to act as a go-between for Connelley, facilitating the purchase of Gregg's memoir and the rights to his story.[7]

Gregg began writing his memoir not long after meeting Connelley. He entitled it "A Little Dab of History without Embellishment." In his book Connelley referred to it as the "Gregg Manuscript," and it is this title that has been subsequently adopted by scholars of the war. The memoir is a bit more than one hundred handwritten pages recalling the guerrilla's time fighting in the bush. As best he could, Gregg remembered and scribbled down his experiences in the war from beginning to end, adding supplements to the memoir that came to mind only after he completed a draft. He was occasionally critical of his fellow guerrillas, but the account is a mostly favorable depiction of his cohort. Gregg clearly wanted to demonstrate that the guerrillas' service to the cause was as legitimate as the service of any other soldiers during the war. When he described combat, the document can be read as an honest and fairly accurate recollection of the events. The memoir can also be read for its omissions, however. Gregg fails to comment on the significance of slavery as a cause of the war or his family's ownership of slaves as a direct motivation for his personal involvement in the conflict. Despite his attempts to communicate the "whole truth," his own deeply imbedded morals and wartime politics clearly continued to shape his narrative.[8]

Whatever their biases, Connelley complimented Gregg as a patriot and a man and commended his memoir as a historical source. In a footnote in *Quantrill and the Border Wars,* the author reports that Gregg's memoir "is faithfully written and very accurate to have been written from mem-

Every bit a guerrilla, William H. Gregg is sketched here as he appeared in his prime. His beard was long, with a mustache draping over his lips. Although his hair was short, his dress—flashy bow-tied necktie, white shirt, and guerrilla shirt under a frock coat—was that of the flamboyant bushwhacker. (William E. Connelley, *Quantrill and the Border Wars* [Cedar Rapids, IA: Torch Press, 1910], 341)

ory alone." Moreover, Connelley opines that "the accounts are modest and truthful, and they are entirely devoid of the spirit of boast and brag." He calls Gregg "a worthy citizen" and states that "when the war was over it was over forever with Captain Gregg, and he immediately returned to his farm and took up the pursuits of peace, which he ever after cherished and followed." A genuine tone seems to emanate from Connelley's words.[9]

Gregg quickly became Connelley's authority on all things Quantrill and guerrilla. Connelley found Gregg to be an appealing ally in his research because the old guerrilla would give his work the credibility that came with an insider's testimony. For a man who had glorified the exploits of Jim Lane and John Brown in print, this sort of access was a hard thing to come by. Connelley used Gregg to get at all of the murky and near-mythical parts of the guerrillas' past. For instance, he was interested in John Noland, the black man who was rumored to have assisted the guerrillas. After numerous attempts to pin him down, Gregg got Noland to tell his story despite the old black man's wariness of outsiders like Connelley. Gregg told Connelley that at the beginning of his tale Noland stopped and interjected, "But . . . Befoh you go any further, sah, tell me of this might create any trouble sah."

Only after Gregg assured him "that it was only for the purpose of perpetuating history" did Noland tell his story.[10]

Noland's suspicions were well founded, however. The way that his story was used by Connelley points to a major flaw in the method through which *Quantrill and the Border Wars* was produced. Noland told his old comrade Gregg that he was sent by Quantrill "to find out the number of soldiers quartered in Lawrence." Once in Lawrence, Noland "counted one hundred and forty soldiers camped . . . but a portion of those left the day I was there." On his way back to meet with Quantrill, he was captured by Union soldiers and taken to Independence, where, he said, he "was offered $10,000 to betray Quantrill and his men, but refused." In custody, Noland was unable to tell Quantrill what he found at Lawrence. While he offered no evidence to back his claim, Connelley made the old man out to be a liar, saying in the text of his book that Noland "*insists* that Quantrill had gone on to raid before he returned." Connelley further asserted his implication by saying that Noland "seems afraid he might yet have trouble if he should admit that he saw Quantrill after he returned from Lawrence and before the raid. That Quantrill had accurate information of the situation at Lawrence there is no doubt."[11]

Gregg demonstrated in his handling of Connelley's inquiries that he would not dabble in embellishment. For example, Connelley asked Gregg what he knew of the affair at the Morgan Walker plantation when Quantrill first arrived in Jackson County. The old guerrilla responded by first telling Connelley, "I think I can tell you the facts in the case, not from participation, for I was not there." Then he went on to say, "But, before giving you a full rehearsal of the affair, I will try to find out the whereabouts of Andy Walker, son of Morgan, and get particulars from him." Deferring to an actual participant of the event before speculating or offering some falsehood says everything about Gregg's unwillingness to sway even slightly outside his principle that he could only report on what he had personally experienced. He does add one final word on the Walker affair, saying that he had "some doubts of the truth of the story" concerning an unnamed woman. Gregg was referring to Connelley's unfounded assertion that Quantrill engineered the Walker raid to impress Morgan Walker's daughter, Anna Slaughter.[12]

The affair at the Walker farm is one of the more mysterious and controversial events of the Quantrill story. Despite the darkness that surrounds the event, it has long served as a touchstone for the general denunciation of

Quantrill and the proslavery guerrilla war effort more generally. The "facts" as Gregg may have recounted them in the early twentieth century would have gone something like this: on December 10, 1860, Quantrill walked onto the Walker farm, where he found Andrew Walker. He told Walker that he had a proposition for his father, Morgan. Quantrill disclosed to Morgan Walker that he was a jayhawker and that his cohort planned to rob and kill Walker. Together with his neighbors and sons, Morgan Walker ambushed the three jayhawkers when they arrived, killing one and wounding another, while the third escaped untouched. To explain his actions, Quantrill told the Missourians a fabricated story composed of two major lies: that he was originally from the slave state of Maryland, even though he was from the free state of Ohio, and that he had a brother who was killed in Kansas by the same men whom he now betrayed, even though no such brother had been killed. The next day Quantrill was arrested for his own protection but was eventually released into the custody of the Walker family, who took him into their household.[13]

Connelley investigated, then speculated and ultimately contrived a tale as dishonest as Quantrill's backstory. He then dressed the new story up in the apparatus of historical scholarship: cited sources. Rather than abide by Gregg's wishes and defer to Andrew Walker on this point, Connelley used sources that lacked firsthand knowledge of the event in question. While Connelley cited a description of the raid produced by Walker, he immediately discounted it. Certainly, Walker's description was informed by his own pro-southern bias, but to push it aside completely was to ignore the only firsthand account in existence. Instead, Connelley relied upon the accounts of two men, John Dean and Albert Southwick, who were most likely *not* present at the Walker farm. The information that comes from Dean and Southwick presents Quantrill's cohort of Charles Ball, Chalkey Lipsey, and Edwin Morrison as benevolent Quakers out to save the world from the evils of slavery. Dean asserts that Quantrill pushed for the Walker raid for some time, and once at the Walker farm he found an excuse to leave his cohort and sell out his companions. That night, when they went to rob Morgan Walker, it was Quantrill who initiated the ambush on his companions, himself firing on Ball. According to Connelley, Morrison was killed at the farm that night. Ball and Lipsey escaped into the woods during the firefight, and Dean and Southwick escaped back to Kansas in a wagon. A day or two after the raid, Ball was shot down in the brush around the Walker farm and Lipsey was executed by Quantrill, who put his revolver in

Lipsey's mouth and pulled the trigger, leaving no one to tell his backstory but himself.[14]

Because of the sources he valued, Connelley's telling of the Morgan Walker raid differed from Andrew Walker's account, the most authoritative source on the event. Interestingly enough, Dean actually claimed that he was not present during the raid, removing any credibility from his words, and Southwick either was killed two days after the raid, in the brush around the Walker farm, or was simply not there. This left Walker's story as the most reliable one. He said that Quantrill did in fact come up to him and tell him what the other jayhawkers had planned and that he wished to betray them. However, that night, according to Walker, Quantrill did not even fire his weapon, nor did he kill Lipsey (who was actually named Southwick in Walker's rendition of the tale) two days later in the brush. It seemed that Quantrill was not all that desperate to cover up his past, as Connelley asserted. On Quantrill's lies, enough speculation has been published. It is significant to report, though, that once he gained entry into the southern community of Jackson County he confided the truth in Walker, revealing that his parents "had settled at Canal Dover, Ohio. Here he was born and grew up."[15]

Unlike the information Connelley acquired from Gregg, Walker's statement was originally procured by W. W. Scott. Having grown up in Canal Dover, Ohio, Scott was a boyhood acquaintance of Quantrill and an early researcher of the infamous guerrilla's career. After the war, he contacted participants and got them to speak on the more interesting events that occurred during the war. Scott, however, passed away before he could write his book, and Connelley was able to obtain his correspondence with the ex-guerrillas.[16]

In addition to Walker's letters, Connelley also grabbed up Fletch Taylor's letters from the Scott estate. He used one of Taylor's letters as evidence that Quantrill "kidnapped a girl named Kate Clarke and made her his mistress," subjecting her to a life well beyond the accepted norms of society and ultimately ruining her and turning her to prostitution. While he had little love for Quantrill, Taylor verified the existence of the girl but contradicted Connelley's assertions about Kate and Quantrill's relationship, saying that "she went willingly." Not letting Taylor have the final word, Connelley ended the note by stating, "*Others* say he kidnapped this girl and that it took her some time to become reconciled to the life to which he doomed her, but that she became infatuated with him, even wearing a man's clothing and riding in the ranks to be near him." The "others" were never cited or named.[17]

The rest of Taylor's letter, which exists in Connelley's papers but is not referenced in his book, described his commander as anything but a kidnapper or abuser of women. Taylor shared an interesting description of Quantrill's actions during the winter of 1863–1864, when many of the men spent their time and money in brothels in Sherman, Texas. Of Quantrill, Taylor noted that "he staid in camp most all the time while the rest of his officers were having a good time in riding in Gen Blunts buggy [and] ambulance." According to Taylor, Quantrill did not go to the brothels with his other, joy-riding captains, and he even discouraged such behavior. Along with confrontations with his own fun-loving men, notably Bill Anderson and George Todd, Quantrill, according to Taylor, had disagreements with other men in Texas, in particular Jim Crow Chiles. Chiles was a Missourian who owned the Sherman saloon and brothel from where most of the guerrillas' troubles that winter seemed to emanate. The sources Connelley collected during his research and even cited in making his argument actually illustrated that whatever the guerrillas' problem was with Quantrill, it was not his treatment of women.[18]

We do not know how Scott might have used Taylor's and Walker's correspondence or what sort of assurances, if any, he gave the two men regarding their stories. Connelley, however, in no uncertain terms made promises to Gregg about the type of history he would write. In a letter toward the end of their correspondence, dated June 30, 1909, Connelley told Gregg the lengths he had gone to in writing a fair history of the war. Connelley said, "I also say that the honor of no woman was violated at Lawrence, and I enumerate instances where many guerrillas interposed and saved lives. . . . I have tried to state just the facts." He made sure to reiterate that he did not "believe the raid was justifiable . . . and many of the guerrillas were needlessly brutal and murderous," but noted that, to provide balance, "instances of kindness and manliness must be credited to even them if they did any."[19]

While Connelley's papers reveal a great number of discrepancies between his sources and the way he presented information from them in his book, the Gregg memoir was pillaged more than any other. This looting can best be seen in the way in which Connelley handled Gregg's description of the massacre at Lawrence, Kansas, where, on August 21, 1863, several hundred guerrillas killed around 180 unarmed men and boys, set a few hundred buildings on fire, and took money, stock, and household goods from the town's residents. Rather than attempt to understand how such an atrocity came about, Connelley omitted from his book what Gregg called the "dastardly acts . . . that caused the raid on Lawrence." In his memoir, Gregg described what he called "one circumstance in illustration of a hundred other similar ones," in which Union soldiers and jayhawkers went to the homes of two southern-sympathizing families, put their houses to the torch, abused the white women, and assassinated two old men for aiding the guerrillas. These attacks, according to Gregg, became so prevalent that dozens of men flocked to Quantrill's banner in the summer of 1863 and clamored for a counterstrike. Connelley, who turned a blind eye toward the series of events that culminated in the raid, presented the guerrillas as unprovoked monsters lusting after blood.[20]

When he was not omitting portions of the Gregg memoir, Connelley actually used Gregg's words to denounce the guerrillas' motives. Gregg recorded that Quantrill told his officers, "'We can get more revenge and more money [in Lawrence] than anywhere else in the State of Kansas,'" which Connelley used and cited accurately. Ripping this quotation from context, however, he expounded on these motives, saying, "Revenge was well enough for the others of the band. For [Quantrill], money, money." In this way, Connelley depicted the guerrillas as men who were driven exclusively by self-interest. But when this quotation is returned to its proper context, Quantrill and his cohort do not appear quite as much the money-hungry, bloodthirsty demons Connelley depicted. Gregg stated that Quantrill told his officers that "all the plunder, (or the bulk of it) stolen from [Missouri] will be found stored away in Lawrence." In taking the war to their enemies' households, the guerrillas hoped to recover what had been taken from their own homes. Furthermore, Gregg recalled that Quantrill said to him, "I want to compensate the people who have and, still will divide their last biscuit with us" and "whatever money that may be gotten at Lawrence will be divided among the men with instructions to give to those people very liberally." This final statement appears in Connelley's work. Rather than position it with the overall motivations for going to Lawrence, however, Connelley tacks it to the very end of the section regarding the raid.[21]

Connelley also suppressed important evidence regarding the massacre itself. In what would appear to be an exhaustive, 130-page description of the events at Lawrence, Connelley painted the citizens of the town as innocent victims. However, the Gregg memoir illustrated the direct involvement of the townspeople of Lawrence in jayhawking, or the raiding of Missouri

William E. Connelley presented himself as a professional scholar. He wore the uniform of a principled and bona fide historian with a dapper haircut, kempt mustache, white shirt, necktie, and suit jacket, reaffirming his promises of measured and academic research. (William E. Connelley, *A Standard History of Kansas and Kansans,* vol. 1 [Chicago: Lewis Publishing Company, 1918], frontispiece)

to liberate enslaved people, steal anything of worth, and kill slaveholders and their kin. During the massacre, Gregg claimed to have "found about forty shanties, built, three sides boards, the fourth a hay stack and covered with hay, all of these shacks were filled with household effects, stolen from Missouri." According to Gregg, inside the shacks were "feather beds, quilts, blankets [etc.] stacked in them higher than I could reach, [and] fine bedstands, bureaus, sideboards, bookcases and pianos that cost thousands of dollars." He knew the goods that filled these shanties were from Missouri because he recognized them. The treasure trove of the jayhawkers' loot was under the care of some black women whom Gregg recognized as well. One woman he remembered "distinctly, was the property of Col Steel who lived near Sibley Jackson County, Missouri." Not only was Lawrence a refuge for liberated and runaway slaves, but it served as a depot for the household goods taken from the guerrillas' homes. From Gregg's perspective, the citizens of Lawrence were complicit in the violence unleashed by jayhawkers and were the direct beneficiaries of their booty, a perspective based on the evidence he had seen with his own eyes.[22]

In a move that appears to have been both premeditated and vindictive, Connelley successfully buried Gregg's recollection of the events surrounding the Lawrence raid. While Gregg's letters showed that he believed that the rights to his story were owned by Connelley all along, documents reveal that Arnold, the pension examiner, was actually the first owner of the memoir. In 1902 Arnold offered Gregg ninety dollars for his memoir, and the old, impoverished guerrilla took him up on the offer. The contract required that "Gregg was not to write another either directly or indirectly." In January 1908 Connelley finalized his purchase of the rights to the Gregg memoir from Arnold for "the sum of one hundred and fifty dollars ($150)," which would be paid out of whatever profits he might earn from sales of the memoir. Years later, in a document that was intended to trace his legal ownership of the memoir, Connelley said, "As there never were any profits I suppose he will never get his money."[23]

Gregg's reaction to being buffaloed by Connelley was predictable: his frustration quickly turned to anger, and his anger manifested as a fervent and self-righteous defense of his wartime actions. Preceding the publication of *Quantrill and the Border Wars,* Gregg had respected the terms of his contract and maintained a conciliatory tone toward his old enemies. After the book was released the old guerrilla's attitude darkened. In a 1910 edition of the *Kansas City Times,* Gregg proclaimed, "I was at Lawrence. . . . I never denied it. We went there to burn and kill and we did it." He continued, "They said we killed citizens in Lawrence. . . . That's not so. There wasn't a citizen in the whole state of Kansas." Rather, he explained, "They were all soldiers—every man big enough to carry a gun was a soldier—and we killed them in retaliation for the killing by the Redlegs."[24]

Gregg died in 1916, some six years after the publication of Connelley's book, assuming that his story died along with him. Obviously, Gregg's memoir was not lost. It eventually came to be held by the manuscript collection at the State Historical Society of Missouri, where it has remained only partially excavated. The original manuscript has been cited and presumably read by a number of historians of the guerrilla war. However, these scholars tend to recycle the same passages of the memoir that appear in Connelley's work or to use excerpts from Gregg's postpublication diatribes that appeared in the newspapers rather than the memoir itself. Certainly these oft-cited passages from Gregg's memoir and the newspapers have important value and are deserving of reexploration with the tools of modern historical analysis, which they have received. However, it is easy to see that as long as the same passages serve as the linchpins of guerrilla histories, the narrative of the guerrilla war will continue to be held together by these anecdotes. Such self-imposed research limits restrict the shape of the guerrilla in guerrilla history to something eerily close to Connelley's caricature.[25]

Generally speaking, guerrilla memoirs like Gregg's are not taken seriously by modern scholars. Michael Fellman, in *Inside War,* argues that guerrillas like Gregg used their postwar memoirs and recollections to construct a memory narrative of the war in which they were forced, as a last resort, to act violently in defense of themselves and their loved ones against the true antagonists, the jayhawkers and their Yankee allies. He further contends that these memoirs were an attempt by the guerrillas to justify unjustifiable acts of violence in order to wipe clean their guilty consciences. Guerrilla-produced sources were infected by the same amnesia that was so contagious during the infamous period of sectional reunification. In his seminal work, *Race and Reunion,* David Blight argues that "the forces of reconciliation overwhelmed the emancipationist vision in the national culture" and "the inexorable drive for reunion both used and trumped race." Blight points to the resulting narrative of the war at the turn of the century that was accepting of the southern perspective on the war and made Confederate leaders into national heroes, even if a few writers, like Connelley, were able to resist this force. In keeping with the literary fashion of the day, the guerrillas' recollections were inlaid with Lost Cause imagery and void of almost any discussion of slavery.[26]

While they have discarded the guerrillas' memoirs as rotten, modern scholars continue to accept the fruit of Connelley's historical bushwhacking. It is possible that Connelley's personal politics and sense of morality, both of which were admirable, have endeared him to modern historians of the war who tend to look past the obvious flaws of his work. For instance, in the very same footnote in which Castel points out his predecessor's extreme bias, he adds, "Fortunately, however, Connelley reprinted in the book most of the documentary material and interviews he had obtained. . . . Except where otherwise indicated, this information provides the basis for this chapter." It is possible that he did not realize the selective nature of his predecessor's reprinting. Nevertheless, the continued popularity of Castel's work has ensured the survival of Connelley's ideas over the years. Although more modern scholars do not as explicitly defer to Connelley as Castel does, his work continues to be cited without caveat, his ideas seemingly swallowed whole.[27]

Castel's first chapter, the one in which the above footnote appears, is merely a condensed version of Connelley's "seriously impaired" work. Castel presents Connelley's questionable material immediately before or after what can only be insincere qualifications. An example is Castel's statement that "we no longer believe in the hereditary transfer of character traits. *But if we did,* we could make much out of Quantrill's immediate ancestry." He then goes on to point out a few rogues in Quantrill's lineage. Then he reports, "The meager records which have come down to us concerning Quantrill's childhood depict a juvenile monster." After detailing the acts of this monster, he says it would be wise to take these reports with "more than a little skepticism." He follows Connelley in portraying the "criminal tendencies on Quantrill's part," when he went out to the West. Castel sums up Quantrill by saying he was a young man "who desired wealth and success, but who was impatient and impotent in their quest; who came to resent his failure and the world which caused it." In Castel's mind, Quantrill was a paranoid, to which he added, "And paranoids make history—which is unfortunate for mankind." Finally, Castel implies that the Missourian's cause during the Civil War was an extension of Quantrill's outlaw past. He contends that "Quantrill's year of banditry in Kansas was his apprenticeship," presumably for his success as a guerrilla chieftain. Whatever the caveats in which Castel wraps the observations regarding Quantrill that he has essentially lifted from Connelley, a bell cannot be unrung, and the ringing echoes into the present day.[28]

Castel believes that his view of the war is located in some objective place. In the 1999 edition of *William Clarke Quantrill,* Castel proclaims victoriously that, unlike Connelley and Edwards, in his first edition he "was able to remain objective and avoid partisan writing. . . . Although a native of Kansas, I had no prejudice against Missouri." He then channels Abraham Lincoln, citing a letter from the president to one of his generals in which Lincoln advised the general on how to deal with being in the middle of two opposed political groups. Lincoln contended that he would prefer to be abused by both factions or by neither faction, but, he warned, "Beware of being assailed by one and praised by the other." Castel then goes on to say of the first publication of the biography, "some have denounced its characterization of Quantrill and the guerrillas as too harsh, whereas others have condemned it for being too lenient."[29]

Unfortunately, this practice of writing a caveat into works of history on Missouri's guerrilla war continues with seemingly every work published on the topic. Whether the authors are themselves protecting against criticism or whether they actually believe that they could be objective, the whole matter is problematic. Castel's self-positioning in some locationless place is a false turning point in the way that scholars of the guerrilla war view their subject. There is no doubt that a move away from the old partisan histories characterized by the North vs. the South or Kansas vs. Missouri was a necessary step to advance the field. However, because it is human beings who write history, it is a given that each scholar will bring a certain perspective to his or her work, either explicitly or implicitly. This perspective guides what sources we use, how we read those sources, and the choice of any methodological or analytical framework we might apply to our study. Each time that a scholar claims to be studying the guerrilla war from an inherently impossible "objective" place, a famous line from Shakespeare's *Hamlet* comes to mind: "The lady doth protest too much, methinks." Preemptive defenses against bias in the early pages of a book make it difficult to trust what follows. Viewing the past from some nowhere place makes everything that Castel sees an extension of where he sits. In this case, Castel seems to be sitting on what he believes to be the more legitimate position. With this in mind, it makes sense that he brackets the body of his work in between a prologue titled "The Border Ruffians" and an epilogue titled "The Bandits." From Castel's perspective, the origins and the results of the guerrilla war were illegitimate.[30]

Even though the cracked and weakened foundation laid down by Connelley's narrative created a number of flawed themes that continue through the histories of the war, much of the base is strong and must remain. We must not completely undercut a critically important correction in the path on which the history of the guerrilla war was moving. *Quantrill and the Border Wars* is a massive tome and an impressive undertaking of research, even if it is not completely transparent in its presentation of research. Although it must be treated with care and viewed almost as a primary source itself, Connelley's work has important contributions to make even today. As a history, *Quantrill and the Border Wars* certainly captured a view of the guerrillas from the perspective of the Kansan. Furthermore, when considering the context in which Connelley wrote his book, his methods were not that far out of step. Conventional historians—trained academics—had only recently begun to practice professional history in America, and untrained amateurs coexisted alongside their degree-carrying counterparts without an obvious indication of which practice would come to dominate the study of the past.[31]

However, in his history of the war, Connelley's presentation of the *actual* guerrillas amounts to little more than a blurry rendering, framed by the trappings of professional history. A close inspection of *Quantrill and the Border Wars* reveals that little substance is used to prop-up this flimsy façade. Connelley so scorched the essence of the information from his guerrilla-supplied sources that when the words of the guerrillas do appear in the book, it is too often in the form of empty, offhand remarks and footnotes. What substance there is in the book was cobbled together from documents that were written on county byways, in garrisoned towns, and from the hills of eastern Kansas, all places high above the dark guerrilla haunts down in the Missouri brush and river bottoms. Writing from great temporal, physical, political, and moral distances, Connelley had to strain to see into the Missouri woods. Despite claiming to write the history of Quantrill and his guerrilla band, he could not bring himself to join them in the brush, so to speak.[32]

It is ironic, then, that the men who had the best view of Quantrill and his guerrilla band were cut from Connelley's history. It is possible that this irony was lost on the amateur historian. While it is evident that Connelley worked to push rival narratives of the war out of the historical conversation, it is unclear how conscious he was at the time he was writing of the power of his own perspective on the narrative he wrote. What is clear is that the very same memoirs and postwar recollections of the guerrillas that have been all but eliminated as credible sources for use by scholars also happen to hold the keys to unlocking the misunderstood inner workings of the guerrilla war. The very nature of guerrilla warfare as unconventional, informal, organic, free, and highly mobile made oral communication the preferred method. Written orders, reports, ledgers, and any other records or correspondence were both unnecessary and difficult to regulate or maintain. As such, very little primary source material was produced inside the guerrilla movement *during* the war and most of what there was did not survive. Instead, whatever orders, conversations, gestures, or debates were communicated, heard, and otherwise observed out in the brush were left as imprints on the minds of men. Very few of the guerrillas survived the war and lived long enough to convert those memories into written words. Gregg, Walker, John McCorkle, Cole Younger, and a handful of others recorded their recollections of the war. These sources need to be read with a critical eye, and if we intend to understand the guerrillas as they understood themselves—and not just an outsider's image of them—they must be used. Whatever their flaws—omissions, hyperbole, the occasional outright lie—they are the best record we have of the mysterious inner world of the guerrillas.[33]

In trying to contribute to the history of the Civil War, Gregg was bushwhacked by Connelley. He went out looking to set the record straight, was lured in, and was ambushed. Like an experienced bushwhacker skulking through the densely wooded timber bottoms of Missouri, Connelley sensed that his prey was out of his depth, moving in unfamiliar country for the first time. Gregg had neither the skill nor the resources to influence the shape of Civil War history. Even though he was present in the brush with Quantrill, Gregg's own naïveté, lack of education, and desperation made his efforts worse than futile. He had unwittingly helped his enemy kill off and bury a piece of history.[34]

Connelley bushwhacked Gregg because his story was dangerous. Gregg believed that "the whole truth [was] going to be told" and that his story would contribute to it. His lengthy narrative was meant to fill in the many blank spots left in the record by the documentary silence on the part of the guerrillas during the war. With contributions like his own, the old guerrilla believed, "Even Quantrill's men will be spoken of more in accord with their just deserts." Given the substance of Gregg's memoir and his correspondence with Connelley, by "just deserts" Gregg did not mean that his cohort should be thought of as heroes. Instead, he wanted readers to understand the death and destruction his people faced, while he conceded that the guerrillas had killed and destroyed the people they believed to be their enemies. Most of all, Gregg wanted readers—his peers, the postwar generation, and outsiders to the guerrilla conflict—to see the war through his eyes. The Gregg memoir was lost to them, but it has been found and awaits us in its box in the basement of Ellis Library. For those who are willing to read it with some measure of historical empathy, it can serve as a knothole through which we might see the unique world of the guerrilla. The risk, of course, in reading the memoir in this way is that we might come away seeing the guerrillas as human beings—ugly, imperfect, bloody, slaveholding, and proud—but human nonetheless.[35]

Notes

1. William H. Gregg to William E. Connelley, December 8, 1903, McCain Library and Archives, University of Southern Mississippi, Hattiesburg.

2. Peter Novick, *That Noble Dream: The "Objectivity Question" and the American Historical Profession* (Cambridge: Cambridge University Press, 1988). Novick

demonstrates the futility of the quest for objective truth and the evolution of the profession toward an acceptance of history as a construction. Nevertheless, the profession created standards along the way so that the methods and presentation of research by professional historians would prevent the deliberate falsification of history. William E. Connelley, *Quantrill and the Border Wars* (Cedar Rapids, IA: Torch Press, 1910), 5, 6, 7, 222. For archival location of the source material used in this paper, see William Elsey Connelley Collection, Denver Public Library; William C. Quantrill Collection, McCain Library and Archives, University of Southern Mississippi; William H. Gregg, "A Little Dab of History without Embellishment," memoir, Western Historical Manuscript Collection, State Historical Society of Missouri, Columbia; William H. Gregg to William E. Connelley, December 8, 1903, McCain Library and Archives, University of Southern Mississippi.

3. Connelley, *Quantrill and the Border Wars.* In addition to Castel's biography, for works on the guerrilla war by modern scholars, see Michael Fellman, *Inside War: The Guerrilla Conflict in Missouri during the American Civil War* (New York: Oxford University Press, 1990); Daniel Sutherland, *A Savage Conflict: The Decisive Role of Guerrillas in the American Civil War* (Chapel Hill: University of North Carolina Press, 2009); Robert Mackey, *The Uncivil War: Irregular Warfare in the Upper South, 1861–1865* (Norman: University of Oklahoma Press, 2004).

4. Albert Castel, *William Clarke Quantrill: His Life and Times* (New York: F. Fell, 1962), 23. Although she takes a very different stance than Castel in her study of the guerrilla war, LeeAnn Whites agrees with Castel in this particular observation of Connelley. She says that Connelley, "a Kansan, was not particularly positive in his evaluation of the guerrillas and their war, especially their leader, William Clarke Quantrill." Whites, "Forty Shirts and a Wagon Load of Wheat: Women, the Domestic Supply Line, and the Civil War on the Western Border," *Journal of the Civil War Era* 1, no. 1 (March 2011): 56–78, 69.

5. Brian McKnight, *Confederate Outlaw: Champ Ferguson and the Civil War in Appalachia* (Baton Rouge: Louisiana State University Press, 2011); McKnight, *Contested Borderland: The Civil War in Appalachian Kentucky and Virginia* (Lexington: University Press of Kentucky, 2006). For specific mentions of Johnson County, Kentucky, see McKnight, *Contested Borderland,* 89, 98, 156, 192. For a description of internal divisions within a community similar to the one in which Connelley grew up, see Ralph Mann, "Ezekiel Count's Sand Lick Company: Civil War and Localism in the Mountain South," in *The Civil War in Appalachia: Collected Essays,* ed. Kenneth Noe and Shannon Wilson (Knoxville: University of Tennessee Press, 1997), 78–103. Without making too much of it, the personal nature of Connelley's distain for Quantrill was also shaped by his strange connection with his subject in that, up to a point, they shared the same life track. Both men were born into families with northern or Unionist leanings. Quantrill had a passion for learning that was fed by his schoolmaster father. Despite working at manual labor with his father, an equally inquisitive Connelley was able to educate himself.

Like Quantrill, Connelley went on to teach school at a young age near his home. Both men were forced to teach in an effort to help support their single parents and siblings—whereas Connelley lost his mother at an early age, Quantrill lost his father as a teenager. Again, unwittingly following in the footsteps of Quantrill, Connelley decided to set out to make his way in the West and arrived in Kansas a little more than two decades after the guerrilla chieftain had. Once in Wyandotte County, he too taught school, just as Quantrill had done in the years before the Civil War. It was at this point that the two paths diverged. Quantrill defected to Missouri and became a rebel guerrilla, while Connelley was left without any great cause for which to fight. History became Connelley's way to fight the war that had done so much harm to his family and to elevate his decision to stay the course over Quantrill's choice to turn his back on his people. See "William Elsey Connelley," in *A Standard History of Kansas and Kansans* (Chicago: Lewis, 1918), transcribed at KSGenWeb.com, http://www.ksgenweb.com/archives/1918ks/bioc/connelwe2.html.

6. While the praise can be found throughout, see especially Edwards's first chapter, on Quantrill, in *Noted Guerrillas; or, The Warfare of the Border* (St. Louis: H. W. Brand, 1879), 31–49. For those who have offered less negative images of the guerrillas, see Richard S. Brownlee, *Gray Ghosts of the Confederacy: Guerrilla Warfare in the West, 1861–1865* (Baton Rouge: Louisiana State University Press, 1958); Donald R. Bowen, "Guerrilla War in Western Missouri: 1862–1865: Historical Extensions of the Relative Deprivation Hypothesis," *Comparative Studies in Society and History* 19 (January 1977): 30–51; Bowen, "Quantrill, James, Younger, et al.: Leadership in a Guerrilla Movement, Missouri, 1861–1865," *Military Affairs* 41 (February 1977): 42–48. Also see a representative example of amateur history on the subject in Donald Hale, *We Rode with Quantrill: Quantrill and the Guerrilla War as Told by the Men and Women Who Were with Him, with a True Sketch of Quantrill's Life* (Kansas City: D. R. Hale, 1992). Matthew Hulbert discusses Edwards's role in the creation of Missouri's unique Lost Cause ideology and offers helpful perspective and depth in the discussion about the significance of Edwards. See Hulbert, "Constructing Guerrilla Memory: John Newman Edwards and Missouri's Irregular Lost Cause," *Journal of the Civil War Era* 2, no. 1 (March 2012): 58–81.

7. William E. Connelley Papers, McCain Library and Archives, University of Southern Mississippi.

8. For information about the origins of Gregg, "Little Dab of History," see the finding aid for the document at American Civil War collection Descriptions, Manuscript Collection, State Historical Society of Missouri, http://shs.umsystem.edu/manuscripts/invent/1113.pdf. The historical society also puts the completion date at 1906, some three years after Gregg first gave the piece to Connelley. The most likely reason for this presumption is that a letter dated 1906 accompanies the manuscript, although the letter in no way refers to the manuscript or its completion. If anything suggests 1906 as a completion date it is the fact that the memoir

was apparently written by Gregg in two installments, in addition to other, smaller supplements that accompany the bulk of the memoir, all of which may not have been finished until 1906 or even later.

9. Connelley, *Quantrill and the Border Wars,* 222.

10. Gregg to Connelley, May 14, 1903, November 26, 1904, McCain Library, University of Southern Mississippi.

11. Gregg to Connelley, November 26, 1904, McCain Library, University of Southern Mississippi; Connelley, *Quantrill and the Border Wars,* 310 (emphasis added).

12. Gregg to Connelley, December 2, 1904, McCain Library, University of Southern Mississippi; Connelley, *Quantrill and the Border Wars,* 197–98.

13. Joanne Chiles Eakin, ed., *Recollections of Quantrill's Guerrillas: As Told by A. J. Walker of Weatherford, Texas to Victor E. Martin in 1910* (1910; reprint, Independence, MO: Two Trails, 1996), 3–9; 1860 U.S. Federal Manuscript Census, Jackson County, MO, pp. 112, 161. According to the 1860 census, Morgan Walker's household had four white members: Morgan; his wife, Polly; his son Zachariah; and a boy named John Carroll, who may have been a grandson. Morgan Walker owned twenty-five slaves. Andrew Walker lived nearly next door, and his household consisted of only him and his wife. He did not own any slaves.

14. Connelley, *Quantrill and the Border Wars,* 140–65. This section of Connelley's work contains transcribed letters from Walker to Scott that predate Walker's published recollections by some twenty years, but Walker's story remains consistent on the important points discussed here. Eakin, *Recollections of Quantrill's Guerrillas,* 1–12.

15. Eakin, *Recollections of Quantrill's Guerrillas,* 1–12. Walker refers to one of Quantrill's travelling companions as Gillespie, who most likely is the same man as Connelley's Lipsey.

16. Connelley, *Quantrill and the Border Wars,* 6. The Connelley Collection at the Denver Public Library has an extensive pile of notes and transcriptions showing what Connelley pulled from Scott's research.

17. Connelley, *Quantrill and the Border Wars,* 282–83. For a history of Kate Clarke, see LeeAnn Whites, "The Tale of Three Kates: Outlaw Women, Loyalty, and Missouri's Long Civil War," in *Weirding the War: Stories from the Civil War's Ragged Edges,* ed. Stephen Berry (Athens: University of Georgia Press, 2011), 73–94.

18. Connelley, *Quantrill and the Border Wars,* 282–83; Fletch Taylor letters to W. W. Scott, file 3, box 1, series 1, Connelley Collection, Denver Public Library; Eakin, *Recollections of Quantrill's Guerrillas,* 80–83; John McCorkle, *Three Years with Quantrill: A True Story Told by His Scout,* written by O. S. Barton (1914; reprint, Norman: University of Oklahoma Press, 1992), 144; Gregg, "Little Dab of History," 86–88; Union general James G. Blunt's buggy and ambulance were taken in the wake of the guerrillas' successful ambush of Blunt's column at the Battle of Baxter Springs.

19. Connelley to Gregg, June 30, 1909, McCain Library, University of Southern Mississippi.

20. Gregg, "Little Dab of History," 51, 52. For another work that demonstrates the lasting influence of Unionist politics on Connelley, even at the turn of the century, see Connelley, *John Brown* (Topeka: Crane, 1900).

21. Connelley, *Quantrill and the Border Wars,* 298–99, 308–9, 419–20; Gregg, "Little Dab of History," 47, 76. For a more developed discussion of household-centered warfare, see Victoria Bynum, *Unruly Women: The Politics of Social and Sexual Control in the Old South* (Chapel Hill: University of North Carolina Press, 1992), 130–50; Kristen Streater, "'She-Rebels' on the Supply Line: Gender Conventions in Civil War Kentucky," in *Occupied Women: Gender, Military Occupation, and the American Civil War,* ed. LeeAnn Whites and Alecia Long (Baton Rouge: Louisiana State University Press, 2009), 11, 88–89; also see Whites, "Forty Shirts."

22. Gregg, "Little Dab of History," 59–60.

23. Gregg to Connelley, February 26, 1907; contract between Arnold and Connelley, January 18, 1908, Topeka, Kansas; and Affidavit by William E. Connelley, March 30, 1918, McCain Library, University of Southern Mississippi.

24. *Confederate Veteran,* May 1907, 279; *Kansas City Times,* August 20, 1910.

25. For an example of the ways in which modern scholars have used Gregg's memoir, "Little Dab of History," see Fellman, *Inside War,* 247–63. In making his argument that guerrilla-produced sources cannot be trusted, as they were filled with romantic embellishments, Fellman augments the document with his own words. He states that Gregg recounts the attacks by Union soldiers on the Saunders and Crawford families, and in response to these attacks, "Gregg had disregarded all danger, whipped out his pistols, and killed both men," pursuant to the claim that "defense of womankind was Gregg's retrospective justification for having acted as a killer." In reality, Gregg makes no such claim about killing anyone in the manner described above in that part of his manuscript. Moreover, there is no mention by Gregg anywhere in his manuscript of actions that resemble the description offered by Fellman. As guerrillas begin to take center stage alongside the traditional actors of the Civil War's grand narrative, it is critical that the underpinnings of scholarly research on the topic be planted in firm ground and that the standards of the historical profession be closely observed. See Fellman, *Inside War,* 255–56, 307n; Gregg, "Little Dab of History," 47–52. The following is a side-by-side comparison of Fellman's use of this particular passage of the Gregg memoir and the memoir itself. The passage from Fellman's work reads, "William Gregg claimed that one day he had been standing by while Union men burned Mrs. Crawford's house. When two of the Union men had 'snatched a lace cap from [her] head and threw it into the flames of the burning building,' Gregg had disregarded all danger, whipped out his pistols, and killed both men." However, the following is from Gregg, "Little Dab of History," 51–52 (which Fellman erroneously cites as pages 48–49):

> The scout arriving at the house of Saunders first, divided, one half going to

Crawfords. Mrs. Saunders and her daughter prepared dinner for the half stopping there, the Col. Furnished feed for their horses. All went well until dinner was over, (mind you the snow was fourteen inches deep with the mercury 10 below zero) when Col Saunders was placed under guard the house burned, the women not allowed a bonnet or shawl. On leaving Saunders place, they told the wife they were going to take Col. to Independence, and, make him take the oath. On the arrival of this party at Crawfords, practically the same scenes were enacted, except, they snatched a lace cap from the head of Mrs. Crawford and, threw in the flames of the burning building, they also told Mrs. Crawford that the men would not be hurt. On their way to Independence arriving at the house of James Burrus, they dismounted Crawford and, Saunders and shot them to death. It was such dastardly acts as the foregoing that caused the raid on Lawrence.

26. Fellman, *Inside War,* 247–63; David Blight, *Race and Reunion: The Civil War in American Memory* (Cambridge: Harvard University Press, 2001), 2–3; Castel, *William Clarke Quantrill,* 23; Sutherland, *Savage Conflict,* 307, 377, 397.

27. Ibid. Fellman cites Connelley without qualification; see *Inside War,* 295n95.

28. Castel, *William Clarke Quantrill,* 23, 24, 27, 42, 43 (italics added).

29. Albert Castel, *William Clarke Quantrill: His Life and Times* (Norman: University of Oklahoma Press, 1999), x, xi. Like Castel, more modern historians of the guerrilla war believe that they write from a locationless place or that their location will not adversely influence their work. Fellman promises a new, more evolved brand of historical analysis. He says, "I seek to describe, without romanticizing them but also without degrading or dismissing them, ordinary nineteenth-century Americans going through terrible times." Continuing, he states, "Becoming contemptuous is a danger for peaceful academics deploying their cool medium to discuss violence. My subjects were neither heroic nor contemptible but ordinary people trying to sort out personal and cultural experience and meaning in an overwhelmingly stressful situation." See Fellman, *Inside War,* xx.

30. Castel, *William Clarke Quantrill,* 1–21, 216–32. While she contains her discussion of Susan Bordo's "view from nowhere" to gender in the writing of history, LeeAnn Whites offers a helpful framework for understanding how perspective and perception play out in power relations in *The Civil War as a Crisis in Gender: Augusta, Georgia, 1860–1890* (Athens: University of Georgia Press, 1995), 1–14. For the original location of the idiom, see William Shakespeare, *Hamlet, Prince of Denmark,* act 3, scene 2.

31. Peter Novick lays out the early history of the profession in *That Noble Dream.*

32. Connelley, *Quantrill and the Border Wars,* 140–65.

33. Beyond Gregg's memoir there are a number of others that contain important historical insights, including McCorkle, *Three Years with Quantrill;* Hamp Watts, *Babe of the Company: An Unfolded Leaf from the Forest of Never-to-Be-Forgotten Years* (Fayette MO: Democrat-Leader Press, 1913); James Cummings, *Jim*

Cummins, the Guerrilla (Excelsior Springs, MO: Daily Journal, 1908); Eakin, *Recollections of Quantrill's Guerrillas;* Harrison Trow, *Charles W. Quantrell: A True History of his Guerrilla Warfare on the Missouri and Kansas Border during the Civil War of 1861 to 1865,* ed. and written by J. P. Burch (Vega, TX: J. P. Burch, 1923); Cole Younger, *The Story of Cole Younger, by Himself* (St. Paul: Minnesota Historical Society Press, 2000). For additional analysis of the guerrilla memoirs, see Matthew C. Hulbert's chapter on the subject, "Rebooting Guerrilla Memory in the Twentieth Century," in "Guerrilla Memory: Irregular Recollections from the Civil War Border Lands" (PhD diss., University of Georgia, 2015).

34. Gregg, "Little Dab of History."

35. William H. Gregg to William E. Connelley, December 8, 1903, McCain Library and Archives, University of Southern Mississippi.

Afterword

Victoria E. Bynum

Guerrilla warfare—brutal, savage, and frequently characterized as "uncivilized" (particularly when practiced by one's enemies)—was long treated by historians, if treated at all, as a deviant slice of the American Civil War. Michael Fellman's groundbreaking study of Missouri guerrillas, *Inside War* (1989), changed that. Today, historians increasingly emphasize "irregular" activities by civilians, along with overt and covert resistance by slaves, as crucial to the outcome of the war. *The Civil War Guerrilla* continues that trend, repositioning the "inside wars" waged by men (variously labeled as bushwhackers, jayhawkers, partisan rangers, deserters, or outliers) and their home-front allies (including women, children, and slaves) as central to our understanding of the larger Civil War.

The eight essays in this volume offer no single answer as to why sporadic eruptions of guerrilla rage occurred throughout the Civil War South. Were guerrilla raiders vicious defenders of threatened institutions (like slavery), or were they common people desperately defending their rights (such as the right to remain in the Union)? Clearly, guerrillas were both and much more.

Several authors reveal the critical importance of geography and local conditions to the force and nature of internal wartime conflicts. In Union-held Missouri, for example, pro-Confederate raiders continued the ongoing Kansas-Missouri border struggles over slavery, while North Carolina's yeoman-dominated Quaker Belt waged a bloody inner war against Confederate forces throughout the war. To better track the location and movement of guerrilla bands across the Civil War landscape, Andrew Fialka introduces an innovative "spatiotemporal" method—the use of digital, "animated" maps. In contrast, David Brown and Patrick Doyle employ the tried-and-true method of comparative analysis to demonstrate why the North Carolina Piedmont became a hotbed of dissent while South Carolina's Piedmont region remained relatively loyal to the Confederate government.

Megan Kate Nelson follows the eruption of irregular warfare beyond Confederate boundaries and across ethnic lines. Just as slaves collaborated with anti-Confederate guerrillas, Indian nations reacted to the Civil War from their own historical vantage point. Nelson recounts efforts by Confederate leaders to forge alliances with far western tribes who specialized in raiding warfare, especially Comanches, Apaches, and Navajos, in hopes they would inflict a "wholesome terror" on New Mexico and Arizona Territories. Noting that Indians "make the very best guerrillas," as indeed they did, these Confederate leaders sorely misjudged Indian loyalty, to the utter ruin of their Far West campaign.

In shifting their research from conventional battlefields to guerrilla terrain, historians enter a world of myths and legends as fully entrenched as those long associated with the larger war and its heroes. Accordingly, a sampling of nearly a century of popular writers who were equally fascinated by guerrilla warfare—so much so that they created a cottage-industry guerrilla literature—enlivens several of the essays.

Matthew Hulbert locates this literature within a "guerrilla memory industry" that coincided with national postwar efforts to commemorate both the Confederacy and the Union. From the earliest years of the Civil War, in fact, guerrilla narratives provided an important arsenal of weapons from which journalists, novelists, and amateur historians drew to fight and refight the war on paper rather than in the theaters of irregular battlefields. Writing with unabashed bias, their authors relied on highly selective sources and, as Joseph Beilein Jr. reveals in the case of William E. Connelley's *Quantrill and the Border Wars* (1910), weren't above twisting the words of their interviewees to push their own perspective on the war. Connelley, writing to refute John N. Edwards's *Noted Guerrillas* (1877), countered images of pro-Confederate guerrillas as unsung heroes by presenting them as savage murderers. And so it went in narrative after narrative; whether one was a hero or a coward depended on which side of the war the author favored.

In service to partisan goals, narrative authors presented readers with one-dimensional characters motivated by either noble ideals or unmitigated evil. There were no shades of gray in these stilted, predictable plots delivered in florid prose. With minor variances, readers encountered the same stock characters over and over again. If the author was pro-Confederate, then the guerrillas' trusty slave spy was likely not interested in freedom (since the war was allegedly not about slavery); if the author was pro-Union, then the slaves were freedom fighters who recognized the supposedly abolitionist goals of the Union. Women were assigned two basic roles: to be rescued from their ravishers or to fight like hell on the side of their avengers. As for the protagonist, regardless of which side he was on, he was dedicated to the protection of women, children, and the old and to avenging the atrocities committed by the other side.

Such standard guerrilla tropes are deconstructed by John Inscoe, who contrasts three examples of nineteenth-century guerrilla fiction. The earliest of them, John Dabney McCabe's 1862 pro-Confederate play *The Guerrillas,* foreshadows the Myth of the Lost Cause. Noble though they are, McCabe's righteous guerrillas are forced by the savagery of their Unionist adversaries to fight fire with fire. Inscoe contrasts McCabe's work with two pro-Union novels, John Townsend Trowbridge's *Cudjo's Cave* (1864), and Edmund Kirke's *Among the Guerillas* (1866). Favoring the opposite side from McCabe, Trowbridge denounces Confederate guerrillas as "fierce hordes," while Kirke likens them to terrorists. Such is the wearying dualism—and long history—of Civil War debates that still pop up among online forums today: one side, then the other, is brave, heroic, and right with God; one side, then the other, is cowardly, vicious, and in league with the devil.

Considering all this, one might ask why historians (including myself) are so fascinated with guerrilla narratives—almost as much as with guerrillas themselves. To begin, they're great fun to read and to analyze, while allowing us to indulge in (ultimately to debunk) the kind of stories known to entertain the masses. High drama prevails, particularly among those published for mass consumption, and is generally unburdened by objectivity and nuance. Good and evil are sharply etched and—always—in direct combat with one another. But most important of all, guerrilla narratives are primary sources, however imperfect, that confirm the irregular bands of men who operated outside the boundaries of battle.

Therein is their value to historians. For all their flaws, guerrilla narratives include what is often missing from Civil War histories: the broader world of people and places outside the official scenes of battle. By abandoning conventional battlefields for the swamps, woods, deserts, and borderlands of partisan rangers and outliers, and despite their bombast and ideological bias, the narratives suggest a broader, more inclusive, and more complicated Civil War than we're likely to find elsewhere. And, although most uncritically repeat myths and legends, they also report much that is true. It's up to the historian to determine which is which.

When narrative authors transformed men like "Bloody Bill" Anderson and William Quantrill into larger-than-life hero/demon figures, individual character and personal motivation generally slipped out of sight. As Rod Andrew Jr. points out in regard to South Carolina's infamous guerrilla Manse Jolly (who was mythologized in both fiction and nonfiction), "the myth and the history are in constant tension, at various points reinforcing, refuting, or modifying each other." Through interviews and careful research in military records, federal manuscript censuses, and the rare discovery of a cache of letters left by the guerrilla himself, Andrew illuminates the real Manse Jolly, in the process telling a more plausible story than the "thrilling exploits and adventures" amid "Yankee tyranny" and "Negro rule" in which Jolly's legend is embedded. This is hard work, requiring both literary deconstruction and tedious research in local records, but well worth the historian's time.

Once the Civil War was formally ended, political and social leaders sought to create a kinder, gentler image of the war, one that would enable the nation to heal its wounds and reconcile its halves. Guerrilla narratives, with their heavy-handed judgments of guilt and innocence, were problematic for that process. In a cultural environment bent on sentimentalizing the war with images of soldiers on both sides as brave and noble, the standard guerrilla narrative left only the victims and vanquishers of guerrillas capable of being on the side of God. How, then, was one to address the barbarous excesses of war without derailing conciliatory accounts of the American Civil War?

Matthew Hulbert notes that Thomas A. Goodman pondered this very question in 1868 as he wrote his first-person account of "Bloody Bill" Anderson's two horrific massacres of Union soldiers at Centralia, Missouri. Writing at the earliest stage of national reconciliation, Goodman worried, writes Hulbert, that the gory events he described, especially the ignoble deaths of almost 150 Union soldiers at the hands of "savage" guerrillas, would be "wholly at odds with idealized concepts of the Civil War soldier or proper notions of Victorian battle and the 'good death.'" Goodman met the challenge by simply insisting that the men's deaths were no less honorable and noble than those suffered on regular battlefields. But did saying so make it so? The mass slaughters committed by Bloody Bill's men, who then proceeded to degrade and scalp their victims, hardly reinforced the romantic notion that martyrdom sanctified the bloody sacrifices of war.

Goodman's dilemma suggests why historians are fascinated—and they should be—with the literature of guerrilla warfare. Virtually all narrators of "thrilling" Civil War guerrilla tales strove to advance fixed truths for the side they favored. Pro-Confederate authors insisted that the noble cause was protection of the Constitutional rights of slaveholding states; pro-Union authors cited emancipationist goals by the federal government as the same. Though at odds with one another, when shorn of guerrilla violence, South and North versions could be massaged into an ideological construct that suited conciliatory commemorations of the Civil War. The problem was that neither version adequately explained the war's causes or outcomes. Nor did commemorative history acknowledge important questions raised by internal dissent, of which guerrilla warfare was only the most dramatic example.

The limits of Civil War guerrilla narratives and commemorative history demonstrate why we need scholarly studies of the sort offered by *The Civil War Guerrilla.* Guerrilla wars, whether generated by home-front conflicts or the hotly contested lands of the western frontier, underscore the complexity of popular resistance to authority as well as the horrific violence and tragic dimensions of the American Civil War. The essays here take us onto the lands and into the homes of citizens and noncitizens alike, enabling us to perceive more fully the sweep of war.

Daniel Sutherland's award-winning *A Savage Conflict* (2009) argued persuasively that guerrilla wars played a "decisive" role in the outcome of the Civil War. As new and in-progress studies provide ever more widespread and detailed knowledge of inner civil wars and their participants, a grand synthesis is surely on the horizon, one that will continue Sutherland's efforts to fold internecine warfare, to borrow a phrase from Christopher Phillips, into the "broader regular war trajectory."

Acknowledgments

A first book is a milestone that can happen only once. Thanking everyone who helped make it possible is especially important, and this is remarkably true in our case. Anne Dean Dotson, the University Press of Kentucky, our anonymous peer reviewers, and our contributors all took a great leap of faith: they placed immense trust in a pair of headstrong junior scholars who wanted to edit an anthology about one of the more controversial topics in Civil War history. Our respective doctoral advisors, John Inscoe and LeeAnn Whites, echoed that trust; we couldn't have asked for better guides through the publication process. Finally, we thank our families—the Hulberts, the Beileins, and our academic clans—for making it possible to raise our own version of the black flag. It's our sincerest hope that we've been worth the trouble . . . guerrilla shirts and all.

For Kylie and for Joe, Addie, Jane, and Clark Azar.

Contributors

Rod Andrew Jr. is professor of history at Clemson University. His previous works include *Long Gray Lines: The Southern Military School Tradition, 1830–1915* (2001) and *Wade Hampton: Confederate Warrior to Southern Redeemer* (2008).

Joseph M. Beilein Jr. is assistant professor of history at Penn State–Erie, The Behrend College, where he teaches Civil War history as well as early American history. His manuscript "Household Warriors: Guerrillas, Violence, and Manhood in Civil War Missouri" is currently under review with Kent State University Press. "Household Warriors" is a masculinity study in which he argues that antebellum concepts of gender structured, guided, and infused discipline into the guerrilla war effort in Missouri. He is also the author of "The Guerrilla Shirt: A Labor of Love and the Style of Rebellion in Civil War Missouri," *Civil War History* (June 2012) and several book reviews for *The Civil War Monitor* and *Civil War History.*

David Brown teaches American history at the University of Manchester in the UK, where he is senior lecturer in American Studies. He is the author of *Southern Outcast: Hinton Rowan Helper and The Impending Crisis of the South* (2006), coauthor of *Race in the American South: From Slavery to Civil Rights* (2007), and coeditor of *Creating Citizenship in the Nineteenth-Century South* (2013). He is completing a study of yeomen and poor whites in the mid-nineteenth-century South.

Victoria E. Bynum is Distinguished Professor Emeritus of History at Texas State University and has published widely on pro-Union guerrillas of the Civil War. Her publications include *The Long Shadow of the Civil War* (2010) and *The Free State of Jones* (2001).

Patrick J. Doyle is lecturer in modern American history at Royal Holloway, University of London, UK. He is currently at work on a study of the South Carolina upcountry during the American Civil War.

Andrew William Fialka, a PhD student at the University of Georgia, works at the Center for Virtual History (ehistory.org) on projects such as "CSI: Dixie," "*Compendium of the War of the Rebellion* Events Dataset," and "Of Methods and Madness: A Spatial History Approach to the Civil War's Guerrilla Violence."

Matthew C. Hulbert is a doctoral candidate in history at the University of Georgia and a 2014–2015 dissertation fellow with the Harry Frank Guggenheim Foundation. His articles on guerrilla warfare and social memory in the western borderlands have appeared in the *Journal of the Civil War Era, Civil War History, Common-Place: The Interactive Journal of Early American Life, Journal of the West,* and the *New York Times.*

John C. Inscoe is Albert B. Saye Professor of History and University Professor at the University of Georgia. He has written widely about nineteenth-century Appalachia, and *Race, War, and Remembrance in the Appalachian South* (2008) is included among his many works.

Megan Kate Nelson is a writer, historian, and cultural critic. She is the author of *Ruin Nation: Destruction and the American Civil War* (2012) and *Trembling Earth: A Cultural History of the Okefenokee Swamp* (2005). She writes regularly for *JSTOR Daily, Civil War Times* magazine, and the *New York Times.* Her blog, Historista, examines the surprising, cool, and weird ways that people engage with history in everyday life.

Christopher Phillips is professor of history and department head at the University of Cincinnati, where he teaches courses in the era of the American Civil War and Reconstruction. His seven published books have focused particularly on the border slave states, and his essays have appeared in such publications as the *Journal of the Civil War Era* and the *New York Times.* His latest book, *The Rivers Ran Backward: The Civil War on the Middle Border and the Making of American Regionalism,* from which his chapter is derived, will be published in 2015.

Index

New Directions in Southern History

Series editors
Michele Gillespie, Wake Forest University
William A. Link, University of Florida

The Lost State of Franklin: America's First Secession
Kevin T. Barksdale

The Civil War Guerrilla: Unfolding the Black Flag in History, Memory, and Myth
edited by Joseph M. Beilein Jr. and Matthew C. Hulbert

Bluecoats and Tar Heels: Soldiers and Civilians in Reconstruction North Carolina
Mark L. Bradley

Becoming Bourgeois: Merchant Culture in the South, 1820–1865
Frank J. Byrne

Cowboy Conservatism: Texas and the Rise of the Modern Right
Sean P. Cunningham

A Tour of Reconstruction: Travel Letters of 1875
Anna Dickinson (J. Matthew Gallman, ed.)

Raising Racists: The Socialization of White Children in the Jim Crow South
Kristina DuRocher

Lum and Abner: Rural America and the Golden Age of Radio
Randal L. Hall

Mountains on the Market: Industry, the Environment, and the South
Randal L. Hall

The New Southern University: Academic Freedom and Liberalism at UNC
Charles J. Holden

Entangled by White Supremacy: Reform in World War I–Era South Carolina
Janet G. Hudson

Bloody Breathitt: Politics and Violence in the Appalachian South
T. R. C. Hutton

Cultivating Race: The Expansion of Slavery in Georgia, 1750–1860
Watson W. Jennison

De Bow's Review: *The Antebellum Vision of a New South*
John F. Kvach

Remembering the Battle of the Crater: War as Murder
Kevin M. Levin

The Political Career of W. Kerr Scott: The Squire from Haw River
Julian Pleasants

The View from the Ground: Experiences of Civil War Soldiers
edited by Aaron Sheehan-Dean

Reconstructing Appalachia: The Civil War's Aftermath
edited by Andrew L. Slap

Blood in the Hills: A History of Violence in Appalachia
edited by Bruce E. Stewart

Moonshiners and Prohibitionists: The Battle over Alcohol in Southern Appalachia
Bruce E. Stewart

The U.S. South and Europe: Transatlantic Relations in the Nineteenth and Twentieth Centuries
edited by Cornelis A. van Minnen and Manfred Berg

Southern Farmers and Their Stories: Memory and Meaning in Oral History
Melissa Walker

Law and Society in the South: A History of North Carolina Court Cases
John W. Wertheimer

Family or Freedom: People of Color in the Antebellum South
Emily West